This volume, the second in an annual series, contains sixteen essays summarizing the scholarship in American literature during the calendar year 1964. Half are devoted to individual authors; the rest to general topics, and each is written by a specialist in the subject assigned. Because the annual MLA bibliography now carries more than 1,500 items in the American literature section and many additional periodical items appear each year in journals not searched by the MLA bibliographical committee, it no longer is possible for any student or teacher in American literature to keep up with the bibliography in any more than a few areas of special interest. This series is planned as a service to the profession and brings to bear on the unmanageable quantity of current American literary scholarship some selective evaluations. Published under the sponsorship of the American Literature Group of the Modern Language Association, the series already has become an essential tool for research.

The editor, James Woodress, who is on leave as dean of the School of Letters and Science at San Fernando Valley State College, is currently a Fulbright lecturer in Italy. He has served both as bibliographer and as secretary-treasurer of the American Literature Group.

American Literary Scholarship

1964

American Literary Scholarship

An Annual / 1964

Edited by James Woodress

Essays by John Clendenning, Hyatt H. Waggoner, Willard Thorp, Edward F. Grier, John C. Gerber, B. R. McElderry, Jr., Richard P. Adams, Frederick J. Hoffman, Richard Beale Davis, Louis J. Budd, J. Albert Robbins, C. Hugh Holman, William T. Stafford, Ann Stanford, Oliver Evans, Malcolm Goldstein.

Indexed by Joseph M. Flora

Duke University Press, Durham, North Carolina, 1966

810.8
A512d
1964

Foreword

When the first volume of *American Literary Scholarship: An Annual, 1963* was projected, my contributors and I hoped to make the venture a continuing enterprise. That hope now seems well on its way toward being realized. The appearance of the second volume in this series ought to convince skeptics that the project is both feasible and that the initial head of steam has not yet given out. Originally I had hoped that the first volume would make its appearance before winter ended, but spring flowers had come and gone before the book actually materialized. This year, however, the process from editing through manufacturing has gone faster—an auspicious sign for the continuing vitality of the series. Since thirteen of the original seventeen contributors have stayed with the venture, Volume II does not suffer from any lack of continuity.

The reception of Volume I has been very generous and favorable. The work obviously fills a gap in the ordinary tools of scholarship and already is finding its place as a supplement to the quarterly checklists and annual bibliographies previously available. Users of the book not only have been complimentary, but they also have submitted useful suggestions for improving the work. In general, however, it has seemed desirable to retain the present format and contents and to get the series well started before considering such matters as reorganization of the contents. There certainly will be changes from time to time. It may be useful at some point to add additional general topics, shift dates enclosing the general topics, combine two or more of the authors presently treated separately, or separate the authors now treated in composite chapters. Also in lean years it may be desirable temporarily to drop a single author completely. The only change or addition to the book this year is an index, which should make Volume II considerably more useful than Volume I. An index to Volume I is also included.

The contributors to the present volume have received the same general instructions they were given last year. That is, they were asked to do the best job possible summarizing the scholarship in their areas for the year 1964. I continue to feel that each chapter presents different problems and that no rigid format should be imposed. Hence some chapters are more evaluative than others, some more selective than others. It probably is inevitable that as the novelty of this project wears off there will be increasing criticism of specific details in the mechanics of the operation.

Once again the form of bibliographical notation used follows closely the style adopted by the MLA bibliography. In general the articles reviewed give the author of the article, the title, the journal, the volume, and the pages. It may be assumed that in every case, unless otherwise stated, the year is 1964. When articles are cited from journals that page each number separately, the number of the issue is included. The periodicals in which the articles appear are represented by abbreviations or acronyms, and a key to the periodicals may be found in the front matter. Books cited are listed with author, title, place of publication, and publisher. The dates, as with journal citations, are 1964 unless otherwise noted.

I am greatly indebted to the sixteen contributors who have written essays for this second volume. Once again their efforts represent a large expenditure of time and energy in the service of fellow scholars. I also am very much indebted to Professor C. Hugh Holman, who saw the book through the press while I was in Europe, and his colleague, Professor Joseph Flora, who compiled the index. A final debt is due Mrs. Marion Magee, whose secretarial services to this project are too numerous to recount.

James Woodress

San Fernando Valley State College
Northridge, California

Table of Contents

Table of Contents

Key to Abbreviations

ABC	American Book Collector	Critique	(Paris)
AGR	American-German Review	CritQ	Critical Quarterly
AHR	American Historical Review	CWH	Civil War History
		DA	Dissertation Abstracts
AL	American Literature	DR	Dalhousie Review
ALaR	Alabama Review	DramS	Drama Survey (Minneapolis)
ALS	American Literary Scholarship: An Annual	EA	Etudes Anglaises
AN&Q	American Notes & Queries	EIC	Essays in Criticism
AQ	American Quarterly	EIHC	Essex Institute Historical Collections
AR	Antioch Review		
ArQ	Arizona Quarterly	EJ	English Journal
AS	American Speech	ELN	English Language Notes
ASch	American Scholar	ES	English Studies
AULLA	The Australasian Universities Language and Literature Association	E&S	Essays and Studies by Members of the English Association
BAASB	British Association for American Studies Bulletin	Essays and Studies	Herbert H. Petit, ed., Essays and Studies in Language and Literature, Duquesne Studies, Philological Series (Pittsburgh, Duquesne Univ. Press)
BB	Bulletin of Bibliography		
BNYPL	Bulletin of the New York Public Library		
BuR	Bucknell Review		
BYUS	Brigham Young University Studies	ESQ	Emerson Society Quarterly
		ETJ	Educational Theater Journal
CathW	Catholic World		
CE	College English	EUQ	Emory University Quarterly
CEA	CEA Critic		
ChS	Christian Scholar	Expl	Explicator
CL	Comparative Literature	Festschrift Hübner	Dieter Riesner and Helmut Gneuss, eds., Festschrift für Walter Hübner (Berlin, Schmidt)
CLAJ	College Language Association Journal (Morgan State College, Baltimore)		
ClareQ	Claremont Quarterly	FHS	French Historical Studies
CLQ	Colby Library Quarterly	FN	Fitzgerald Newsletter
CM	Carlton Miscellany	FQ	Four Quarters (La Salle College)
Com	Commentary		
CRAS	The Centennial Review of Arts & Science	FuS	Furman Studies
		GaHQ	Georgia Historical Quarterly
Crit	Critique: Studies in Modern Fiction	GaR	Georgia Review

HC	The Hollins Critic	MTJ	Mark Twain Journal
HLQ	Huntington Library Quarterly	Muk	Maske und Kothurn
		NA	Nuova Antologia
HSE	Hungarian Studies in English	N&Q	Notes and Queries
		NCF	Nineteenth-Century Fiction
HudR	Hudson Review		
IMA	Indiana Magazine of History	NEHGR	New England Historical and Genealogical Register
ISHSJ	Illinois State Historical Society Journal		
JA	Jahrbuch für Amerikastudien	NEQ	New England Quarterly
		NHQ	The New Hungarian Quarterly
JAAC	Journal of Aesthetics and Art Criticism	NJHSP	New Jersey Historical Society Proceedings
JEGP	Journal of English and Germanic Philology	NR	New Republic
JHI	Journal of the History of Ideas	NS	Die neuren Sprachen
		PAAS	Proceedings American Antiquarian Society
JPH	Journal of Presbyterian History	PBSA	Papers of the Bibliographical Society of America
JRUL	Journal of the Rutgers University Library	Per	Perspective (Washington Univ.)
JSH	Journal of Southern History	Person	Personalist
KN	Kwartalnik Neo Philologiczny (Warsaw)	PH	Pennsylvania History
		PMASAL	Papers of the Michigan Academy of Science, Arts, and Letters
KR	Kenyon Review		
LC	Library Chronicle (Univ. of Pa.)	PMHB	Pennsylvania Magazine of History and Biography
L&P	Literature and Psychology	PMHS	Proceedings of the Massachusetts Historical Society
LitR	Literary Review (Fairleigh Dickinson Univ., Teaneck, N. J.)		
MASJ	Midcontinent American Studies Journal	PMLA	Publications of the Modern Language Association of America
MCR	Melbourne Critical Review	PQ	Philological Quarterly
MD	Modern Drama	PR	Partisan Review
MdF	Mercure de France	PrS	Prairie Schooner
MdHM	Maryland Historical Magazine	QQ	Queen's Quarterly
		Reality and Myth	W. E. Walker and Robert E. Welker, eds., Reality and Myth: Essays in American Literature in Memory of Richmond Croom Beatty (Nashville, Vanderbilt Univ. Press)
MFS	Modern Fiction Studies		
MHSB	Missouri Historical Society Bulletin		
MissQ	Mississippi Quarterly		
MLN	Modern Language Notes		
MLQ	Modern Language Quarterly		
MLR	Modern Language Review	Ren	Renascence
ModA	Modern Age (Chicago)	Review	the Review: a magazine of poetry and criticism (Oxford)
MQ	Midwest Quarterly (Kans. State College at Pittsburg)		
MR	Massachusetts Review	RLC	Révue de Létterature Comparée

RLV	Revue des langues vivantes (Bruxelles)	TSE	Tulane Studies in English
SA	Studi Americani	TSLL	Texas Studies in Literature and Language
SatR	Saturday Review	TUSAS	Twayne United States Authors Series (New York, Twayne)
SAQ	South Atlantic Quarterly		
SB	Studies in Bibliography: Papers of the Bibliographical Society of the University of Virginia	TWA	Transactions of the Wisconsin Academy of Sciences, Arts, and Letters
SDR	South Dakota Review	UFMH	Univ. of Florida Monographs, Humanities Series
SELit	Studies in English Literature (Eng. Lit. Soc. of Japan, Univ. of Tokyo)		
		ULR	University of Leeds Review
SFQ	Southern Folklore Quarterly	UMPAW	Univ. of Minn. Pamphlets on American Writers
SGG	Studia Germanica Gandensia		
ShawR	Shaw Review	UMSE	University of Mississippi Studies in English
SIR	Studies in Romanticism		
SR	Sewanee Review	UR	University Review (Kans. City)
SSF	Studies in Short Fiction (Newberry College, Newberry, S. C.)		
		UTQ	University of Toronto Quarterly
STL	Studies on the Left (New York)	VC	Virginia Cavalcade
Studies	(Dublin)	VMHB	Virginia Magazine of History and Biography
SWR	Southwest Review		
SZ	Stimmen der Zeit	VN	Victorian Newsletter
TamR	Tamarack Review (Toronto)	VQR	Virginia Quarterly Review
		WF	Western Folklore
TCL	Twentieth Century Literature	WHR	Western Humanities Review
TCSM	Transactions of the Colonial Society of Massachusetts	WMQ	William and Mary Quarterly
		WSCL	Wisconsin Studies in Contemporary Literature
Thoth	(Dept. of Eng., Syracuse Univ.)		
		WWR	Walt Whitman Review
TLS	Times Literary Supplement	YR	Yale Review
TM	Temps Modernes	YULG	Yale University Library Gazette
TQ	Texas Quarterly		
TSB	Thoreau Society Bulletin	ZAA	Zeitschrift für Anglistik und Amerikanistik
TSBooklet	Thoreau Society Booklet		

Part I

1. Emerson, Thoreau, and Transcendentalism

John Clendenning

i. Emerson

The scholarly productivity in Emerson studies during the year has been most impressive. Three major editions, three new books of criticism, and an abundance of articles will keep Emersonians busy for some time.

a. **Bibliography and genealogy.** Although scholars must still labor without a complete bibliography—Cooke's work of 1908 now proving inadequate—they will find assistance in Jackson R. Bryer and Robert A. Rees, *A Checklist of Emerson Criticism, 1951-1961* (Hartford, Conn., Transcendental Books—reprinted in *ESQ*, No. 37)—an annotated list of 420 items with a detailed index. A briefer list is Kenneth Walter Cameron, "Current Bibliography on Ralph Waldo Emerson" (*ESQ*, No. 37, pp. 88-92). Cameron has also published a note on "The Wider Emerson Family" (*ESQ*, No. 37, pp. 76-87), which examines the records of a collateral branch of the Emerson clan, presents the evidence of a family Bible, and prints a manuscript autobiography of Charles Noble Emerson to show the intellectual interests of Emerson's distant relatives.

b. **Editions.** Among the most important publications is Alfred R. Ferguson, ed., *The Journals and Miscellaneous Notebooks of Ralph Waldo Emerson*, Vol. IV, *1832-1834* (Cambridge, Mass., Harvard Univ. Press, Belknap). The eight journals and three notebooks that comprise this volume are edited with the great care and intelligence that has characterized the entire project. Two of these journals, "Q" and "A," are personal and meditative. Here Emerson reveals the influence of his now favorite authors—Montaigne, Goethe, Carlyle—and seeks finally to resolve his conflicting beliefs, to define his status as a Christian minister. But unlike some of the earlier journals where Em-

erson seemed quite baffled by doubt, now he appears to attack problems with more serenity and to write in a more deliberate, self-confident, forceful style. Most of the remaining journal material shows
Emerson's recorded impressions of Europe, his enthusiasm for the
art of the High Renaissance, his visits with Landor, Carlyle, Coleridge, and Wordsworth. Emerson was a thoughtful traveler whose
observations were often trenchant, but like many of his contemporaries, he was still an innocent abroad.

As Ferguson's *Journals* vastly improves our understanding of Emerson's inner life, Joseph Slater's new edition of *The Correspondence
of Emerson and Carlyle* (New York, Columbia Univ. Press) throws
important light on his letter-writing. The many omissions for which
Charles Eliot Norton was responsible in his edition of 1883 are now
fully restored. Slater may be overstating his case when he maintains
that this is the most famous correspondence of the nineteenth century, but its importance and its intrinsic interest are undeniable. Now
the story of their valuable friendship is before us, their first mutual
enthusiasm, their inevitable differences and cooling of affection, and
their abilities to see the best in each other despite the differences.
This edition is the fruit of many years of hard labor, and one is
obliged to say to Slater, as Carlyle said to Emerson after reading *The
Conduct of Life*, "Well done." A minor addition to the canon of Emerson's letters is edited by Walter H. Murphy in "A Letter by Emerson" (*AL*, XXXVI, 64-65). In this letter to J. R. Leeson, May 17, 1870,
Emerson commented upon his Harvard lectures, thus confirming, according to Murphy, Holmes's claim that these lectures cost Emerson
"a great deal of labor."

A third major publication of primary materials is the second volume of *The Early Lectures of Ralph Waldo Emerson* (Cambridge,
Mass., Harvard Univ. Press, Belknap), edited by the late Stephen E.
Whicher, Robert E. Spiller, and Wallace E. Williams. Printed here
in full are the two lecture series, "The Philosophy of History" and
"Human Culture," that Emerson presented in successive winters,
1836-1837 and 1837-1838, plus an "Address on Education" delivered
in June, 1837. Although much of this material has been printed elsewhere, a great deal is now widely available for the first time, and
only now do we have the two series collected in a complete and coherent form. Those interested in American public address will find
this volume indispensable; those concerned with Emerson's intellectual development will find these pages repeatedly suggestive. A

point, however, regarding the proper use of these lectures may be in
order. It is clear that Emerson did not consider them complete, finished, and publishable. Most of the passages which did turn up in
his two series of *Essays* were revised and assembled in vastly different forms. We must, therefore, use these lectures with caution,
resisting the temptation to treat them as Emerson's views as he intended they should be presented to the reading public. Careful editing is clearly evidenced throughout the volume. Further information
about Emerson's career as a lecturer is provided by Paul O. Williams,
"An Unnoticed Emerson Lecture" (*AN&Q*, III, 5), and by Lynda
Beltz, "Emerson's Lectures in Indianapolis" (*IMH*, LX, 269-280).

c. **Criticism.** Especially acute to the critic of Emerson is the problem of approach. If we see him as a poet, we tend to employ the techniques of literary analysis; if we see him as a figure in the history of
ideas, we want to discover where he stands and to submit his views to
the test of scrutiny. Fundamentally different Emersons are bound to
develop.

To Jonathan Bishop, *Emerson on the Soul* (Cambridge, Mass.,
Harvard Univ. Press), he was a literary artist whose essays might be
explicated and judged as one treats a poem or short story. Matters of
tone, metaphor, and rhythm interest Bishop more than Emerson's
"philosophy"; a well turned phrase or a striking image can excuse a
trivial or contradictory opinion. The result is a useful book, possibly
the best of the "literary" studies. If after reading it one still does not
know where Emerson stands, if Bishop's writing is sometimes obscure, if not simply meaningless, one has seen the best, the most art-
ful of Emerson examined by a sophisticated and responsive critic. A
similar approach may be found in Josephine Miles's *Ralph Waldo
Emerson* (UMPAW, No. 41, Minneapolis, Univ. of Minn. Press).
Professor Miles projects Emerson into the tradition of wisdom literature; he takes his place with Jesus, Confucius, Marcus Aurelius, Montaigne, and Bacon, whose heritage is that of the maxim, the proverb,
the aphorism, not a systematic philosophy. *The Conduct of Life, Representative Men,* and *English Traits*—Emerson's most successfully
organized works—are discussed in some detail; his other works similarly illustrate his important style—active, predicative, simple, and
economical.

If these books by Bishop and Miles emphasize stylistic considerations and only incidentally treat Emerson's ideas, Maurice Gonnaud,

Individu et société dans l'oeuvre de Ralph Waldo Emerson (Paris, Didier), is somewhat different in purpose and broader in scope. He has set out to write a full-scale "biographie spirituelle" of Emerson's ideas seen against the backdrop of American social, religious, educational, and political history. Like Bishop, whose book is dedicated to the memory of Stephen Whicher, Gonnaud has been profoundly influenced by *Freedom and Fate*; in general, his analysis is Whicher's: Emerson's early conformity was followed by an intellectual crisis that resulted in the first phase of Transcendentalism, which in turn was followed by a second personal crisis that brought about a more sober, more mature writer. One might feel that Gonnaud's work derives too much from previous studies and that too many obvious facts are needlessly repeated, but we should recognize that this book was written for a French audience, not for American scholars. Emerson was always interested in the French, and the fascination has been returned. The writings of Regis Michaud still rank high among Emerson studies; now Gonnaud's book will certainly become the standard work on Emerson written in French. A further indication of foreign scholars' interest in Emerson's ideas is evidenced by Leyla Goren, "Elements of Brahmanism in the Transcendentalism of Emerson" (*ESQ*, No. 34, Sup.—a reprint of a book published abroad in limited edition during 1959). Professor Goren maintains that Emerson's great interest in Indian thought derived from his contemplative nature. In her first chapter, she summarizes clearly the various systems of Brahmanism from the period of the Upanishads (*ca.* 800 B.C.) to the modern thought of Tagore and Gandhi. The second chapter traces the development of Emerson's Orientalism, which began in 1818, but which came to maturity after 1845. "Brahma," "Hamatreya," and *The Conduct of Life* are seen as his most thoroughly Eastern works; each is discussed with careful and suggestive comparisons between Emerson's writings and the Hindu scriptures. A useful bibliography concludes this thoughtful study.

Among the best work recently published are articles which clarify special features of Emerson's art and ideology. Roland F. Lee, "Emerson's 'Compensation' as Argument and as Art" (*NEQ*, XXXVII, 291-305), suggests that Emerson's confusions led to the failures of the essay. As argument, the theory of compensation is absurd and even pernicious; as art, the essay fails to sustain a unified purpose. But Lee maintains that these problems are inherent: Emerson was trying to state the incommunicable and thus failed to see that his belief was existential. At one point—in stating that there is something deeper than compensation, namely, its own nature—he was expressing an idea that many modern existentialists, such as Marcel, have more clearly seen and effectively said.

Four brief articles should have important consequences in future scholarship. Robert Detweiler, "The Over-Rated 'Over-Soul'" (*AL*, XXXVI, 65-68), warns us against using the handy, but vague, term "Over-Soul" to describe Emerson's concept of God. Detweiler demonstrates that, contrary to most accounts, Emerson seldom used the term. Three possible meanings are suggested: (1) over-the-soul or the idea of transcendence, (2) super soul (*Über-Seele*) or the idea of immanence, and (3) general (all-pervading) soul or the idea of unity. Stephen S. Conroy, "Emerson and Phrenology" (*AQ*, XVI, 215-217), shows that Emerson took a dim view of phrenology, but his belief in the correspondence between physical and spiritual reality caused him to admit that even a pseudoscience can possess an important truth. Two thoughtful explications appeared in 1964: George Arms, "The Dramatic Movement in Emerson's 'Each and All'" (*ELN*, I, 207-211), and Sister Paula Reiten, "Emerson's 'The Snow-Storm'" (*Expl*, XXII, Item 39). Both are stimulating readings.

A single dissertation appears to be a work of considerable significance. Wallace Edward Williams, "Emerson and the Moral Law" (*DA*, XXIV, 4204-05), argues that the concept of a moral law is central throughout Emerson's writings. His early belief in Christian morality gave way to a Transcendental dualism of the inner and the outer laws. This belief was reformulated in *The Conduct of Life*, Fate and Power now being the terms of the dualism. In the 1860's political issues forced him to enlarge his private ethics to include a social dimension, and finally in the 1870's he resolved his original dualism by proposing a psychological metaphysics, resembling somewhat the philosophy of C. S. Peirce.

Works of less importance are perhaps inevitable. Joel Porte, "Nature as Symbol: Emerson's Noble Doubt" (*NEQ*, XXXVII, 453-476), argues that Emerson adopted an Ideal theory because he found sense experience distasteful, not because he honestly doubted the reality of the physical world. The hypothesis, though interesting, is not easily proved, nor are its assumptions self-evident. As Emerson made clear in *Nature*, he did not adopt Idealism as a true theory of reality; he merely suspended his judgment, maintaining that neither the Ideal nor the Material theory is conclusive. Idealism, Emerson suggested, is *useful*, not necessarily true, because it shows the relationship between God and man. Further, if Emerson found sense experience distasteful, one wonders why he was so drawn to the beauties of nature and why he so constantly employed natural images in his poems and essays. These uncertain assumptions, together with several errors of fact, would seem to question the value of this article. William Drummond's *Academical Questions*, for instance, is described as "Lockean," though the work contains a devastating critique of Locke. The "crack" seen in *Nature* (see the letter to William Emerson, August 8, 1836) was not identified by Emerson, though Porte says otherwise, as a structural flaw between "Discipline" and "Idealism." Therman O'Daniel, "Emerson as a Literary Critic" (*CLAJ*, VIII, 21-43, 157-189, to be continued), seeks to prove that Emerson is more important in the history of literary criticism than has been supposed. The central principles of Emerson's discrimination, O'Daniel maintains, are (1) nature, (2) the moral purpose of art, and (3) the love of beauty. Although the fact that Emerson did hold to such principles is obvious, it is not clear that these are proper criteria of literary judgment. The article contains extended discussions of Emerson's opinions about Milton, Landor, Carlyle, Montaigne, Shakespeare, Goethe, Burns, Parker, Thoreau, Lincoln, Plutarch, and others, but little light is shed upon those subjects. Nothing is said about Emerson's theoretical criticism, his concept of the nature of literature, or his ideas about the relationship between art and inspiration, though one would suspect that he made his most impressive contributions to criticism as a theoretical, not as a practical, critic.

d. **Emerson and others.**   Emerson has been seen repeatedly as a focal point in American letters. Many of the articles which appeared in 1964 clarify his relationships with others, historical antecedents, contemporaries, and later figures of the nineteenth century. Only one of these is a study of Emerson's sources. John Clendenning, "Emerson and Bayle" (*PQ*, XLIII, 79-86), suggests that Emerson may have read Pierre Bayle's *Dictionary* in the 1820's and that this may be the source of his later skepticism regarding man's abilities to comprehend God.

The *ESQ*, No. 35, contains an important "Critical Symposium on American Romanticism," edited by Carl F. Strauch. Emerson's ideas and works are frequently mentioned throughout these papers; in two of them he is a major subject of discussion. Luther S. Mansfield, "The

Emersonian Idiom and the Romantic Period in American Literature"
(pp. 23-28), suggests that the American Romantic period might better be called the age of Emerson or of the Emersonian idiom, for a
reading of his essays—*Nature*, "Self-Reliance," "The Poet," "Experience," and "Fate"—is essential if we would deal with the other authors of the period. This idiom is expansive, inclusive, fluid, and thus
useful. Thoreau, Hawthorne, Melville, Whitman—all learned the
idiom, possessed it, even when they doubted its truth, and it made
them great. Carl F. Strauch, "The Problem of Time and the Romantic Mode in Hawthorne, Melville, and Emerson" (pp. 50-60), studies
the ways in which Hawthorne, Melville, and Emerson solve the painful question of the relationship between time and personality. Hawthorne is most "average"; he escapes time by entering a timeless present of love. For Melville the problem becomes a cosmic battle, and
the only redemption is achieved in the aesthetics of tragedy. Emerson escapes time by harmonizing the suffering and thus by rising
above it. In "Experience" both time and suffering are ephemeral. In
Nietzsche's terms, therefore, Emerson and Melville share a great
deal: one is Apollonian, the other Dionysiac.

The relationship between Emerson and Melville is studied further by Barbara Ruth Nieweg Blansett in "Melville and Emersonian
Transcendentalism" (*DA*, XXIV, 2904). Self-reliance, optimism, and
individualism are discussed as the major themes of the Transcendental movement. *Mardi*, according to this definition, presents a belief in Transcendentalism, and Taji is the Transcendental man. But
in *Pierre* the theme is inverted. The Transcendental doctrines are still
the major themes, but the hero is now doomed; his obsession with absolute truth leads to his destruction.

Two articles show Emerson's more positive relationships with his
fellow Transcendentalists. Hazen C. Carpenter, "Emerson and Christopher Pearse Cranch" (*NEQ*, XXXVII, 18-42), reviews Emerson's
influence on Cranch in chronological order, bringing to our attention
an abundance of unpublished material. The evidence indicates that
Emerson was an important, if not the most important, influence on
Cranch's intellectual development, but it shows also that Cranch was
not an uncritical disciple. Paul O. Williams, "Emerson Guided: Walks
with Thoreau and Channing" (*ESQ*, No. 35, pp. 66-68), notes that
Emerson's journal descriptions of his walks with Thoreau and Channing reveal that he learned from them two strikingly different lessons.
From Thoreau he received facts of nature particularized and botani-

cal; from Channing he received impressions of nature generalized
and aesthetic. Williams adds that Emerson eventually grew dissatisfied with Thoreau's view of nature and suggests, therefore, that Channing's influence was the more enduring and important.

Emerson's relationship with England's men of letters is the subject of two articles. Robert N. Hertz, "Victory and the Consciousness
of Battle: Emerson and Carlyle" (*Person*, XLV, 60-71), depicts Emerson as the apostle of victory who joyfully affirms his spiritual affinity with all nature, whereas nature for Carlyle is a persisting ob-
stacle, a fact of experience which cannot be transcended, but which
provides a consciousness of battle. Hertz unfortunately deals only
with *Nature*; a reading of *Essays* (Second Series), *Representative
Men*, and *The Conduct of Life* would suggest that the differences between Emerson and Carlyle, in their views of nature, are not so
distinct as this article maintains. A more scholarly effort is William J.
Sowder, "Emerson's Rationalist Champions: A Study in British Periodicals" (*NEQ*, XXXVII, 147-170), which demonstrates that Emerson had strong supporters among certain iconoclastic sects: the
Secularists and the Theosophists. The Secularists saw Emerson as a
courageous heretic, a spokesman for the new religion of science. The
Theosophists, on the other hand, tried to reconcile the mysticism of
Eckhardt and Bohme with the science of Darwin; to them Emerson
was not simply anticlerical, but rather one who sought the same reconciliation.

Three articles clarify Emerson's influence on later writers. Earl
Rovit, "James and Emerson: The Lesson of the Master" (*ASch*,
XXXIII, 434-440), reconsiders James's ambivalent feelings about Emerson. Rovit suggests that the early criticism is evasive: because
James could not resolve his conflicting feelings about America, he
could not give a just estimate of Emerson. But the later James was a
better man, a more self-confident writer whose fiction became a celebration of aesthetics as morality. This is also Emerson's major theme.
Maurice F. Brown, "Santayana on Emerson: An Unpublished Essay"
(*ESQ*, No. 37, pp. 60-70), prints with a brief introduction Santayana's
unsuccessful Bowdoin Prize Essay of 1886 entitled "The Optimism
of Ralph Waldo Emerson." Here the young philosopher condemns
Emerson for failing to state and justify his views with clarity and
logic. Emerson claims to be an optimist, yet his beliefs would seem to
lead to pessimism. His melancholy view of experience, his doubts of
immortality, his denial of progress—all this, Santayana observes,

sounds like Schopenhauer! Thus, he concludes, Emerson's optimism is merely an idle hope, not an adequate theory of reality. Edgar L. McCormick, "Higginson, Emerson, and a National Literature" (*ESQ*, No. 37, pp. 71-74), counters the argument that T. W. Higginson was a narrow traditionalist and a superficial romantic. He was instead an important and a farseeing critic who recognized that American letters had achieved an authentic voice in Ralph Waldo Emerson.

ii. Thoreau

Compared with the great work done on Emerson during 1964, a review of the scholarship on Thoreau may be disappointing, yet several works of considerable importance appeared.

a. **Bibliography, biography, manuscripts.** In the past several years Walter Harding and Kenneth Cameron have patiently attended to these basic necessities. Harding keeps us abreast of bibliographical matters with his "Additions to the Thoreau Bibliography" (*TSB*, No. 86, pp. 2-3; No. 87, pp. 1-3; No. 89, pp. 2-4), which lists more than 150 publications. Harding also, with "Thoreau and Kate Brady" (*AL*, XXXVI, 347-349), identifies the Irish girl with whom Thoreau was supposed, by Alcott, to have fallen in love. Harding maintains that Alcott overstated the case, but in examining the available evidence suggests that Thoreau took more than a mild interest in the young lady. Cameron, "Thoreau Manuscripts—Ungathered and Migrant" (*ESQ*, No. 35, pp. 84-86), excerpts from dealers' catalogs which list, with brief descriptions, six manuscripts.

b. **Editions.** Three facsimile editions of Thoreau material were published in 1964. Harding's edition of "Sophia Thoreau's Scrapbook: From the Collection of George L. Davenport, Jr." (*TS Booklet*, No. 20) is a miscellaneous notebook first used by John Thoreau as a poetry copy book and later by Sophia as a memorial to John and Henry. Included are family mementos and tributes of various kinds. In 1876 Sophia gave the volume to Ellen Sewell Osgood, who continued to keep it as a scrapbook of Thoreau material. Cameron's edition of *Thoreau's Literary Notebook in the Library of Congress*, Facsimile Text (Hartford, Conn., Transcendental Books), is another miscellaneous notebook containing Henry's copyings from English authors, Greek and Oriental mystics, and friends. The introductory material to this volume is printed also in *ESQ*, No. 37, pp. 55-59. Finally, "Anti-Slavery Song Books in Thoreau's Library" (*ESQ*, No. 36, pp. 52-121), is an interesting and sometimes amusing set of photographic reproductions.

Of greater consequence is the enlarged edition of *Collected Poems of Henry Thoreau*, edited by Carl Bode (Baltimore, The Johns Hopkins Press), which reprints the 1943 text without revision, plus some thirteen new poems. It is perhaps unfortunate that a complete revision has not been possible, for the many questions raised by Francis H. Allen ("Thoreau's *Collected Poems*," *AL*, XVII, 1945, 260-267) are still unanswered. We now know that "Carpe Diem" and "Therefore a current of sadness deep" were not the work of Thoreau and are disturbed to find them still in the canon. Bode's editing is so generally excellent that it is distressing to have the book flawed by these few important errors. As a final note of caution, it should be observed that "The Centaur," presented here as a new poem, is quite clearly, as Raymond Gozzi has already pointed out, a variant of "Life," published in the original edition.

c. **Criticism.**   In a sense, more attention has been paid to Thoreau's poetry than to any other aspect of his thought and art. Besides Bode's edition, two articles appeared in 1964. Paul O. Williams, "The Concept of Inspiration in Thoreau's Poetry" (*PMLA*, LXXIX, 466-472), sees that inspiration is a major theme in Thoreau's writing, but unlike some of his contemporaries, he insisted that his inspiration must be founded in fact and action. He feared the Transcendental tendency to get lost in the ether of vague mystical enthusiasm. Basic images of inspiration reflect this: sounds, dawn, dew, rain, fog, mist, and ascension. Prose, he eventually thought, is a better medium for inspiration, for, unlike verse, prose is more nearly based on fact and action. Williams has also offered an explication of "Thoreau's 'It is no dream of mine': A New Proposal" (*TSB*, No. 86, pp. 3-4).

Among the most impressive critical studies is Howard Mumford Jones's "Thoreau as Moralist," first printed in the *Atlantic* (CCX, Sept., 1962) and now included in *History and the Contemporary: Essays in Nineteenth-Century Literature* (Madison, Univ. of Wis. Press). Differing with those who portray Thoreau as a primitivist, an oddity, or a Transcendentalist, Jones sees him as a social being who viewed with horror the image of man confronting raw nature without the aid of civilized institutions. *Cape Cod* and *The Maine Woods* are

Jones's poignant examples. Thoreau is, in fact, a moralist in the tradition of Plutarch, Montaigne, Voltaire, and others—sophisticated, aph-
oristic, personal, discursive, insightful, satirical, skeptical, and even
cynical. Like the great moralists, his major themes are human nature,
conduct, and psychology. The moral side of Thoreau is further studied by Joel Porte, "Thoreau on Love: A Lexicon of Hate" (*UR*, XXX,
111-116). Porte defends Thoreau against critics who feel that he
failed to understand love and insists that Thoreau, like certain modern psychologists, saw that love and hate must exist together in every
love relationship.

Charles Calvin Kopp, "The Mysticism of Henry David Thoreau"
(*DA*, XXIV, 5409-10), disagrees with Jones's thesis. Exploring the
relationship between Thoreau and the great mystics of the Christian,
Hindu, and Buddhist traditions, Kopp maintains that Thoreau was a
mystic of the highest order and insists that no proper reading of his
works can ignore this fact. A similar thesis is proposed by Frank Mac-
Shane, "*Walden* and Yoga" (*NEQ*, XXXVII, 322-342), who argues
that Thoreau was, quite literally, a *yogi*. Suspecting that much of the
controversy over Thoreau's Orientalism has resulted from misunder-
standings, MacShane carefully distinguishes between different types
of Yoga and maintains that Thoreau consistently followed Karma-
yoga (the path of action) and Jnanayoga (the path of knowledge).
Yoga is not equivalent to the debasement of the self or the twisting
of the body into grotesque knots. Indeed nothing, to a *yogi*, is more
important than the self, and the essence of this philosophy is that
each man must follow his own path.

Walden continues to interest scholars more than Thoreau's other
works. Bruce King, "Thoreau's *Walden*" (*EA*, XVII, 262-268), sees
the work as a rendering of the various meanings of nature that
Thoreau experienced. This view of nature, King insists, is wholly unlike Emerson's, for Thoreau had a sensual feeling for physical nature
and a knowledge that human improvement must be found in a certain violence of the will, not in a mere hope for enlightenment. A
more specialized study is Raymond D. Gozzi's "The Meaning of the
'Complemental Verses' in *Walden*" (*ESQ*, No. 35, pp. 79-82). The
lines of Thomas Carew quoted at the end of "Economy" were taken
from *Coelum Britannicum*, a courtly masque intended to please
Charles I. In this context, the lines are a repudiation of the pretended
virtues of poverty. Gozzi suggests that Thoreau may have considered
these verses as "complemental" either as criticism or as clarification of

his own position. He may have selected Carew's lines because he felt that his own defense of poverty needed a counterstatement, or he may have wished, by warning his readers against concluding that he was advocating an apathetic and self-satisfied poverty, to make it clear that he was not interested in ordinary poverty or in the ordinary virtues of poverty. Another valuable note is Walter Harding, "A Source for a *Walden* Anecdote" (*TSB*, No. 87, p. 4), which identifies the source (*Yeoman's Gazette*, Nov. 22, 1828) for the swamp-bottom story in the final chapter of *Walden*.

Additional facts are offered in three brief articles. After examining all available evidence, Charles Boewe, "Thoreau's 1854 Lecture in Philadelphia" (*ELN*, II, 115-122), establishes that Thoreau lectured on "The Wild" at the Spring Garden Institute in Philadelphia on November 21, 1854. Ruth Robinson Wheeler, "Thoreau and Capital Punishment" (*TSB*, No. 86, p. 1) examines a petition upon which Thoreau's signature, along with those of four hundred other citizens of Concord, appears, protesting the execution of a Negro seaman convicted of murder. Albert E. Lownes, "Arthur Fifield and Thoreau's 'Civil Disobedience'" (*TSB*, No. 86, p. 3), explains that Thoreau's famous essay was largely ignored until Fifield issued it in a cheap edition in 1903. Lownes hazards the guess that this pamphlet introduced Thoreau to both Tolstoi and Gandhi.

iii. Transcendentalism and Minor Transcendentalists

As Walter Harding indicated in the last volume of this work, it is unfortunate that Transcendentalism, important as it is in the history of American thought and literature, has attracted so little scholarly interest.

Two studies of the movement in general appeared in 1964. Perry Miller's "New England's Transcendentalism: Native or Imported?" was originally given as a lecture at Rice University, 1962-1963; now it is printed in *Literary Views: Critical and Historical Essays*, ed. Carroll Camden (Chicago, Univ. of Chicago Press). Miller recognizes that the movement was both native and imported, but insists that it took a uniquely American direction as a revolt against commercialism, materialism, and business ethics. The Transcendentalists did not, like their European counterparts, express a desperate view of civilization or a disgust with reason, but rather turned to nature as an act of resistance. Robert Charles Albrecht, "The New England Tran-

scendentalists' Response to the Civil War" (*DA*, XXIV, 4687-88),
notes that although most members of the movement had liberal the-
ologies before and after the war, they reverted to the language and
ideas of orthodoxy during the war. Thus their attitude was distinctly
religious; this was a holy war in which the sins of the nation, slavery
and disunion, must be remitted in a sacrifice of blood. Many Transcendentalists saw the conflict between North and South as a specific
instance of God's war with Satan. Though many were pacifists before
the outbreak, most joined the cause enthusiastically.

Of the minor Transcendentalists, only Margaret Fuller was
adequately studied in 1964. Arthur W. Brown, *Margaret Fuller*
(TUSAS), has presented a first-rate critical biography. Miss Fuller
is portrayed as a "promise of great things never to be fully accomplished." Brown lays his narrative before the reader in clear, effective prose. Her family milieu, her education, her friendships and
literary associations with Emerson, Clarke, and others, her teaching
at Alcott's Temple School and at Fuller's Greene Street School in
Providence, her editing of the *Dial*, her journalistic work on Gree-
ley's *Tribune*, her love affairs with James Nathan and the Marchese
Ossoli, her experiences during the Roman revolution of 1849, her
tragic death—all these are discussed and evaluated with scholarly
precision and insight. With balanced judgment Brown sees Margaret
as a gifted, but not a flawless critic. Francis E. Kearns, "Margaret
Fuller and the Abolition Movement" (*JHI*, XXV, 120-127), suggests
several reasons why she failed to take an active role in the antislavery
movement: (1) like Emerson, she found radical reformers distasteful; (2) she disliked platforms and parties; (3) she died before the
movement entered its activist phase; (4) she was primarily interested
in feminine rights and feared that the Abolitionist cause would inter-
fere. Kearns maintains, however, that Margaret's opposition has been
exaggerated and that she was personally committed to the principle
of human freedom.

San Fernando Valley State College

2. Hawthorne

Hyatt H. Waggoner[1]

i. The Centenary

We expect centenaries to be solemn occasions, but they ought not to induce melancholy. The recent Hawthorne centenary, though, does just that, to those who still care for Hawthorne. There were of course many things printed that do not have that effect at all—new editions, some excellent criticism, some small but significant contributions to biographical knowledge, all of which are heartening. But of the three printed commemorative volumes, the largest and most ambitious, *Hawthorne Centenary Essays* (Columbus, Ohio State Univ. Press), does provoke melancholy reflections, in this reader at least.

The work is full of signs that in avant-garde academic circles Hawthorne is no longer in favor. Over and over the contributors cite James on Hawthorne to buttress their own doubts about him or to remind us of James's doubts about the validity of Hawthorne's way of writing. Last year's blast against Hawthorne by Martin Green ("The Hawthorne Myth: A Protest," *E&S*, XVI, 1963, 16-36) was, as I said at the time, a straw in the wind. No one in *Hawthorne Centenary Essays* appears to agree with all of Mr. Green's arguments for Hawthorne's unimportance, but something of Green's attitude is often discernible. Several of the contributors who do not stress Hawthorne's faults still appear to find their subject somewhat uncongenial, to be embarrassed, as James was, by their relationship with him. Others find him congenial enough, but in their own terms, not his. Several confess their inability to establish any relation with him at all. Robert Lowell first sounds this note, in a poem that is surely not one of his best, by admitting that he "cannot resilver the smudged plate," by concentrating on "the disturbed eyes," with their look "furtive, failed,

1. When teaching duties at Breadloaf prevented my getting to a large library to examine a number of hard-to-find items I had not yet read, George Monteiro came to the rescue by sending me brief summaries of the content of the following items (the numbers are those of the *PMLA* listing): 6068, 69, 83, 84, 85, 86, 98; 6102, 05, 07, 08.

dissatisfied," and by ending his poem with the lines "from meditation on the true/ and insignificant." *Insignificant* thus gets the major emphasis in a poem which is chiefly devoted to confessing that to Lowell, Hawthorne is remote and unreal, or "real" only in being "disturbed." (Just so, James had insisted on Hawthorne's remoteness, his archaic and provincial quality, preferring not to recognize his own great indebtedness to so old-fashioned an ancestor.)

Lionel Trilling, whose "Our Hawthorne" concludes the volume, reinforces the impression initiated by Lowell's poem and only partially countered by the pieces in between. Taking a New Critically oriented textbook, *The Hawthorne Question,* as his straw man to demolish, he makes it *almost* clear that "our" Hawthorne, the darling of lesser critics, is not *his* Hawthorne; but then, neither is James's Hawthorne *quite* satisfactory either; so that in the end, when he has finished balancing his ambivalences, there is in effect *no* Hawthorne. "Our judgment of Hawthorne," he concludes, "may have to be that he is not for today, or perhaps not even tomorrow. He is, in Nietzsche's phrase, one of the spirits of yesterday—and the day after tomorrow."

In between Lowell and Trilling, the two "name" contributors, one seldom feels the excitement of discovery. In the first essay Terence Martin, writing on "The Method of Hawthorne's Tales," summarizes the several aspects of Hawthorne's attempt to achieve imaginative freedom and to blend past and present. Charles Feidelson, Jr., in the next piece, analyzes the moral meanings of *The Scarlet Letter,* working chiefly from the characters outward to the largest meanings and relating the work to the Puritan mind. Marcus Cunliffe, after admitting that *The House of the Seven Gables* is a work "of high interest," places his final emphasis on its defects. "Why, then, all the bother about Evil and Lineage?" Like Faulkner, Hawthorne "sought meaning," Mr. Cunliffe believes, "in a tenuous heritage he could neither wholly admire nor wholly deplore. . . . To me, *The Seven Gables* is a flawed book, whose strengths are somewhat incidental to its plot."

Robert C. Elliott thinks even less well of *Blithedale.* Hawthorne's subject, he believes, "cried out for detailed, novelistic treatment." James was right when he complained of the absence of satire in the book. Elliott finds Hawthorne evading the responsibility of moral judgment: "Neither Blithedale nor the man who tells of Blithedale is finally placed in the moral (which is to say, the fictive) structure of the book." Mr. Elliott finds it "impossible not to wish" Hawthorne had written a different kind of book.

Harry Levin, writing of Hawthorne's use of setting in *The Marble Faun* ("Statues from Italy"), and Edward H. Davidson, writing on "The Unfinished Romances," complete the section devoted to individual works.

In the following section of the volume, Hyatt H. Waggoner, in "Art and Belief," surveys the difficulties encountered when one tries to define Hawthorne's religious beliefs, finds these difficulties related to Hawthorne's own resistance to doctrinal formulations of faith, and relates his conclusions on these matters to Hawthorne's practice as an artist. When Hawthorne had no doubts, he tended to write allegory, as in "Lady Eleanore's Mantle" or "The Great Carbuncle." By contrast, on matters more distinctly theological, where he wavered and resisted commitment, he wrote more ambiguously, more in the vein of "My Kinsman" and *The Scarlet Letter*. In the next piece, "Myth, Romance, and the Childhood of Man," Daniel Hoffman, disagreeing sharply with several earlier writers in the volume, finds that by "building verisimilitude upon a structure of myth" Hawthorne "could be faithful both to the truth of the human heart and to the laws of art."

Roy Harvey Pearce, in "Romance and the Study of History," approves of Hawthorne for understanding that "History is a means to moral understanding" and that "History is the past in the present about to become the future," but regrets that in *The House of the Seven Gables*, Hawthorne's most ambitious effort to show the past living in the present, "the romancer does not carry through his role as critical philosopher of history. Yet he could have. He should have." The ending is false, Pearce thinks, because Hawthorne lets Holgrave off without suffering. Larzer Ziff, in the following piece, "The Artist and Puritanism," is also concerned with history, this time not so much with Hawthorne's symbolic interpretation of it as with the effect of the past on Hawthorne: Hawthorne's imagination was deeply marked by the Puritans, as we have long understood.

R. W. B. Lewis, in "The Tactics of Sanctity: Hawthorne and James," starting from the known similarities between *The Bostonians* and *The Blithedale Romance*, goes on to explain James's debt, especially but not solely in *The Bostonians*, to other Hawthorne works, especially *The Scarlet Letter* and *The House of the Seven Gables*.

James carried on Hawthorne's idea of "the sanctity of the human heart." Mr. Lewis reads Hawthorne as an antinomian—correctly, I think. "In *The Bostonians*, James made his comment upon the American scene by casting a Hawthornian eye upon a non-Hawthornian world: by reassembling themes and motives and devices and language from Hawthorne and then . . . twisting and [often] reversing them." Very different from this sort of literary-historical investigation is Edwin Fussell's "Neutral Territory: Hawthorne on the Figurative Frontier," drawn, as the author says in a note, from his forthcoming book, to be called *Frontier*. "Hawthorne was at heart a Western writer. . . . Hawthorne apparently made a real Western tour, perhaps as far as Detroit. . . . By a judicious use of the Romantic imagination . . . he transformed New England into an available prototype of the West. . . . 'Young Goodman Brown' is about American advance to the West, penetration into the dark forest of the unmapped future, which is also the buried past. . . . [Hawthorne's] gradual and accelerating decline after *The Scarlet Letter* conceivably reflects the disappearance of the frontier. . . ." Conceivably.

The last section of the book, entitled "Discovery and Rediscovery," contains some of the most useful pieces. Edwin H. Cady's history of Hawthorne's nineteenth-century reputation in " 'The Wizard Hand': Hawthorne, 1864-1900" is a boon to any serious student of Hawthorne. The continuation of this historical survey to the present, first assigned to the late Randall Stewart and then, as his health worsened, completed by Seymour L. Gross, is less satisfactory than Cady's, but still useful. Perhaps "The Hawthorne Revival" is too close to us, and Mr. Gross himself too much involved with it, for the author to avoid the lacunae and occasional biases that mar an otherwise admirable piece. The essay that follows, by Roger Asselineau of France, "Hawthorne Abroad," contains some useful information but also some misinformation. Mr. Asselineau was excellent, recently, on Whitman, whom he greatly likes, but not so good on Hawthorne.

The final essays in the volume, before Trilling's concluding "Our Hawthorne," reflect special interests. Matthew J. Bruccoli writes on "Hawthorne as a Collector's Item," citing recent prices paid for Hawthorne editions and noting the chief Hawthorne collection; Fredson Bowers, textual editor of the Centenary Edition, discusses "Hawthorne's Text." The remaining essay, Trilling's, closes the volume as it began, with doubts, hesitations, reservations, and an admitted inability to bring Hawthorne into satisfactory focus.

Nineteenth Century Fiction and the *Essex Institute Historical Collections* also observed the centenary by putting out special Hawthorne issues, but I shall discuss their contents under the appropriate analytical headings that follow.

ii. Editions

The Blithedale Romance and Fanshawe (Columbus, Ohio State Univ. Press), the third volume of the Centenary Edition to appear, continues Ohio State's laudable project of getting Hawthorne's text in order. The general format is that of the earlier *Scarlet Letter*. What I said of that volume in last year's report on Hawthorne would apply, in part, to this new volume as well; I shall not repeat it. I have no doubt that the text here presented ("essentially an exact transcript of the Pierpont Morgan Library manuscript in its fully revised state except for . . . [certain] restorations. . . .") is as correct as it is humanly possible to make it, and that it will remain the standard text for the foreseeable future.

The general Introduction, by Roy Harvey Pearce, consists of a brief summary of facts about the composition of the book, Hawthorne's response to its sale, and his use of his experiences at Brook Farm—this last topic verging, I fear, on "criticism," which the editors have told us they mean to keep out of the individual volumes. The Textual Introduction by Fredson Bowers announces several important discoveries made in the editing. It seems that Hawthorne deleted three passages at a late stage, one a short clause dealing with liquor, one a sentence emphasizing Zenobia's effect on Coverdale as he pictured her in "Eve's earliest garment," and the last, most of a long paragraph attacking temperance reformers and suggesting that they concentrate their efforts on improving "the general atmosphere of life" instead of trying to take away the only "solace" many sufferers have in "this cold and barren world." The editors decided to restore these passages from the manuscript, despite the fact that Hawthorne's final intention called for their deletion, because they feel that "the causes behind" Hawthorne's intentions "are suspect"—that is, the deletions *may* have been prompted by suggestions made either by Mrs. Hawthorne or by E. P. Whipple, to whom Hawthorne sent the manuscript for a critical reading.

The first two restorations are critically unimportant. The first merely adds that Coverdale had in his room some "proof" beverage as well as his claret. The second is tautological, saying, after Coverdale had just told us that "something in her manner" had "brought up a picture" of Zenobia naked as Eve, that "I almost fancied myself actually beholding it." Obviously, he *was* "beholding it"; where *was* the picture, except in his imagination? One can imagine Hawthorne removing the sentence simply for stylistic reasons.

The third restoration, nearly a page long, presents a somewhat similar problem. Though it seems possible, as Mr. Bowers suggests, that someone, probably Sophia, may have urged this deletion on grounds of taste and expediency, as too forthright a defense of "the custom of tippling," it is also possible that Hawthorne himself saw it as a defect in his work. For one thing, there is almost no distance in the passage between Hawthorne and Coverdale. For another, a briefer passage four paragraphs farther along restates the gist of the longer one in a tone more appropriate to Coverdale. Beginning, "But the true purpose of their drinking," it ends with Coverdale mockingly speaking as a temperance reformer himself: when a "less baneful" way of producing cheer in "this weary world" has been found, then, and only then, "we temperance people may ring out our bells for victory!" Considering the repetition between the two passages and the fact that the second sounds more like Coverdale than the first, one wonders whether the novel is really strengthened by the restoration. Personally, I should have preferred to have it available in a note, but not restored as it is.

I have only one minor quibble with Mr. Bowers' Textual Intro-duction—which perhaps ought to be stated as a *query* rather than a difference of opinion. From my experience with the manuscript of *The House of the Seven Gables*, an experience by no means casual or brief, since it was acquired in the preparation of a new text of the novel about to be mentioned below, I am not persuaded that the pub-lishing partnership of Ticknor and Fields could be said to have had a "house style" at this period, at least not in the sense in which we would interpret that term today. Each printer seems to me to have modified Hawthorne's punctuation as he saw fit. Some were more faithful to Hawthorne's manuscript than others, and they had habits, or followed practices, that seem to have been their *own*, not the re-sult of a set of rules given them by Ticknor and Fields. The whole story about this matter is not yet known. Perhaps it will be when the lang-delayed Centenary Edition of *The House* appears. (It was planned as volume two of the set.) But I suspect that the final truth will have to make room for considerable variation in practice among printers as they did their separate stints. If so, can we properly speak of the imposition of a "house style"?

The other new Hawthorne text produced in 1964 was the present writer's edition of *The House of the Seven Gables* (Boston, Houghton Mifflin, Riverside Series). A textual note, tables of variants, and reproduced sample pages from the manuscript set forth the problems and the process by which decisions were reached that resulted in the new text. It is a "critical text" produced by a collation of the manuscript and the first edition.

The chief discovery having *critical* significance to emerge from the editing process is that late in the course of copying his first draft to make the "fair copy" now in the Houghton Library at Harvard, Hawthorne realized that Hepzibah had grown beyond his initial conception of her, so that his constant reference to her by the derisive epithet "the Old Maid," which he was copying from his earlier version, was a false note. She had ceased to be for him a comic abstraction, a grotesque specimen of decayed gentility, and had become a *person*, and moreover a person for whom he felt both sympathy and admiration. He went back and systematically crossed out "the Old Maid" and wrote above it such sympathetic or neutral ways of referring to her as "cousin Hepzibah," "poor Hepzibah," "the old gentlewoman," "her cousin," and so on. This discovery should be considered in relation to Marcus Cunliffe's statements, in the centenary essay referred to above, that "Hawthorne traced the ramifications of his germinal idea [in *The House*] with scrupulous care. We never feel that he has taken himself by surprise. . . . In Henry James's phrase, 'Hawthorne always knew perfectly what he was about.' "

iii. Biography and Miscellaneous

The most important single source of biographical information to come out in 1964 was the "Special Hawthorne Issue" (*EIHC*, C, 235-305). Except for one critical essay, to be mentioned later, the whole issue concerns biography. Norman Holmes Pearson leads off in "The Pynchons and Judge Pyncheon," bringing together all the evidence, previously scattered or unavailable, on the affair of the several Pyncheons (or "Pynchons") who protested to Hawthorne that he had traduced their family by using their name in *The House*. In "Dickens and Hawthorne," Ghulam Ali Chaudry writes that Hawthorne was aware of Dickens, and Dickens of Hawthorne; that Dickens decided he could not approve of Hawthorne's work; and that, conscious of their differences, they went their separate ways. Maurice Bassan, in "Julian Hawthorne Edits Aunt Ebe," further documents what, in a general way, we have known, that Julian suppressed all references to himself in the letters and documents he worked with, that he felt free to substitute words and phrases, and that he "edited" with a view to preserving the family reputation.

Edward C. Sampson, in "The 'W' in Hawthorne's Name," decides, after surveying the evidence, that Hawthorne added the "w" to preserve the original pronunciation at a time when American speech habits were changing rapidly and the flat "a" was becoming dominant. The change was apparently connected with Hawthorne's concern with family history: he did not wish to have his name pronounced differently from the way it *had* been pronounced, he believed, in England. In "A 'Good Thing' for Hawthorne," Norman Holmes Pearson draws on Elizabeth Peabody's letters about Hawthorne to document further some points we associate with Stewart's biography—that Hawthorne hoped to solve his financial problems by political appointment, that he used what influence he could to get an appointment, and so on. His wife's sister helped him get his early post at the Boston Custom House, though she feared the influence of such associations on "our Ariel," "one of Nature's ordained priests," who would, she hoped, vindicate Transcendental ideals by writing great things.

Apart from these articles in the *EIHC* Hawthorne issue and from those in the *Hawthorne Centenary Essays* volume already mentioned (Asselineau, Cady, Gross and Stewart, Bruccoli, Bowers), only a few items call for classification in this "Biographical and Miscellaneous" category. Douglas Grant, in "Sir Walter Scott and Nathaniel Hawthorne" (*ULR*, VIII, 1962, 35-41), argues that Scott's influence on Hawthorne was "first and longest." Grant believes that Hawthorne would have chosen to follow Scott, who had in *Waverley* "at a blow vindicated the history, types, manners, customs, speech, and scenery of his own country as eminently suitable for romance." Following Woodberry, Grant sees, specifically, the influence of Scott's *Peveril of the Peak* and *The Heart of Midlothian*, both "deeply concerned with the Puritan conscience," upon *The House of the Seven Gables* and *The Scarlet Letter.*

Arlin Turner, in "Nathaniel Hawthorne in American Studies"

(*CE*, XXVI, 133-139), believes that "our major American authors, even the most alienated of them, must have a major place in American Studies" and that "American Studies . . . benefits most from literary works if they are considered in their full [literary] distinctiveness and in their complementary relation to other documents and artifacts belonging to an era. Literary works reach beneath the surfaces and toward the essentials of a culture." Using Hawthorne, in some respects an "alienated" artist, to illustrate these ideas, he finds that "Hawthorne's major contribution to the study of American culture is distinctive to him . . . [growing] from his peculiar questioning of contemporary affairs, the play of his skeptical, speculative mind on events and attitudes around him."

Alfred Weber ("Hawthornes Briefe über *The Old Manse*," *Festschrift Hubner*, Berlin, Schmidt, pp. 234-238), quoting from Hawthorne letters in the Berg Collection, New York Public Library, traces Hawthorne's difficulty in writing a sketch to lead off the first volume of *Mosses from an Old Manse*. Hawthorne writes (July 1, 1845): "It was my purpose to construct a sort of frame-work, in this new story, for the series of stories already published, and to make the scene an idealization of our old parsonage, and of the river close at hand, with glimmerings of my actual life—yet so transmogrified—that the reader should not know what was reality and what fancy." Interpretation of the sketches, the author thinks, may well begin with a consideration of Hawthorne's autobiographical comments in these letters.

George Monteiro ("First Printing for a Hawthorne Letter," *AL*, XXXVI, 346) shows that of the "Three Unpublished Letters by Nathaniel Hawthorne to Epes Sargent" (ed. Edward C. Sampson, *AL*, XXXIV, 1962, 102-105), the one dated Oct. 21, 1842, had appeared earlier in an anonymous note, "Hawthorne upon Thoreau" (*Harper's Weekly*, XXIII, Nov. 1, 1879, 863).

Marshall A. Ledger, in "George Eliot and Nathaniel Hawthorne" (*N & Q*, XI, 225-226), has found an earlier comparison of Hawthorne and George Eliot than we have known about. The two were compared in a review of *Adam Bede* in the *Edinburgh Review* (CX, July, 1859, 114-25): "minute description" and "'passages of wit which charm us by their poetry, or make us smile by their humour.'" This item antedates "The Author of *Adam Bede* and Nathaniel Hawthorne" (*North British Review*, XXXIII, Aug., 1860, 183), hitherto considered the earliest such comparison.

William M. Gibson, in "Faulkner's *The Sound and the Fury*" (*Expl*, XXII, Item 33), writes that "Faulkner found the germ for the basic motivation of Quentin Compson . . . either in Dante's *Inferno* or in Hawthorne's *The Scarlet Letter*." He believes that there is a stronger case for the latter. "Quentin's perverse wish for love sanctioned by special divine punishment may thus have arisen in Faulkner's mind from his memory of Mistress Prynne's dreaming of love after death in the midst of 'endless retribution.'"

Matthew G. Bruccoli, in "Negative Evidence About 'The Celestial Rail-Road'" (*PBSA*, LVIII, 290-292), finds that collation of the two pirated imprints (1843) of "The Celestial Rail-Road" reveals that they are probably two printings of the same edition (there are no textual differences) and that there is "no internal evidence to indicate the order of issue."

Eleonora Taglioni Natale, in "Solitudine di Hawthorne" (*NA*, CCCXCI, 373-386), discusses the origins and effects of Hawthorne's inveterate solitude, isolation, and melancholy [*sic*]. One wonders whether the author has read any recent biographies.

iv. Criticism

Overlooked last year by the bibliographers of the *PMLA* bibliography and by the present writer was Franz H. Link's *Die Erzahlkunst Nathaniel Hawthornes* (Heidelberg, 1962). I find the title ("Narrative Art") a little misleading as the book is centered on Hawthorne's moral and theological meanings. An example of the type of contribution the book makes: In Hilda and Kenyon, in *The Marble Faun*, Hawthorne found a way of letting the "head" develop without destroying the "heart" and, therefore, without sin. Critical articles in the *Hawthorne Centenary Essays* have been discussed in the opening section of this survey. I turn now to the third commemorative work, the "Hawthorne Centenary Issue" of *NCF* (XIX, 103-211). These writers, unlike several of those in the *Hawthorne Centenary Essays*, generally speak from within and represent the fruits of "the Hawthorne revival" of the fifties; as a group, they have much that is fresh and interesting to offer.

Robert Emmet Long leads off with an article that interestingly parallels, in some ways, R. W. B. Lewis' contribution to the *Hawthorne Centenary Essays*. Hawthorne's influence on James, the author believes, as exemplified in *The Blithedale Romance* and *The Bos-*

tonians, goes much deeper than mere similarity of subject matter and characterization. Hawthorne and James share the same view of American life; both are moralists concerned with the illusive nature of the society of their day, which they see as a kind of "mock-life" in which the characters deceive themselves by playing parts and hiding their true identity behind public masks. James finds in Hawthorne's portrayal of the disguise of the self in *The Blithedale Romance* "an unconscious allegory of democracy," and he incorporates and interprets this in his own novel, *The Bostonians*.

In "Hawthorne's 'Bell': Historical Evolution through Symbol," Gretchen Graf Jordan writes that in "The Bell's Biography" Hawthorne uses the bell not only to symbolize the evolution of European history in the American wilderness, but also to express his philosophy of history, which has never been studied by critics of Hawthorne and which derives largely, according to the author, from the new interpreters of Biblical history, particularly the German scholars, Herder and Strauss, whose ideas on moral evolution were appearing in American journals during the 1820's and 1830's. This theory of history, the author believes, affects the tone and the symbolism of many of Hawthorne's greatest stories. Compare with this the article by Ely Stock on Hawthorne's use of history and the Bible, below; the two tend to confirm each other.

Peter L. Thorslev, Jr. ("Hawthorne's Determinism: An Analysis") discusses, from the vantage point of contemporary philosophic distinctions, determinism, free will, and fatalism in Hawthorne's work, concluding that in his major tales and novels Hawthorne was not a fatalist but a determinist. ("Determinism," as here defined, allows for human decision and its results, though the decision itself may have been determined; "fatalism" looks to events that fall outside the realm of human decision.) Moments of decision are de-emphasized in Hawthorne's works. Natural psychological laws and causal sequences move his stories, but he also offers his readers alternative, fatalistic interpretations. The author calls this Hawthorne's "ambiguous supernaturalism."

"Hawthorne and the Fiction of Sensibility," by Otis B. Wheeler, argues that it is not true, as has been alleged, that Hawthorne outgrew, in his mature work, the conventions of the fiction of sensibility. Rather, conventions (such as the outward, physical expression of emotion) that were used awkwardly and derivatively in the early work, came to be used, later, in new contexts that gave them validity and life. In the greatest works we are hardly aware of them because they have been revitalized and transmuted.

In "Journey into Moral Darkness: 'My Kinsman, Major Molineux' as Allegory," Arthur T. Broes presents evidence to show that in this tale Hawthorne borrowed heavily from Dante, Spenser, and Bunyan for allegorical patterns and episodes. The author feels that when the tale is read in the light of its "sources," it presents very little suggestion of the possibilities of spiritual regeneration found in Hawthorne's later works. (Earlier writers on this story have treated it as a myth, not allegory, and have found evidence of psychological, moral, or spiritual growth in it.)

In another new view of a much discussed story, Oliver Evans ("Allegory and Incest in 'Rappaccini's Daughter'") argues that since Eve was made, in the Genesis story, from Adam's rib, she is at once his offspring and his wife. This incestuous motif he finds repeated in the tale in the unnatural relation of Rappaccini with his daughter, in the "brother-sister" relation between Giovanni and Beatrice, in the "sisterly" relation between Beatrice and the plant, and in what he finds to be an atmosphere of unnatural forbidden sexuality pervading the garden dedicated to Rappaccini's "commixture" of plants. (Compare the second article by Crews, below, which also finds sexuality at the center of the tale.) Hawthorne uses the garden story, the author believes, to dramatize the chief nineteenth-century dilemma, the choice between scientific materialism and moral idealism.

In the two final articles in the issue, Bruce Ingraham Granger ("Arthur Dimmesdale as Tragic Hero") calls Dimmesdale "Every-Christian," the true center of the novel, and finds Hester only heroically pathetic; Leo B. Levy ("The Mermaid and the Mirror: Hawthorne's 'The Village Uncle'") finds evidence in the sketch to refute the commonly held idea that in Hawthorne's work creativity leads to alienation. The life of the imagination and the life rooted in the family, in this sketch, the author believes, combine to establish a single order of values.

Turning now to critical articles scattered through other journals, I begin with a piece by Frederick C. Crews that appears to be a part of a systematic effort on his part to reinterpret Hawthorne's work in purely humanistic and naturalistic terms and to show that the moral-religious readings of recent critics are invalid, are read *into* Haw-

thorne, not out of him. In "The Logic of Compulsion in 'Roger Malvin's Burial' " (*PMLA*, LXXIX, 457-465), the author objects to critics
who "by analyzing only those symbols that bear Biblical or sacramen-
tal glossing, succeed in blending Hawthorne into a background of
Christian moralism." The moral meaning, Mr. Crews believes, is a
secondary element "in nearly all of Hawthorne's tales"; "Roger Malvin's Burial" is typical in resting on "an amoral, problematic . . . psychological theory." The ending of the story is "merely psychological
. . . no strictly religious interpretation seems possible . . . . [We should
see in it] an ironic spirit."

These conclusions are based on an analysis of Reuben's motivation. But Reuben did not write the tale. As Mr. Crews generously
admits, the present writer, and others, have "partly anticipated" the
discovery that, at least after his initial act of leaving Roger Malvin,
Reuben moves as one compelled. The question then becomes whether
the story should be read in terms of Reuben's motivation alone. Mr.
Crews, in his zeal to destroy "pious" readings, is in effect proposing
that we ignore the Biblical parallels and allusions Hawthorne scatters
so profusely through his tale. But why should *any* aspect of the tale
be ignored? That "psychological" and "moral" perspectives are not
mutually exclusive alternatives is one of the lessons to be learned
from the work of Eric Erikson and other contemporary psychiatrists
and psychoanalysts. "Psychological laws," I suggest, do not annul
moral responsibilities or mythic patterns of meaning.

The full extent to which Hawthorne *did* draw upon the Bible in
creating "Roger Malvin's Burial" had not been known until Ely Stock
published his "History and the Bible in Hawthorne's 'Roger Malvin's
Burial' " in the Hawthorne issue of the *EIHC*, in the same month
with Mr. Crews's piece. With a wealth of documentation drawn from
both the Bible and other treatments of the historic incident on which
Hawthorne based his tale, Mr. Stock in effect writes an answer to the
reading just discussed. He concludes, in part, that "Paradoxically,
Reuben Bourne, despite his conscious wishes, reenacted by the end
of the tale the movements of the Biblical tradition which [the Biblical Reuben] had first exemplified. By shooting his son, the symbolic
extension of himself, he affirmed the importance of self-sacrifice as
a means of finding 'peace.' Like Roger Malvin he was able, finally,
to find solace in prayer . . . redemption came for him by means of
other than his conscious self, from what a psychologist might call
the workings of the unconscious mind, but what Hawthorne would

have called 'Providence.' " In this writer's view, Ely Stock, in this, and in his later article on the Biblical sources of "Ethan Brand" (*AL*, XXVII, 1965, 115-134), and elsewhere, is producing some of the most useful Hawthorne criticism of our time. One easily tires of re-interpretations wholly dependent on "point of view"; criticism based on sound scholarship, in which the critic subordinates his own point of view to that of his subject, is the kind that lasts.

To return to Mr. Crews's effort to reinterpret Hawthorne in wholly naturalistic terms, in "Giovanni's Garden" (*AQ*, XVI, 402-418), he concludes that "it should be clear that 'Rappaccini's Daugh-ter' neither affirms nor denies Christianity, for except in a few moralizing lines that have a hollow ring, we are never brought out-side Giovanni's subjective plight. . . . Here as elsewhere in Haw-thorne, nothing whatever is asserted about the structure of the universe." For both Rappaccini and Giovanni, the garden represents "sexuality as seen through morbid inquisitiveness."

In an article that should be compared with Harry Levin's in the *Hawthorne Centenary Essays*, Gary J. Scrimgeour treats Haw-thorne's use of art and the Italian scene in *The Marble Faun* ("*The Marble Faun*: Hawthorne's Faery Land," *AL*, XXXVI, 271-287). Hawthorne found in Italy the "Faery Land" "he had tried to create in the American romances. . . . Many of the improbabilities of the plot . . . can be explained by referring them to the very real social and political conditions of mid-nineteenth century Italy. . . . *The Marble Faun* is as new to the American fiction of 1860 as *The Scarlet Letter* was to that of 1850 . . . only through immersion in [the Ital-ianate] details [can we] . . . enter into the world of *The Marble Faun* and so approach the problems of theme, characterization, and mean-ing."

The Marble Faun has attracted much critical attention recently. In "The Problem of Theme in *The Marble Faun*" (*NCF*, XVIII, 393-399), Sidney P. Moss concludes that "the doctrine of the fortunate fall is deliberately left unresolved. . . . In the romance Hawthorne remained within his usual orbit, refusing to resolve complex matters simply." Gene A. Barnett, in "Hawthorne's Italian Towers" (*SIR*, III, 252-256), finds the tower symbol, especially that of Monte Beni Castle, less ambiguous and far more consistent than have earlier critics. A close reading of Chapters XXIV, XXVIII, XXIX reveals that Donatello has *not* lived in the tower since childhood, but only *since* the death of the monk in Rome. "The tower symbolizes Dona-

tello's attempt to reach through his guilt to God; by the same token
it symbolizes an attempt to escape the world and its responsibilities,
both of which had assumed the realities of sin." Robert L. Gale, in
"The Marble Faun and the Sacred Fount: A Resemblance" (*SA*, VIII,
1962, 21-33), sees in the novel another foreshadowing of a work of
James. (These keep on piling up, but they have not all been found
yet, by any means.) Mr. Gale writes: "The dramatic circumstances
surrounding the Guido painting in *The Marble Faun* [chap. xv] and
the pastel portrait [chap. iv] in *The Sacred Fount* are similar. . . .
Each picture polarizes an opposition: the one, that of an archangel
and the devil, hence good and evil; the other, that of a livid face and
an elaborate mask, hence perhaps life and death, or appearance and
reality. . . . Both novelists, then, use challenging pictures, hung in
deceptive light, to elucidate character and implement plot, while the
postures within the frames are thematically symbolic."

Finally, some miscellaneous pieces of criticism: William G. Carleton, in "Hawthorne Discovers the English" (*YR*, LIII, 395-414),
writes in appreciation of *Our Old Home* and *English Notebooks* that
they are "less analytical, but superior in imagination, description, and
. . . nuances" to Taine's *Notes on England* in the light they throw on
English life and character. Richard C. Carpenter (*UR*, XXX, 1963,
65-71) argues that the happy ending of *The House* is well prepared
for by the horticultural imagery, which suggests "a typically American view of life—that out of old evil new good can grow, provided
that the soil has been suitably prepared." H. Alan Wycherley, in
"Hawthorne's 'The Minister's Black Veil'" (*Expl*, XXIII, Item 11),
writes that the shuddering of the young girl's corpse, in "The Minister's Black Veil," when the veil fell forward and revealed the minister's features, should be interpreted in connection with "the ancient
belief that a dead person will give some sign when in the presence of
the one who caused his death." Robert L. Gale (*SA*, IX, 1963, 83-87)
believes that there are hints throughout the story that Baglioni "deliberately murdered Rappaccini's daughter."

Leo B. Levy ("Hawthorne's 'Middle Ground,'" *SSF*, II, 56-60)
believes that "The Canterbury Pilgrims" can be interpreted "in
thematic terms, without recourse to a concept of structure or to . . .
symbolism. . . ." In "Hawthorne's 'The Canal Boat': An Experiment
in Landscape" (*AQ*, XVI, 211-215), the same writer interprets "The
Canal Boat" as contrasting nature and civilization and implying that
there may be decay in both. William L. Vance ("The Comic Ele-

ment in Hawthorne's Sketches," *SIR*, III, 144-160) finds Hawthorne's sketches rich in humor and irony, with an occasional touch of gentle satire; they lack the tragicomic element so important in the greater tales and novels. Alfred S. Reid ("Hawthorne's Ghost-Soul and the Harmonized Life," *FuS*, XII, i, 1-10) believes that Hawthorne's use of ghost lore reveals "his idealistic or other-worldly orientation, his Platonic-Christian dualism," and that the *way* he treats it reveals his "belief in the harmonized life [of body and soul], the . . . balanced life. . . ." David H. Karrfalt, writing on "Anima in Hawthorne and Haggard" (*AN&Q*, II, 152-153), finds parallels in character, setting, and motif between "Rappaccini's Daughter" and H. Rider Haggard's *She*; they suggest "a common origin in the archetypal symbols that are bound into the collective subconscious."

This was the Hawthorne year. He would no doubt have been gratified by the quantity of the writing on him. About the quality, he would almost certainly have entertained mixed feelings. As usual, he would have been justified in doing so.

Brown University

3. Melville

Willard Thorp

i. Editions and Book-Length Studies

In Charles Feidelson, Jr.'s edition of *Moby-Dick* (Indianapolis, Bobbs-Merrill) we have at last an annotated *Moby-Dick* suited for close study as well as general reading. More than any other American work this novel needs full annotation if the reader is to understand Melville's creative use of quotations and allusions. My edition has been out of print for some time (and out of date for as long). The Mansfield-Vincent Hendricks House edition is possibly too heavily annotated for general use. Mr. Feidelson has naturally taken what information he needed from this edition, but he has gone beyond it in some particulars. He has made use of the glosses which have appeared since 1952, and he suggests in some of the notes possible interpretations of difficult passages. The text has been prepared with care. The three maps and five drawings are clear and accurate. The brief Introduction (pp. ix-xxvi) is largely factual. Mr. Feidelson invites the reader to interpret *Moby-Dick* as he wishes, but gives him this excellent piece of advice. "Certainly no interpretation is adequate that fails to take into account the multiplicity of possible meanings in . . . *Moby-Dick* as a whole. Like the story it tells, our reading of this book is a kind of quest. The point at which we emerge, the conclusion we reach, is largely determined by the point at which we enter, the assumption from which we start."

Hennig Cohen's edition of *The Confidence-Man* (New York, Holt, Rinehart and Winston) is not annotated. (The "Rinehart Editions" do not supply notes.) This is a pity, because *The Confidence-Man* is Melville's most riddling book and, as Miss Elizabeth Foster's 1954 edition showed, notes can help us to unlock the riddles. Mr. Cohen's Introduction wastes no time in seeking esoteric interpretations of the novel. He is concerned rather with its adroit, if sometimes baffling, structure, the range of character-delineation, the ways in which the animal imagery defines character, the use of foreshadowing, the cyclical form, and the geographical identifications in "the pattern of moral imbalance." (All sections of the country are represented.)

A principal merit of Mr. Cohen's *Selected Poems of Herman Melville* is the fullness of the selections offered. (The hardcover edition was issued by Southern Illinois University Press. The paperback edition is in the Doubleday Anchor Books series. The editions are identical in contents and pagination.) We remember how timidly thin earlier selections from the poems were (Plomer in 1943, Matthiessen in 1944). Have we not asked too much of Melville as a poet and forgiven him nothing, while we forgive Whitman his lapses in taste and Emily Dickinson her coynesses? Mr. Cohen risks printing flawed lines and stanzas in order to present poems which are effective as a whole. He has also made a bold stroke in printing excerpts from *Clarel* that stand up as complete in themselves when taken out of context. His annotations give the thread of the story and place the episodes sufficiently well.

I failed to mention in *ALS, 1963*, the edited text of a work which, though not by Melville, is of the utmost interest to Melville scholars. This is the *Narrative of the Most Extraordinary and Distressing Shipwreck of the Whaleship Essex* by Owen Chase (1821). The present edition was prepared by B. R. McElderry, Jr., and published as a paperback in 1963 by Corinth Books (The American Experience Series). The importance of Chase's *Narrative* as a source for the climax of *Moby-Dick* has been known, of course, but few scholars can have seen the original work since it is a great rarity. Fortunately Mr. McElderry had access to the Harvard copy, procured for Melville by his father-in-law in April, 1851, when the writing of *Moby-Dick* was well along. It contains his valuable notes on "General Evidences," "What I know of Owen Chace [*sic*] &c," reproduced here in facsimile and in transcription. Mr. McElderry has further enriched his edition by printing two supplementary narratives, Thomas Chapple's *An Account of the Loss of the Essex* and Captain Pollard's "Narrative," contained in Tyerman and Bennet's *Journal of Voyages and Travels* (1832).

Only one full-length study of Melville's work was issued in 1964, John Bernstein's *Pacificism and Rebellion in the Writings of Herman Melville*. This volume is the first in the series, Studies in American Literature, published by Mouton & Co. of The Hague. It was Mr. Bernstein's aim "to show that pacificism or rebellion appear as themes in virtually all of the author's writings, that they emerge as polarities in Melville's major works, and that an understanding of the issues involved in the conflict between these two themes is essential to an understanding of Melville as a thinker and as an artist. Often, however, pacifism and rebellion, far from being antithetical, are complementary." I wish Mr. Bernstein had defined his terms more completely and carefully. He runs into difficulties because the terms are so open-ended. Any variety of revolt for whatever cause is taken account of. In his search for rebels Mr. Bernstein sometimes stretches a point. Though he admits that the text will not support his conclusions, he agrees with D. H. Lawrence that Tommo quits the Happy Valley of the Typees in order to "fight against the forces of injustice." Since the definition of pacifism is also wide open, the pacifists are a very miscellaneous company: Babbalanja, Starbuck, the Reverend Mr. Falsgrave, Bartleby, Nehemiah, and Derwent. Mr. Bernstein's study suffers from a fallacy by which thesis writers are too often deluded. Once a leading idea in an author's work has been isolated and described, it must be hunted down in everything the author wrote. One could wish Mr. Bernstein had not felt obliged to comment on *Redburn* and *The Confidence-Man*, for example, about which he has little of importance to say in line with his thesis, and had studied at greater length the conflict between Ahab and Starbuck and the conflict in Melville's mind and heart over the Civil War. In the sections dealing with these matters his thesis works very well.

ii. Articles Published in 1964

a. **Early novels.** In 1964 *Moby-Dick*, the tales, and *Billy Budd* were in the ascendant as subjects for study. I have come on only two articles which are concerned with the early novels. Richard M. Fletcher's "Melville's Use of Marquesan" (*AS*, XXXIX, 135-138) is highly entertaining, but it also reveals the Melville we know as an inventive and often sly and cryptic manipulator of language. He remembered enough Marquesan to make some use of it in *Typee* and considerably more in *Omoo*. (There is only one Marquesan word in *Mardi*.) Mr. Fletcher finds several categories of use. Melville often reproduces the language with reasonable accuracy and uses it "straight." He also inserts words of his own devising, endowing them with alternate meanings for the fun of it. There are borderline cases which can be taken comically or seriously. We cannot be sure whether Melville is being accurate or is fooling us. Sometimes he gets deliber-

ately vulgar effects by playing on Marquesan words. Of curious interest, at least, is George Perkins' "Death by Spontaneous Combustion
in Marryat, Melville, Dickens, Zola, and Others" (*Dickensian*, LX,
57-63). Here is all one needs to know about this pseudoscientific belief as it was treated by these novelists. Mr. Perkins states that Melville possibly got his idea for the death of the sailor Miguel in
Redburn from John Mason Good's *The Book of Nature* (New York,
1831). He probably knew the book, for he puts it in the man-of-war's
library in *White-Jacket*.

b. Moby-Dick. In "Ahab and Bartleby: Energy and Indolence"
(*SSF*, I, 291-294), Jack B. Moore attempts to relate the themes of
the two works to a two-stanza poem published in *Timoleon*, "Fragments of a Lost Gnostic Poem of the Twelfth Century." Baffled by
the meaning of the poem, Mr. Moore does not carry his argument
very far. In view of the fact that Melville was much interested in
Gnosticism, one could wish he had gone farther. There is something
here worth exploration.

The thesis of Robert A. Watts' "The 'Seaward Peep': Ahab's Trans-
gression" (*UR*, XXXI, 133-138) is that the ocean in *Moby-Dick* represents a concept which is known by many names. One may call it
the Platonic Absolute, or ultimate reality, or the Oversoul. Mr. Watts
prefers to equate it with the Oversoul because this was "a concept
contemporary to Melville and important in the American Romantic
tradition." All goes well until Mr. Watts begins to explore the ocean-
symbols in detail. By the time he is saying that the sea "lures man
but always threatens to destroy him" the Emersonian Oversoul has
been left far behind. We are on solid ground again in Carl F.
Strauch's "The Problem of Time and the Romantic Mode in Hawthorne, Melville and Emerson" (*ESQ*, No. 35, pp. 50-60), one of the
best of the articles contributed to *ESQ*'s "Critical Symposium on
American Romanticism." European and American Romantics con-
fronted the dual problem of time and personality, a problem that
may also be stated as art *vs.* history. In *Moby-Dick* the problem of
time and personality becomes a cosmic battle. "The whale is . . . the
incarnation of time and the cetology chapters give us a comprehensive unfolding of the time-beast in man's experience." The weight
of epochs crushes Ahab. But Melville also provides a sense of the
simultaneity of epochs through his use of the doctrine of metem-
psychosis, explicitly referred to in Chapter XCVIII. "Ishmael does

hover over Descartesian vortices, but the plain narrative fact is that the vortex shoots him up, with Queequeg's coffin, for survival. Life refuses to die, and belief is woven into the very fabric of life." Taking as his text the "Mat-Maker" chapter in *Moby-Dick*, Luther S. Mansfield, in "Some Patterns from Melville's 'Loom of Time'" (*Essays on Determinism in American Literature*, ed. Sydney J. Krause, Kent State Univ. Press, pp. 19-35), discusses the many passages in Melville's fiction in which he meditates on the limitations on man's freedom. This well-reasoned article is difficult to summarize, but one sentence states the general theme. "As a man of feeling and an artist, he never accepted the demands for consistency a general formulation would entail, but mused on fate and free will in the more concrete terms of characters and situations."

André Le Vot's "Shakespeare et Melville: le Thème Impérial dans *Moby Dick*" (*EA*, XVII, 549-563) brings new insights to an old subject. Most accounts of Shakespeare's influence have studied allusions and verbal echoes. M. Le Vot moves out on a new path. Melville professed to delight in Shakespeare as a thinker and poet rather than as a dramatist. He was particularly struck by "the imperial theme" as Shakespeare developed it in *Macbeth*. In *Moby-Dick* this becomes the theme "des responsabilités humaines d'Achab consideré, non plus comme un rebelle, un révolté luciférien, mais dans sa fonction de meneur d'hommes, dans sa fonction de chef ou de roi." What might have been a drama of revolt (allusions to Prometheus, Job, and Faust echo in the novel) is transformed into another kind of action. "Ici, le thème faustien de la révolte métaphysique est relayé par le thème impérial des responsabilités historiques." M. Le Vot comments at length on an interesting paradox. Having spoken lightly of Shakespeare as a dramatist, Melville was forced to use dramatic techniques in creating his novel, particularly in arranging the grandly staged crowd scenes and in revealing character through stance and gesture. M. Le Vot believes that Melville was indebted to *The Scarlet Letter* for the symmetrical placing of the crowd scenes (chaps. xxxvi-xl, xcix-cxxii). The parallels are indeed striking. Finally, M. Le Vot takes issue with Charles Olson on the question of the paramount influence of *Lear* on *Moby-Dick*. "[Lear] ne cherche pas à transformer l'histoire, il la subit. Enfin, le nihilisme d'Achab, meme lorsqu'il se tempère de pieté, rend impossible la catharsis que sauve Lear."

There is little that is new in Ramiro Páez's "*Moby Dick*, la historia de la persecución de la bellena blanca" (*Atenea*, CLII, 1963, No. 402, pp. 149-155), but it is a good all-purpose article and it has a special significance because it appeared in a journal published under the auspices of the Universitad de Concepción in Chile.

This is a convenient place to review the section in Leo Marx's *The Machine in the Garden, Technology and the Pastoral Ideal in America* (New York, Oxford Univ. Press) in which he discusses *Moby-Dick* (pp. 277-319). This is an impressive book, one of the best which the American studies movement has produced. Mr. Marx shows how pervasive the theme of the conflict between the pastoral ideal and our developing technology has been in American literature, right up to the present time. Much as I admire the book as a whole, I am obliged to say that the pages on *Moby-Dick* strain too hard. The author makes much of too little. Can he rightly say in a climactic statement, "[Ahab] is the perverted, monomaniac incarnation of the Age of Machinery"?

c. Pierre. Floyd C. Watkins' "Melville's Plotinus Plinlimmon and Pierre" (*Reality and Myth*, Nashville, pp. 39-51) observes that "the best and most complex novels by Herman Melville present character relationships of stark contrast between reasonable compromisers and unreasonable absolutists. Those who tolerate the world and its laws and travails are closely associated with those who defy not only this world and its laws but also whatever gods may have made it." Thus in *Pierre* Plinlimmon defines Pierre's tragic error and provides a commentary on almost every fact of Pierre's life. I question Mr. Watkins' conclusion—that "the emotional and skeptical Melville takes the side of the defiant rebel while philosophically Melville . . . seems to adjust himself to the world and its horological mortality."

d. Tales. In "Melville's Chimney Chivy" (*ESQ*, No. 35, pp. 63-65), William Bysshe Stein uses the religious imagery in "I and My Chimney" to make a case for reading this tale as a debate on religious faith. What is Scribe, the master-mason, up to in his plans to rebuild the chimney? Are we to see this as "the disease of unfaith which is rotting out the foundations of Christian unity"? In any event the narrator "fights valiantly for the ease and comfort of a faith which does not tax his devotion too strongly." Hershel Parker, in "Melville's Salesman Story" (*SSF*, I, 154-158), makes the interesting conjecture that "The Lightning-Rod Man" would have been read at the time of

its publication as a story in a well-known genre—the humorous salesman story in which the type-figure is a Yankee pedlar. Melville's
salesman is not a Satanic figure but a character out of the folklore of
the time. As the title indicates, Buford Jones extends earlier discussions of literary influence in his "Spenser and Shakespeare in *The
Encantadas*, Sketch VI" (*ESQ*, No. 35, pp. 68-73). In "Melville's Buccaneers and Crébillon's Sofa" (*ELN*, II, 122-126), Mr. Jones ingeniously brings together Colnett (*A Voyage to the South Atlantic*),
the poet Gray, and Crébillon to explicate the stone-sofa passage in
"Barrington Isle and the Buccaneers." John Gardner, in "*Bartleby*:
Art and Social Commitment" (*PQ*, XLIII, 87-98), sees *Bartleby* as
a study in the uses of the creative imagination. Bartleby himself is the
artist manqué. His vision is not of life but of death, whereas the
story the lawyer-narrator tells is a highly organized literary work.
Mr. Gardner comes up with some wild conjectures when he tries to
see Bartleby as Christ-like, the lawyer as Jehovah-like, Turkey as
Michael, Nippers as Lucifer, and Ginger Nut as Raphael—"perhaps."

Valeria Verucci's " 'The Bell-Tower' di Herman Melville" (*SA*, IX,
1963, 89-120) is a definitive study. One cannot imagine that anything
further need be said about this exciting story, so crucial for an understanding of Melville's thinking in the 1850's. There is space to mention only a few of the insights which the article affords: the symbolic
significance of towers (also mountain-tops "and all the other grand
and lofty things") in Melville's writing; the tale seen as Melville's
commentary on the civilization of his time, two particulars being the
worship of the machine and the increasing isolation of the artist; the
import of Belladonna's sarcastic and disparaging language; the influence of Hawthorne on the theme of the story and the significant
differences between the ways the two authors viewed the relation of
the artist to nature. The most revelatory pages in this study deal with
the use Melville made of Pierre Bayle's observations on the "Golem,"
Albertus Magnus, and Cornelius Agrippa. Possibly these sentences
best state the central argument of this study. "Come a Melville non
si era prospettata soluzione al drammatico contrasto fra la libera
volontá e l'obbedienza a Dio, così non gli si presenta alcuna soluzione
al conflitto fra l'uomo e la macchina, alcuna conciliazione fra i due
termini. La vita dell'uno è la morte dell'altro."

e. Billy Budd.   Leonard Nathanson makes a nice point in "Melville's
Billy Budd, Chapter I" (*Expl*, XXII, Item 75). Billy's thrashing of

Red Whiskers prefigures his killing of Claggart. Both are Satanic figures, though Red Whiskers is in the tradition of the popular folk devil or the Vice. Neal F. Doubleday, in "Jack Easy and Billy Budd" (*ELN*, II, 39-42), writes convincingly of the possible influence of Marryat's *Mr. Midshipman Easy* on *Billy Budd*. Jack Easy has been brought up to believe in the principle of equality. He and his father speak frequently of the "rights of man" and Jack's firm belief in this idea gets him into trouble on his ship, where he is known as "Equality Jack." Lee T. Lemon's "*Billy Budd*: The Plot against the Story" (*SSF*, II, 32-43) makes good use of the distinction between story and plot originated by the Russian Formalist critic, Victor Shlovskij. The *Billy Budd* story is simple and straightforward. The complications are in the plot, which embodies "the conflict in Melville's own mind between the claims of natural moral law and the social law." The increasing attention he gave to Vere as the story grew shows that Melville was forced "to the realization that man, because he must live in the social world, must abide by its laws." Robert Rogers' "The 'Ineludible Gripe' of Billy Budd" (*L&P*, XIV, 9-22) is a Freudian reading, based on the belief that each of the three times Billy stammers he betrays "repressed hostility toward the King and, by extension, toward God and other parental figures."

John C. Sherwood advances the interesting hypothesis that Captain Vere may be the deliberate portrait of a known historical figure whom Melville admired—Cuthbert, Baron Collingwood ("Vere as Collingwood: A Key to *Billy Budd*," *AL*, XXXV, 476-484). Collingwood, vice-admiral and second in command at Trafalgar, was well known in the nineteenth century. Among his admirers were several literary men—Emerson, Thackeray, De Vigny, W. Clark Russell, and Melville himself. Collingwood is praised in *White-Jacket*. Nelson and he are mentioned in *Billy Budd* as officers who were essentially humane. Enough is known about Collingwood as a person so that Mr. Sherwood can list his outstanding traits. There are eight of them which correspond to traits with which Melville endows Vere. There are other points in Mr. Sherwood's argument for the Collingwood-Vere parallel, but they add up to conjecture only. There is no explicit linking of the two names.

f. **Miscellaneous.** Did Melville lecture in Philadelphia, San Francisco, and St. Louis, as J. E. A. Smith says in his biographical sketch? It has now been established that he did not make appearances in

Philadelphia or San Francisco. Francis V. Lloyd's "A Further Note
on Herman Melville, Lecturer" (*MHSB*, XX, 310-312) establishes the
fact that an invitation to lecture was extended by the Mercantile
Library Association of St. Louis. It is not known whether Melville
sent a reply. The title of Victor H. Strandberg's article, "God and the
Critics of Melville" (*TSLL*, VI, 322-333), is misleading. Mr. Strandberg is concerned with one critic and one book, Lawrance Thompson's *Melville's Quarrel with God*. He impugns several of Mr.
Thompson's arguments, but he is most severe in his condemnation of
the chapter on *Billy Budd*. "If, as Mr. Thompson asserts, Melville had
to entrust the narration of his story to a stupid, insensitive speaker so
as to hide his (Melville's) heretical feelings . . . then this was an
extraordinary timid, pussy-footing sort of writer indeed in an age
when everybody from Thomas Huxley to Mark Twain was frankly
trampling down the old certitudes." Mr. Strandberg concludes: "Tre-
mendous possibilities open up if we apply this assumption [of Melville's secretive method] to a host of other writers, from the prophet
Isaiah to Allen Ginsberg." In "Herman Melville and the Craft of
Fiction" (*MLQ*, XXV, 181-186), Herbert S. Donow asserts that Melville was a novelist "only in the vaguest sense of that word." His
knowledge of the craft of fiction "was no match for his vision of metaphysical immensity." As his title shows, Mr. Donow is thinking of
fiction-writing in Jamesian terms only. Robert André's "Melville et
Shakespeare" (*Critique*, XX, 705-715) reads like an essay that might
have been written forty years ago. He says little about Shakespeare's
influence on Melville, but conjectures at length about Melville's relations with his parents. Under the influence of Shakespeare, it seems,
Melville was at last able, in writing *Moby-Dick*, to count "his birth
days as the Hebrews did: a son's years gathered not from the son's
birth but from the father's death." (M. André is quoting from Charles
Olson.) As for his mother, apparently M. André believes that Melville
never escaped from her baneful influence: "C'est elle sans doute qui
incarnait l'impitoyable austerité calviniste, c'est d'elle qu'il tient son
moralisme, son horreur du péché." There is more in the same vein.

Agnes Dicken Cannon's "Melville's Use of Sea Ballads and Songs"
(*WF*, XXIII, 1-16) is one of the best articles of 1964. It provides us
with a new view of Melville as a man who loved ballads, knew many
of them, sang them (we have Toby Greene's testimony to this), and
made subtle use of them in his prose and verse. Mrs. Cannon finds

that Melville used ballads in three ways: to heighten the realism of his descriptions of life at sea, to indicate the emotional state of a character, and to supply the base for ballads of his own. Examples of the third use are found in the poems "Tom Deadlight" and "Billy in the Darbies." Some of Melville's allusions to ballads will be lost on present-day readers. Melville's first readers knew the ballads which he knew.

g. Dissertations. So far as I can determine, two dissertations on Melville were completed in 1964, Marjorie J. Elder's "Transcendental Symbolists: Hawthorne and Melville" (Chicago) and Morris Starr's "Melville's Use of the Visual Arts" (Northwestern). The second of these has been recorded in *DA* (XXV, 2988). Mr. Starr finds that though Melville's aesthetic theory was never formulated into one coherent system, three chief views may be traced. "They range from a facade of verisimilitude to an avowal of organic form and inspiration and then to a late homage to classical form." Melville used art images "as sources of factual information, as foreshadowing devices, as reinforcements of concreteness, as aids to exalt and intensify, and as symbols."

Three dissertations listed in the *ALS, 1963*, as completed in 1963 had not at that time been recorded in *DA*. These are Thomas Edward Lucas' "Herman Melville as Literary Theorist" (*DA*, XXIV, 1963, 2015), Robert Joslin Packard's "A Study of Melville's *Clarel*" (*DA*, XXIV, 1963, 2018-19), and Michael P. Zimmerman's "Herman Melville in the 1920's: A Study in the Origins of the Melville Revival, with an Annotated Bibliography" (*DA*, XXV, 1224). Mr. Lucas contends that at the center of Melville's theory of prose fiction was the belief that the function of art is telling the truth. Melville was soon baffled by the "opacity of the visible world and the conditions of human knowledge." He dismissed religion, philosophy, and science as helpful in solving the problems which concerned him and concluded that "art is able to present a world more real that the world of the senses, and, consequently, more moving." Mr. Packard believes that "metaphysical doubt," the one great consistency of *Clarel*, is viewed by Melville as the midpoint between the polarities of belief and unbelief. Melville therefore attempted "to fix doubt's logical metaphysical status by exploring its psychological consequences for his characters." Mr. Zimmerman's dissertation both describes and

accounts for the astonishing revival of interest in Melville in the
1920's. It was Melville the rebel, the philosopher, and the psychologist who particularly attracted readers at that time.

I failed to mention two dissertations which were completed in
1963: Ken Kirby Kreuter, "The Literary Response to Science, Technology, and Industrialism: Studies in the Thought of Hawthorne,
Melville, Whitman, and Twain" (Wisconsin), and Hershel C. Parker,
"Melville and Politics, A Scrutiny of the Political Milieux of Herman
Melville's Life and Works" (Northwestern). Both have now been recorded in *DA* (XXIV, 1963, 2446; 5390-91). Mr. Kreuter finds some
similarities in the response to science and industrialism of the four
authors he studied. "All saw religion, not nature or culture, as a primary context within which to evaluate the worth of science, technology and industrialism." To some extent each was affected by a
kind of "technological nationalism that gave them some hope that
America might avoid the gross inhumanities that industrialism had
brought in Europe." Mr. Parker's "Melville and Politics" is based on
hitherto unexplored material. His study is "intended as a contribution
to the recent corrective scholarship which seeks to understand Melville, in Howard's words, 'as a human being living in nineteenth-century America.'"

Princeton University

4. Whitman

Edward F. Grier

i. Editions and Texts

The appearance of two volumes of *The Collected Writings of Walt Whitman* (New York, New York Univ. Press) is the most significant event of an otherwise dull year. *The Correspondence of Walt Whitman*, Vol. III, *1876-1885*, ed. Edwin Haviland Miller, maintains the very high level of editorial excellence set by Miller in his two previous volumes. In addition, although the introductions to the earlier volumes were interesting, in this one, which is a major contribution to the understanding of Whitman's personality, Miller devotes himself to the single topic of Whitman's friendship with Harry Stafford. It does not, of course, deal directly with the poetry. *Prose Works, 1892*, Vol. II, *Collect and Other Prose*, ed. Floyd Stovall, completes Stovall's edition of the 1892 *Complete Prose Works* and adds some items not collected by Whitman: "A Backward Glance O'er Travelled Roads" and six short late notes. The textual notes are very full; each item is traced back to the printer's copy, where possible, and to its original appearance in print; and rejected portions are reprinted.

Other manuscripts continue to appear. One almost regrets the reappearance of *Walt Whitman's Workshop*, ed. Clifton Joseph Furness (1928) (New York, Russell and Russell). Despite this rare book's general usefulness and particularly the mine of information in the notes, it is ill-organized and textually unreliable.

The editors of *WWR* continue their agreeable custom of printing a manuscript fragment or other Whitmanian item on the back cover: "Whitman A MS, 'Hegel—To introduce'" (X, 48), "The Poet and Mrs Fels" (X, 79-80), "MS of 'How I Get Around'" (X, 102-103). Edwin Haviland Miller's "A Whitman Letter to Hiram J. Ramsdell" (*WWR*, X, 97-98) is of more consequence, for the letter (of July 19, 1867), while dealing with matters of no great importance in themselves, gives us a glimpse of Whitman as a clerk and poet in Washington. A. L. McLeod has edited nineteen letters (eleven by Whitman) exchanged by Whitman and Bernard O'Dowd in 1890-1891, in *Walt Whitman in Australia and New Zealand: A Record of His Reception* (mimeographed; Sydney, Wentworth Press; Lock Haven, Pa.). O'Dowd was a young rebel poet, and the letters have all the qualities one finds in the letters between Whitman and his young admirers at the end of his life. All but one (Whitman, March 15, 1891) have been previously published in *WWR* (1961).

ii. Biography

Horace Traubel, *With Walt Whitman in Camden*, Vol. V (April 8— —Sept. 14, 1889), ed. Gertrude Traubel (Carbondale, Southern Ill. Univ. Press), continues the slow publication of this important item. There are indexes of names with topical subdivisions and of manuscripts published, but no other critical apparatus. Unreadable, but essential. Florence B. Freedman, in "Caricature in Picture and Verse: Walt Whitman in *Vanity Fair*, 1860" (*WWR*, X, 18-19, 23), reprints a verse parody and caricature from *Vanity Fair* (March 18, 1860). She suggests that the caricature proves that Whitman did not do the professional-looking sketches of himself and others in a manuscript notebook (LC 91, Holloway's No. 6) which have been traditionally attributed to him. She is undoubtedly correct, for the only other sketches assuredly attributable to Whitman show no talent whatsoever. Charles E. Feinberg, in "Walt Whitman and His Doctors" (*Archives of Internal Medicine*, CXIV, 834-842), reviews Whitman's medical history. Harold D. Bradshaw, "Walt Whitman's Physicians in Camden" (*Transactions and Studies of the College of Physicians and Surgeons of Philadelphia*, 4th series, XXXI, 227-230), adds biographical details of his various physicians, his death certificate, and the notice of his death "written on brown paper and posted on the door of 328 Mickle Street. . . ."

iii. Criticism: General

The place due to seniority goes to the seventeen lectures and essays by antipodean enthusiasts between 1892 and 1907 published by A. L. McLeod in *Walt Whitman in Australia and New Zealand* (see above). The most interesting are those by William Gay, though as criticism all are period pieces. In his "Is Poetry an American Art?" (*CE*, XXV, 395-405), Karl Shapiro answers his own question in the negative and cites Whitman as a great prose writer and an innovator in the breakdown of verse in the United States. One does not have to agree with Shapiro that all which is not traditionally metrical is prose to agree with his thesis that our most memorable poetry has been written in varying degrees of disregard of traditional verse practice. Two critics have compared Whitman with his contemporaries. Roland A. Duerksen, in "Shelley's 'Defense' and Whitman's 1855 'Preface': A Comparison" (*WWR*, X, 51-60), finds the two statements in agreement in significant matters. Benjamin T. Spencer, in " 'Beautiful Blood and Beautiful Brain': Whitman and Poe," part of "Critical Symposium on American Romanticism" (*ESQ*, No. 35, pp. 45-49), profitably draws contrasts between the two. Whitman is mentioned in nearly every other contribution to the symposium. Critics have been baffled by the division of "Song of Myself" into fifty-two chants, with the exception of James E. Miller, who suggests that they represent the weeks of the year. In "Whitman's Calendar Leaves" (*CE*, XXV, 420-425), Richard Bridgman claims to detect the existence of a private number system used by Whitman to structure the *Leaves*. For example, the thirty-two poems in the 1856 *Leaves* may represent the thirty-two states. In the 1867 "Song of Myself," the 52 sections and 366 lines give a year divided into weeks and days, with an extra day for leap year or as an introduction. In the 1881-1882 edition of the *Leaves*, we have "a twenty-four hour day preceding a three hundred and sixty-five day year." Although at first thought so rigorous a symbolic patterning seems fantastic, it is not entirely inconsistent with Whitman's expressed ideas about his poetry. Sister Miriam Clare, O.S.F., in "The Sea and Death in *Leaves of Grass*" (*WWR*, X, 14-16), succinctly rejects the thesis that there is a rigid dichotomy between the sea and the land and the death and life they image, but points out rather that there is a close association and that the sea signifies immersion in the Oversoul and "also the Soul's retention of its own individuality." Klaus Poenicke's " 'The Test of Death and Night'—Pose und bewältige Wirklichkeit in Whitmans *Leaves of Grass*" (*Festschrift Hübner*, Berlin, Schmidt, pp. 239-266), attempts to rescue Whitman from the neglect into which he has allegedly fallen in American criticism by means of an elaborate study which demonstrates that *Leaves of Grass* is an honest and successful spiritual autobiography. John D. Magee's "Whitman's Cosmofloat" (*WWR*, X, 43-46) is a useful, if too brief, note on Whitman's "float forever held in solution." Millie D. Jensen, in "Whitman and Hegel:

The Curious Triplicate Process" (*WWR*, X, 34), reargues the case
for Whitman's use of Hegelian logic. C. N. Stravrou's *Whitman and
Nietzsche: A Comparative Study of Their Thought,* University of
North Carolina Studies in the Germanic Languages and Literatures,
No. 48 (Chapel Hill, Univ. of N. C. Press) is, to use one of the author's
favorite words, "perfervid," and the overpowering exuberance of the
style—reminiscent of that of W. D. O'Connor—is somewhat dismay-
ing. Stavrou has obviously written out of personal enthusiasm rather
than cool scholarly curiosity, but he refrains from the extravagances
of thought that characterized O'Connor's work, and personal enthusiasm on an intelligent level is always worthwhile. He finds both
of his heroes to be major prophets and more alike than unlike on
most of the major issues. Stavrou's study is something of a tract for
the times, but it stimulates interesting historical and critical speculations.

The most interesting work of the year on Whitman's poetry at
large has been done by comparatists working from Oriental literature. As far as Whitman's logic is concerned, there now seem to be
two schools: that which claims he was a cosmic intuitionalist and
that which insists that he was a Hegelian. The fact is that Whitman
knew very little about Hegel or, for that matter, about Oriental philosophy, but he liked to refer to both. It seems fairly clear, however,
that his mind was fundamentally intuitional and mystic rather than
dialectical. Such is the claim of three long studies. Som Parkash
Sharma, "A Study of Themes [−] Self, Love, War and Death [−]
in Relationship to Form in the Poetry of Walt Whitman" (*DA*, XXIV,
4703-04), is a mature study, or series of studies, from the point of
view of Vedantic thought. Sharma conservatively follows the 1892
text rather than the current disintegrationist criticism, and some of
his analyses also run counter to current trends, especially his discussions of "Children of Adam," "Calamus," and "Drum-Taps." For example, he defends vigorously and with much conviction the "genuineness" of "Children of Adam." He scorns the Hegelian approach
and is more persuaded of Whitman's psychological wholeness, or
better, of the irrelevance of psychological biography than most
readers. His concept of the Self is central to his critique of the other
themes. Discarding the psychological concept of the Self, he presents a mystical interpretation. The Self is not lyric or dramatic or
existential, but is Revelation, a Cosmos. Although his study is based
on Vedantic concepts, Sharma avoids any attempt to track down

sources or turn Whitman into "an American *saddhu*." One of the most rewarding features of his study is his close analyses of single poems or groups of poems. Walter Karl Malone, in "Parallels to Hindu and Taoist Thought in Walt Whitman" (*DA*, XXV, 4689-90), takes another approach, that of searching out parallels, which is less rewarding to the reader than Sharma's direct approach to the text. The author's writing is substandard, and he adds little to what has been known about Whitman and Indian thought since the theses of Dorothy Mercer, "Leaves of Grass and the Bhagavad Gita" (California, 1933), or, in a related area, Man Mohan Singh, "Emerson and India" (Pennsylvania, 1946). The Taoist parallels are fresh material, although of less significance than those with Vedanta. The parallels between Whitman's individualism, his feminine orientation (the *Yin* principle), his passivity, and his concept of the open road seem to be particularly close.

To one reader at least the mystical interpretation of Whitman (as well as of Transcendentalism) seems more fruitful than a more logical, Western, approach. Therefore it is useful to have a monograph on the subject available in print: V. K. Chari, *Whitman in the Light of Vedantic Mysticism* (Lincoln, Univ. of Nebr. Press). Chari is, like Sharma, convinced that an approach to Whitman via any Western philosophy (except possibly Neoplatonism) is inadequate, especially the approach through the Hegelian dialectic, and his book is, in part, an able critique of this interpretation; indeed, in a quiet bit of bravura, he quotes from "Carlyle from American Points of View," Whitman's most "Hegelian" essay, to prove that Whitman was not a Hegelian. Every study of Whitman's thought must deal with the Self, and Chari's book handles the topic fully, the chapters being entitled, after the introductory one, "Polarity versus Intuition," "Emergent Ego," "The Dynamic Self," "The Paradox of Identity," and "The Self and Reality." One might have a few minor complaints about the text. For one thing, although Chari has tactfully kept Sanskrit to a minimum, a fuller explanation of the Vedantic position would be helpful occasionally to readers meeting it for the first time. The book also loses, in comparison to Sharma's thesis, by its lack of attention to specific poems. One would also like to have some treatment of love or war (there is a discussion of democracy), and certainly one would like to have a fuller treatment of Whitman's doctrine of the body. Moreover, as is also inevitable in a study of ideas, Whitman is, so to speak, flattened out. On the other hand, as Gay Wilson Allen notes in his foreword, the Vedanta is presented as less passive and negative than in older treatments of it, so that its similarity to Whitman is more evident. All reservations aside, however, Chari's book is a thoughtful and useful one.

iv. Criticism: Specific Poems

Melvin W. Askew, in "Whitman's 'As I Ebb'd with the Ocean of Life'" (*WWR*, X, 87-92), analyzes the theme of Transcendental types and "likenesses": "Each principal in the poem becomes a type for all, and all are a type of each, namely a type of poet." Askew points out that the frustration and disappointment so conspicuous in the poem are ultimately transcended, for even as he states his frustrations the poet (and the readers) becomes part and parcel of God. Robert C. Steensma, "Whitman and General Custer (*WWR*, X, 41-42), offers an explanation of revisions made between 1876 and 1881 and relates "From Far Dakota's Canyons" to Whitman's state of mind in 1876. Robert J. Bertholf, in "Poetic Epistemology of Whitman's 'Out of the Cradle'" (*WWR*, X, 73-77), emphasizes the character of the poem as "an expression of the way to poetic knowing. . . ." Beverley Luzietti Strohl, in "An Interpretation of "Out of the Cradle'" (*WWR*, X, 83-87), reads the poem as a symbolic presentation of the dissipation and reunification of the Self characteristic of the Romantic personality as analyzed by Morse Peckham. Alvin Rosenfeld's "The Poem as Dialogical Process: a New Reading of 'Salut au Monde!'" (*WWR*, X, 34-40) deals with the difficult problem of Identification which, in this poem, he sees as expressed by the movement from an internal "Monde" to an external one of "I" and "Thou." As usual, "Song of Myself" finds the most interpreters. Jon Bracker, in "The Conclusion of 'Song of Myself'" (*WWR*, X, 21-22), advances cogent reasons for believing that the omission of the period at the end of the last line in 1855 was deliberate. He is supported by Malcolm Cowley. Steven Foster, "Bergson's 'Intuition' and Whitman's 'Song of Myself'" (*TSLL*, VI, 376-387), finds similarities in the concept of perception and of its significance in time, memory, and creativity held by the philosopher and the poet. He would substitute "perception of process" for "mysticism" in discussions of Whitman. Sydney Krause's "Whitman's Yawping Bird as Comic Defense" (*BNYPL*, LXVIII, 347-360) points out that Whitman was using a comic gambit of being jeered at by a bird to disarm criticism. In "The Respiration Motif in

'Song of Myself'" (*WWR*, X, 92-97), Richard A. Law examines the imagery of breathing as an appropriate and unifying element in the poem, but presses his evidence too hard after his discussion of Chants 1 and 2. Oswald LeWinter's "Whitman's 'Lilacs'" (*WWR*, X, 10-14), although proceeding from traditional critical bases, offers an arresting and unorthodox thesis which defines "When Lilacs" as a poem about the failure of Western orthodoxy, as compared with "Oriental wisdom," to cope with death—a description which does less than justice to the subtlety of LeWinter's argument.

University of Kansas

5. Mark Twain

John C. Gerber

All the important signs indicate that Mark Twain studies are fast reaching their peak, may indeed have reached it. Work on Twain's texts flourishes as never before. In the next few years almost all of his writings, complete and fragmentary, should appear in well-edited volumes. Once done, this huge task should not have to be done again in the foreseeable future. In addition, new and carefully focused accounts of Twain's life are yielding such excellent results that the major gaps in our information about him are fast disappearing. What is more, critical studies of his writing grow ever more numerous. Unfortunately, quantity is never a guarantee of quality. Although helpful and perceptive essays continue to appear, much too much of the criticism is becoming strained and repetitious—and distressingly solemn. Even so, scholarship for the year, when considered as a whole, has been rich and varied.

i. Texts and Editions

Four brief articles add items to the Mark Twain canon. In "Samuel Clemens, Sub Rosa Correspondent" (*ELN*, I, 270-273), Dewey Ganzel reports that three short dispatches by Twain dealing with aspects of the *Quaker City* expedition appeared anonymously in the New York *Herald* on August 20 and 27 and September 18, 1867. Ganzel speculates that their anonymity was due to the fact that Twain at the time was under contract to the *Tribune* for such material. Lawrence E. Mobley, in "Mark Twain and the *Golden Era*" (*PBSA*, LVIII, 8-23), lists sixty items by Twain which appeared in the *Golden Era* up to April 17, 1868. Ten of these pieces have not been included in previous bibliographies. Two letters by Twain to Hjalmar Hjorth Boyesen appear in Marc L. Ratner's "Two Letters of Mark Twain" (*MTJ*, XII, ii, 9, 17). Dated April 23, 1880, and January 11, 1882, the letters thank Boyesen for favorable comments on *A Tramp Abroad* and *The Prince and the Pauper*, respectively. In "Letters from Mark Twain to William

Walter Phelps, 1891-1893" (*HLQ*, XXVII, 375-381), Arthur L. Scott reports on seven letters written by Twain—six to Phelps, U.S. minister in Berlin, and one to his daughter Marian—now in the Huntington Library collection. Light-hearted and humorous, the letters reflect little of Twain's anxiety at that period.

"Revision and Intention in Mark Twain's *A Connecticut Yankee*" (*AL*, XXXVI, 288-297) is an important textual study that no scholar working on the *Yankee* in the future can afford to disregard. After a meticulous study of Twain's manuscript changes, James D. Williams concludes that there is little evidence to support the theory that we can establish points in time and in the text marking changes in Twain's general intention. Taking the cancellations as well as the approved text into account, Williams finds that Twain was writing serious satire and sheer zaniness from 1886 to 1889, from the beginning of the book until the end. Twain's chief aims in revision seem to have been to cut down on the wildest of the burlesque, to eliminate the "vulgar," and to modify attacks on the church that might have been offensive to Protestants. His changes do not indicate any attempt to give order or even sharper point to the thematic material, unless it was to increase the satire on England. Thus Williams is able to conclude that however interested we may be in the historical and social philosophies underlying it, the novel is really "a giddy, shrewd, and violent realization of that ordinary fantasy in which a hostile world is reduced to impotence before the unchanged yet conquering dreamer."

Formal announcements of the two large publishing projects now under way appear in "Twain in Progress: Two Projects" (*AQ*, XVI, 621-623). The new edition of Twain's published works, described by Paul Baender, will attempt by the most reliable principles of editing to establish the texts as Twain intended them to be. The edition of the Mark Twain Papers, described by Frederick Anderson, will include works which either have remained unpublished or have been published in such inadequately prepared editions as to be unacceptable to contemporary scholars. The works will appear in twenty-five volumes, the Papers in twelve (eight different titles). Both Baender and Anderson include the names of those serving on the two editorial boards and the names of those editing the various volumes. In *Books at Iowa* (No. 1, pp. 15-17), John C. Gerber, chairman of the editorial board, describes some of the problems encountered by those working on the new edition of the published works.

ii. Biography

Three extraordinarily competent books provide what well may be
the definitive treatment of three aspects of Twain's life. No one of
them will give heart to those who like to think of Mark Twain as a
genial father-figure chuckling the hours away with heart-warming
anecdotes.

Despite the fact that no complete file of the *Territorial Enterprise*
is known to exist, Paul Fatout puts together a substantial and quite
satisfying account of Mark Twain's experiences in Virginia City from
September, 1862, to May, 1864. His *Mark Twain in Virginia City*
(Bloomington, Ind. Univ. Press) easily supersedes all previous treatments of this period in Twain's life. It is all here, and engagingly told:
Twain's day-to-day life as a reporter for the *Enterprise*, the editorial
feuds, the insults and fights, the visits of Artemus Ward and Ada
Menken, the hoaxes, the silly talk of a duel, and Twain's half-furtive
departure for California. The picture of Washoe in flush times is
especially diverting. For the most part, Fatout reports the facts with
a minimum of interpretation. As a result, Twain emerges as a fairly
unattractive character. But a "character" he undoubtedly was. Ir-
reverent, profane, peppery, he lived, as Joe Goodman said, "by the
Grace of Cheek." Yet in many ways these were the golden days for
Mark Twain. Fatout may be a little too cautious in saying that Twain's
stay in Washoe "was more beneficial than otherwise."

In *Mark Twain and Elisha Bliss* (Columbia, Univ. of Mo. Press)
Hamlin Hill offers not only new information about the publication of
Twain's early books but also fresh insights into the nature of the books
themselves. Basically a study of the relations between Mark Twain
and Elisha Bliss, Hill's volume becomes in part a fascinating com-
pendium of dates, costs, publication statistics, royalty payments, and
business memoranda. What finally comes to light from this careful
detailing is that between 1869 and 1879 Bliss sold 337,902 copies of
Twain's books, paid the author about $73,000 in royalties, and may
have cheated him out of as much as $49,000 if Twain really had a
right to half-profits on *Roughing It, The Gilded Age, Sketches New
and Old,* and *Tom Sawyer.* If the American Publishing Company did
not give Twain his due or make him rich during this decade, however, it clearly provided him with a more substantial income than a
non-subscription house could have made possible.

Even more interesting than the facts of Twain's relations with

Bliss's company are the effects of them on his writing. It was Bliss and the success of *Innocents Abroad*, as Hill makes clear, that diverted Twain from journalism to book-length compositions. It was the subscription house and, more accurately, the mass audience it served that required Twain to write long books, that encouraged him to exploit fact as well as fiction, to indulge in anecdote, and to emphasize the topical, the moral, and the sensational. What is even more interesting, it seems clear that Twain's association with a subscription house increased his sense of inferiority at the same time that it gratified his desire for a substantial income. For some time we have recognized many reasons for Mark Twain's not being able to crack the eastern literary Establishment as he wished to do, but until Professor Hill's book no one has given one of the strongest reasons its due weight: Twain published through a subscription house, and reputable eastern authors simply did not do such a thing. The sources for Twain's disagreements with Bliss and his shrill denunciations of him must be sought, therefore, in Twain himself as well as in Bliss's methods of operation. Starting, then, as a narrative of a business relationship, *Mark Twain and Elisha Bliss* succeeds in illuminating both Twain and his artistic methods. Hill's style is clear, straightforward, and altogether pleasing.

A study that brings out Mark Twain's most unattractive qualities is Margaret Duckett's *Mark Twain and Bret Harte* (Norman, Univ. of Okla. Press). Twain's thirty-year hostility to Bret Harte has been well known but never well investigated. Many literary historians, notably Bernard DeVoto, have been willing to accept Twain's sneers about Harte at face value. But now Miss Duckett contends that Harte has been unfairly maligned. She admits that she may be favoring Harte, but her research has been thorough and her documentation impressive. In the face of the evidence she presents it would be hard to deny her general conclusion that the chief blame for the break between the two must rest with Twain. For whatever reasons—and Duckett suggests many—Twain was violently jealous of Harte, even after Harte's star had dimmed perceptibly. Indeed, it must have been sheer paranoia that led to Twain's shabby treatment of Harte during their collaboration, so-called, on *Ah Sin*; or that led to Twain's attempt to keep Harte, then down and out, from obtaining a government position; or that led to his incredible statement to Howells that Harte was "a liar, a thief, a swindler, a snob, a sot, a sponge, a coward, a Jeremy Diddler, he is brim full of treachery, & he conceals his Jewish

birth as carefully as if he considered it a disgrace." As Duckett tells
the story, moreover, there seems little cause for Twain's charging
Harte with such shortcomings as plagiarism and irresponsibility with
respect to contracts. (In view of the rather startling parallels between the lengthened version of Harte's "M'liss" and Twain's *Tom
Sawyer*, Harte may be the one who had real grounds for flinging a
charge of plagiarism.) The story is a long and unhappy one that does
little to enhance Twain's reputation. But it is good to have it told,
and we are fortunate to have it told with such careful attention to
the available evidence. One comes away from the study believing
that more of Twain's activities than we would like to believe were
motivated by jealousy and sheer spite.

Five short articles provide bits and pieces of information. In
"Mark Twain and Vedder's *Medusa*" (*AQ*, XVI, 602-606), Regina
Soria reports from the unpublished papers of Elihu Vedder that
Twain visited Vedder's studio in Rome in the autumn of 1878 and
later returned with Mrs. Clemens. In a few days he bought the
Young Medusa which subsequently hung for years over the mantel-
piece in the Hartford house. The painting offers further evidence of
Twain's interest in the pre-Raphaelite style. "The Poetaster and the
Horse Doctors" (*MASJ*, V, i, 56-59) is an account by Maurice Bas-
san of Twain's slight role in the vote to accept Will Carleton into the
Author's Club, December, 1885. Though a member of the organization, Twain declared it was no more an author's club than a "horse-
doctor's club." In "Mark Twain, W. T. Stead and 'The Tell-Tale
Hands'" (*AQ*, XVI, 606-612), Joseph O. Baylen describes how Stead
published unidentified photographs of Twain's hands in *Borderland*,
October, 1894, and invited palmists to describe the nature of their
owner. Only four replied, but Twain found their analyses "remarkable." Only one, however, suggested that the owner of the hands had
a sense of humor. Stewart Rodnon, "Mark Twain's Get-Rich-Quick
Schemes: A Balance Sheet" (*MTJ*, XII, iii, 3-5), believes that if
Twain's use of get-rich-quick projects in his novels and short stories
were placed on a balance sheet opposite his actual financial losses in
such schemes, the artistic credits would overbalance his financial
debits. And Myrtle M. Duffy puts forth the possibility, in "Twain in
Howells' *A Modern Instance*" (*AQ*, XVI, 612-614), that the Clemenses
may have been the models for Squire and Mrs. Gaylord.

Two works deal with members of Mark Twain's immediate family. Rachel M. Varble's *Jane Clemens* (Garden City, N.Y., Doubleday)

is without a doubt the most complete account of the life of Twain's mother that we have, or are likely to have for some time. Obviously the author's research has been lengthy and conscientious, for the book contains information found easily nowhere else. "As for the facts," the author says, "I followed them minutely from every source available, even when I wished (sometimes) that the facts had been otherwise, had been more glamorous. And what I could not learn about her, I omitted. So it is a factual book, merely fleshed out with the trappings of life and of the era." The "mere" fleshing out that the author refers to consists of having the characters act and talk as though they were operating in an historical novel. The facts get to us via speeches like this one of John Clemens to Jane Lampton at their second meeting: "There's a farm in Western Virginia to be sold. It's at that famous place where the Kanawha River enters the Ohio. And there are ten slaves that had to be appraised. We four heirs, Betsy and Hannibal and Caroline and I—Pleasants is dead—had to divide the Negroes amongst us so that we would get the same value. It was a puzzle to work out, for we couldn't separate the slave children from their mothers." Rachel Varble should be encouraged to write another version without the "fleshing out" for us stuffy scholars who like our information straight. "My Friend Clara Clemens" (*MTJ*, XII, iii, 116-117) is a pleasant tribute by Avis Bliven Charbonnel. The author first met Clara when they were both studying music in Vienna. Clara's voice, she says, was "of lovely quality, a contralto with mezzo timbre. It was not a big voice but ideal for Lieder."

iii. Criticism

A major attempt at an over-all assessment of Twain's craftsmanship is Robert A. Wiggins' *Mark Twain, Jackleg Novelist* (Seattle, Univ. of Wash. Press). In his preface Wiggins suggests that what he is doing may in its common sense and simplicity irritate "the Mark Twain fraternity"—whatever that may be. The suggestion seems a shade presumptuous, however, since there is little in the book that is new or radical. It is Wiggins' contention that Twain was primarily an improviser and that he was at his best when writing realistically and humorously about folk material out of his life. As a consequence, Wiggins finds *The Gilded Age* too unrestrained and indiscriminate, *Tom Sawyer* more successful, *Huckleberry Finn* the best of them all, the *Connecticut Yankee* marred by burlesque and naive assumptions, and most of the late works aesthetically inferior because of their hortatory character. None of this seems especially surprising. The only aspect of the book that may annoy Twain scholars is the occasional evidence that Wiggins has not done his homework thoroughly. He seems not to know, for example, how grossly "The Mysterious Stranger" manuscripts were altered by Paine and Duneka. Nevertheless, the book is the most substantial and possibly the best of those relatively unchallenging arguments that Mark Twain was an improviser and not a deliberate craftsman.

In a thoughtful essay entitled "Realism as Disinheritance: Twain, Howells, and James" (AQ, XVI, 531-544), Roger B. Salomon describes realism as both a response and a solution to the problem of the past. Since the picturesque had been unable to deal with the present satisfactorily, realism made a religion of it. In doing so, it denied the continuum of time and became, in effect, the aesthetic of disinheritance. Intellectually, as Salomon sees him, Twain was committed to the present, but emotionally he was swept by a nostalgic sense of the past. Except for the equilibrium between observation and memory he achieved in *Huckleberry Finn*, therefore, Twain almost never achieved a workable relation between past and present. One of the best of the year, Salomon's essay not only provides a fresh awareness of the thrust and limitations of realism but also, with respect to Twain, points up the centrality of his too rarely discussed aesthetic.

Three other articles deal with aspects of Twain's work as a whole. In "Mark Twain on Joseph the Patriarch" (AQ, XVI, 577-586), Louis Budd traces Twain's interest in the Genesis story of Joseph, whose climb from rags to riches made him a favorite of the Gilded Age. Irritated by the general praise of the story, Twain tended to satirize it. Once he even turned down an invitation to attend John D. Rockefeller, Jr.'s Sunday School class because Rockefeller was a Joseph fan. "Mark Twain, Mencken, and 'The Higher Goofyism'" (AQ, XVI, 587-594) by C. Merton Babcock suggests that both writers attempted to puncture man's arrogance, but in doing so Twain used verbal prestidigitation and Mencken the direct and villainous snarl. William C. Havard finds all previous criticism inadequate in capturing the full dimension of Twain as a product and purveyor of social and political thought. In "Mark Twain and the Political Ambivalence of Southwestern Humor" (MissQ, XVII, 95-106), he suggests the need for treating Twain as "a personal distillation of the major factors that make up the political myth." Viewed thus, Twain's failures are simply part of the general failure of the social mythology of the time to satisfy the demands of the rational intellect.

a. Quintus Curtius Snodgrass Letters.   These letters would now appear to be permanently excluded from the Mark Twain canon. Since their publication by Minnie M. Brashear in 1934, the belief has persisted that despite internal discrepancies Twain *could* have written them because he was in and out of New Orleans early in 1861 when the letters were appearing in the *Crescent*. Now Allan Bates, "The Quintus Curtius Snodgrass Letters: A Clarification of the Mark Twain Canon" (*AL*, XXXVI, 31-37), shows that Twain was not there at the right times. Furthermore, the letters are obviously part of a running exchange some obscure *Crescent* writer was carrying on with one Whiffles of the New Orleans *Daily Delta*.

b. The Jumping Frog.   Picking up where Paul Schmidt and Kenneth S. Lynn left off, S. J. Krause makes of the "Jumping Frog" a thing of almost incredible complexity in "The Art and Satire of Twain's 'Jumping Frog' Story" (*AQ*, XVI, 562-576). The structure of the story he finds to be "a nest of boxes" with eight levels of interest. All of the proper names, moreover, suggest for him the opposition between East and West. The ultimate conclusion we are to reach is that a blend of East and West is desirable. Twain's humor has seldom been exposed to such far-reaching (or far-fetched, depending upon your point of view) interpretation.

c. The Gilded Age.   Bryant Morey French, in "Mark Twain, Laura D. Fair and the New York Criminal Courts" (*AQ*, XVI, 545-561), shows how Twain and Warner manipulated the facts of the trial of Laura D. Fair in developing the fictional trial of Laura Hawkins. According to French, Mark Twain was primarily responsible for the satirical attacks on the jury system and the insanity plea even though Warner was the author of the trial chapters. In "The American Scene: Dickens and Mark Twain" (*MTJ*, XII, ii, 9-11, 16), Abigail Ann Hamblen finds the same targets in the satirical attacks on America in *Martin Chuzzlewit* and *The Gilded Age*. Dickens, she feels, is bitter, whereas Twain and Warner are good humored.

d. Tom Sawyer.   In "Setting and Theme in *Tom Sawyer*" (*MTJ*, XII, ii, 6-8), William B. Dillingham argues that the setting is suggestive of the conflicting influences on Tom's maturation: Cardiff Hill represents the dream world of youth, Jackson's Island the possibilities of escape in real life, the cave the dark part of life, and the village the involvements of adulthood that Tom finally accepts. "Mark Twain in Shawneetown, Illinois, Home of Tom Sawyer and Colonel Sellers" (*Charlatan*, No. 2) is a piece of speculation in which James B. Anderson can hardly keep from saying that Twain used material from Shawneetown when writing *Tom Sawyer* as well as *The Gilded Age*. It has already been established that Eschol Sellers of Shawneetown and nearby Bowlesville was at least in part the original for Beriah Sellers. Anderson has additionally discovered that the original Sellers was a silk-worm fancier and had mulberry trees around his house— hence, presumably, the Mulberry Sellers of the play. But what really tantalizes Anderson is that in Shawneetown he has found a cave where the Murrell gang hung out, an island off shore, a foundry, a tannery, two churches, a wooden schoolhouse, and a Tom Sawyer Spivey who wrote in his autobiography that he and two of his friends were the originals for the boys in *Tom Sawyer*. Also, it is part of Shawneetown lore that Twain piloted a boat up the Ohio and stopped there. Anderson has yet to discover that he was really there.

e. A Tramp Abroad.   Franklin R. Rogers, in "Mark Twain and Daudet: *A Tramp Abroad* and *Tararin sur les Alpes*" (*CL*, XVI, 254-263), indicates through the use of parallel passages that Daudet borrowed the general outline and several specific incidents from the section of the *Tramp* dealing with the visit to Switzerland.

f. Life on the Mississippi.   The chapters originally printed as "Old Times on the Mississippi" are for Barriss Mills not only a narrative of the cub pilot's initiation into the complexities of the river but are also the archetypal story of youth's initiation into the complexities of the adult world (" 'Old Times on The Mississippi' as an Initiation Story," *CE*, XXV, 283-289). The final realization, according to Mills, is that no security can be found after one has left Hannibal (boyhood). Arthur M. Kompass, "Twain's Use of Music: A note on *Life on the Mississippi*" (*AQ*, XVI, 616-619), provides an interesting gloss on the passage where Mr. Bixby scrapes his boat along the shore of Jones's plantation at night, singing, "Father in heaven, the day is declining." Kompass provides the actual words and music—the piece is entitled *Last Beam*—and shows how it at once pokes fun at the cub pilot and satirizes hymn-singing in general.

g. Huckleberry Finn. The title of "The *Adventures of Huckleberry Finn* as Picaresque" (*MQ*, V, 249-256) makes the point of the article. Charles R. Metzger finds a number of ways in which Huck corresponds to the typical picaro. In *"Huckleberry Finn:* A Study in Structure and Point of View" (*MTJ*, XII, ii, 10-15, 5), Clarence A. Brown keeps the argument over the ending going. He believes it useful as it stands, for the structural frame requires that Huck return to the pastoral world he was forced to leave in the beginning. Besides, this frame adds importantly to the dimensions of the book by providing an ironic contrast to the episodes it encloses. Alfred Kazin, "The Scholar Cornered" (*ASch*, XXXIII, 173-182), maintains that *Huckleberry Finn* makes us realize how seldom elsewhere in American literature children speak to us directly. By contrast, life even in *Tom Sawyer* is fun and games for the children as their activities come to us through the sensibilities of an adult. Kazin regrets that it is the American desire to keep children forever children. In "Huck, Sam and the Small-Pox" (*MTJ*, XII, iii, 1-2, 8), Claude R. Flory mentions a possible source for Huck's small-pox ruse in Harriet Beecher Stowe's *Sam Lawson's Oldtown Fireside Stories.* Those who find Huck a gutty little humanitarian are going to be annoyed by J. R. Boggan, who in "That Slap, Huck, Did It Hurt?" (*ELN*, I, 212-215) debunks the famous decision of Huck to "go to hell." Huck, Boggan contends, evidences no fear of hell before his decision, and no fear of an avenging Providence after it. In short, Huck is not nearly the heroic character that most critics would have us believe.

h. A Connecticut Yankee. The most detailed treatment, yet, of this novel is contained in three lectures delivered by Henry Nash Smith at the University of Puget Sound and now published in a small volume entitled *Mark Twain's Fable of Progress: Political and Economic Ideas in A Connecticut Yankee* (New Brunswick: Rutgers Univ. Press). The lectures are admirably interlocked. In the first, Smith argues that as possessors of the genteel perspective Warner and Howells looked upon the new American entrepreneur with suspicion and even hostility. In the second, he shows that Twain turned his back upon the genteel tradition by deliberately choosing an entrepreneur as his spokesman. Potentially Twain had an epic hero on his hands, a Prometheus to succeed the American Adam of pre-Civil War days. But for a variety of reasons the character's potential was never realized. In accounting for such a failure Smith follows Howard

Baetzhold in detecting changes in tone and intent between a portion of the book written at one time and a portion written at another. Roughly, Smith finds the book to begin as comic burlesque, to move into serious satire, and ultimately to slide down into melodrama. In the third and concluding lecture Smith turns to the thematic content of the novel, arguing that what Twain is essentially trying to do is convert the vernacular common man into a capitalist hero who is both articulate and efficient. Consciously or unconsciously, however, Twain hurls into his hero too many of the contradictory attitudes and values of the time, contradictions that Twain is never able meaningfully to resolve. As a consequence, the book displays a growing uncertainty in concept and tone; ultimately the dream of progress becomes a nightmare.

Mark Twain's Fable of Progress is the most complete analysis that we have of the *Yankee* in terms of the social and political context from which it emerged. It is also one of the most probing treatments of the novel in terms of Twain's apparent purpose or, one should say, purposes. As always, Professor Smith is informative and provocative. Yet one cannot help thinking that this brief volume raises more questions than it answers. One wonders, for example, whether Twain really turned his back on the genteel perspective in writing this novel, or whether there are clear shifts in intent (Williams in the article mentioned above does not think so), or whether the ending is primarily due to a loss of certainty in concept, or whether the book is really deliberate and profound and systematic enough to deserve being called "a philosophic fable which sets forth a theory of capitalism and an interpretation of the historical process that has brought it into being."

Hamlin Hill, "Barnum, Bridgeport, and the *Connecticut Yankee*" (*AQ*, XVI, 615-616), provides a useful gloss on the passage in the early part of the novel where Hank Morgan on seeing Camelot asks if it is Bridgeport. Many contemporary readers with good memories would have understood Hank's confusion since Bridgeport until 1852, when it burned, was the site of P. T. Barnum's "castle" called Iranistan, a fantastic place with serried balconies, shining domes, spires, and other architectural fantasies.

i. **Late Works.** Edgar T. Schell, "'Pears' and 'Is' in *Pudd'nhead Wilson*" (*MTJ*, XII, iii, 12-15), finds *Pudd'nhead Wilson* a book in which Twain piled layer on layer of disguise and misconception, each more improbable than the last, and all held together by the seemingly logical surfaces. The supposition that Mark Twain had Fredonia in mind in writing "The Man That Corrupted Hadleyburg" receives the strongest support yet in Leslie F. Chard's "Mark Twain's 'Hadleyburg' and Fredonia, New York" (*AQ*, XVI, 595-601). In "The Date of Mark Twain's 'The Lowest Animal'" (*AL*, XXXVI, 174-179), Paul Baender assembles persuasive evidence to indicate that Twain began the piece a few days before Susy's death on August 18, 1896, and finished it a month or two after her death. Contrary to what has been believed, therefore, the essay is not a response to her death.

An interesting criticism of Mark Twain criticism occurs in James Hiner's "Mark Twain: Ambivalence Not Disjunction" (*AQ*, XVI, 620-621). Citing the familiar disjunctions he has in mind—East *vs.* West, Tom *vs.* Huck, head *vs.* heart, patterned *vs.* poetic, machine *vs.* garden, realist *vs.* romantic—he contends that inevitably the critic in using one of these oversimplifies and takes sides. A work of art, he argues, objectifies the ambivalence of each preference, for each preference is not only contradictory to its polar opposite but contradictory in its inherent tendencies. The implication throughout Hiner's essay is that Mark Twain deserves a better fate than to be interpreted simply in terms of polarities.

On the silly side is D. J. Hamblin's "Mark (ye) (the) Twain" (*Life*, LXII, July 10, 13-14) in which, to spoof the Baconians, she deduces by their methods that Longfellow wrote the works attributed to Mark Twain. A fantastic number of persons who should have known better took the article seriously. Also, for anyone who cares the year can be remembered as the one in which the argument finally broke into print over whether one may properly say "Twain" or must use the full pseudonym "Mark Twain." John Lydenberg brings up the controversy in a review article in *AQ* (XVI, 627-628) and suggests that Twain himself would have guffawed at it. Since the subject has been raised, I should probably defend the usage of "Twain" in this article. The evidence is clear, it seems to me, that both Clemens and many of his closest friends treated the pseudonym not as a unit but simply as another name with separable parts. Clemens frequently signed himself "Mark." An inspection of his letters indicates that his signatures move from the informal to the formal in the following order: "Sam," "Mark," "Mark Twain," "S. L. Clemens" or "Samuel L. Clemens." According to Lydenberg, the oafish practice of using "Twain" excludes me from "the club." Alas.

University of Iowa

6. Henry James

B. R. McElderry, Jr.

i. Bibliography, Texts, Manuscripts

Reissue of the New York Edition (New York, Scribner's) and Leon Edel's edition of the *Complete Tales* (Philadelphia, Lippincott, 112 tales in 12 volumes) was completed. In the last volume of the *Tales* Edel provides a succinct balancing of their limitations and virtues. S. P. Rosenbaum contributed to a distinguished "casebook" series an edition of *The Ambassadors* (New York, Norton), including relevant passages from the *Notebooks* and letters, detailed textual notes, and ten interpretative essays. William T. Stafford's *Daisy Miller: The Story, the Play, the Critics* (New York, Scribner's, 1963) is another convenient collection of widely scattered materials.

ii. Biography

Rayburn S. Moore continued the discussion of biographical treatment in "The Full Light of a Higher Criticism: Edel's Biography and Other Recent Studies of James" (*SAQ*, LXIII, 104-114), objecting to Edel's sparse documentation, and in particular to his inferences regarding Constance Fenimore Woolson. Moore insists that James's current popularity is chiefly scholarly and critical. Edel published a new and more accurate text, appropriately annotated, of *The Diary of Alice James* (New York, Dodd, Mead), the only previous edition being that of Anna Robeson Burr (1934). Peter Gunn, in *Vernon Lee: Violet Paget, 1856-1935* (New York, Oxford Univ. Press), details James's uneasy relationship with that minor novelist-critic.

Several items made brief comments on incidental points, some very incidental indeed. George Monteiro, "A Contemporary View of Henry James and Oscar Wilde, 1882" (*AL*, XXXV, 528-530), quotes from a contemporary young woman who met both men when they visited Washington, D. C.: Henry James she thought "an excellent young man. Very well meaning but very slow minded." Simon Fleet's

"In Search of Henry James at Rye" (*ModA*, IX, 69-76) brings together some amusing comments by James's neighbors, servants, and a Miss Weld, James's secretary from 1902 to 1905. J. C. Maxwell's "Henry James's 'Poor Wantons': An Unnoticed Version" (*NCF*, XIX, 301-302) finds in Ada Leverson's *The Limit* (1911) a version of an anecdote in Simon Nowell-Smith's *The Legend of the Master*. Louis Auchincloss, "The World of Henry James" (*Show*, Aug., pp. 49-55), assembles several attractive and a few rare photographs.

iii. Criticism: General

Edward Stone's *The Battle and the Books* (Athens, Ohio Univ. Press) is in part a reply to Maxwell Geismar's attack (1963), "a species of literary McCarthyism." More important is Stone's analysis of James's little read early novel, *Watch and Ward*; his perceptive comparison of *Daisy Miller* and *The Tragic Muse* with earlier analogues known to James; and his lively chapter on James Thurber's considerable knowledge of the Master whom he satirized so well. Laurence Bedwell Holland's *The Expense of Vision: Essays on the Craft of Henry James* (Princeton, Princeton Univ. Press) is a more pretentious but less valuable study of seven novels, rather arbitrarily selected and over-reverently treated. D. W. Jefferson's *Henry James and the Modern Reader* (London, Oliver and Boyd; New York, St. Martin's Press) maintains that James is "accessible" and not "difficult." Jefferson rightly points out that Blackmur's influential estimate overlooks James's considerable sense of humor. Jefferson's comments on many stories will not be clear to the "modern reader" who has not yet read them, as was pointed out in a somewhat ungenerous review (*TLS*, August 13).

Barbara Hardy devotes two chapters of *An Appropriate Form* (London, Univ. of London, Athlone Press) to James, illustrating her general thesis that the concept of form should be more flexible than it often is. James's form was appropriate to his material and purposes, though Miss Hardy finds in the conclusion of *The Ambassadors* and elsewhere examples of "dearly purchased economy." James's complaint (in the preface to *The Tragic Muse*) about "the large loose baggy monsters" such as Tolstoi's *War and Peace*, Miss Hardy rejects; James's formal precepts do not apply to such works. In her analysis of fiction, Miss Hardy confines herself to the essential story.

Symbolic relevance of detail, she feels, has been exaggerated and has moved us "too far away from the actual experience of responding to fiction."

Three volumes give incidental treatment of James and his fiction. Maurice Beebe's *Ivory Towers and Sacred Founts* (New York, New York Univ. Press) develops the general thesis that "the artist is detached from one kind of life only that he may accept more fully and participate more completely in a different kind of life." Beebe finds a thematic affinity between *The Blithedale Romance* and *The Sacred Fount*, and echoes of the latter in *The Ambassadors*. In *The Examined Self: Benjamin Franklin, Henry Adams, Henry James* (Princeton, Princeton Univ. Press), Robert F. Sayre analyzes the friendship between James and Adams and its bearing on such stories as "The Point of View" and "Pandora." C. B. Cox, in *The Free Spirit* (New York, Oxford Univ. Press), includes essays on George Eliot, James, Forster, Virginia Woolf, and Angus Wilson. The central theme is the failure of "liberalism" to deal with essential ethical problems. Jamesians may be surprised at the emphasis (p. 39) that Maggie Verver, in *The Golden Bowl*, was a practicing Catholic.

Bruce Lowery's *Marcel Proust et Henry James* (Paris, Plon), without claiming "influence" in either direction, skilfully develops many parallels in social environment, personality, technique, aesthetic principles, and style. Due allowance is made for differences, with intelligent appreciation for both writers. An article similarly titled (*Revue de Paris*, LXXI, 74-82) is an extract from this book.

Several articles work out relationships between James and other writers. J. Oates Smith, "Henry James and Virginia Woolf: The Art of Relationships" (*TCL*, X, 119-129), finds that both authors recognized the subjective nature of reality. In James, knowledge is gained through "relentless witnessing"; in Woolf, knowledge is gained through "the desperate effort to transcend time." Alan Holder, "T. S. Eliot on Henry James" (*PMLA*, LXXIX, 490-497), points out that while Eliot sometimes misrepresents and underestimates James's critical views, he consistently valued James's fiction. Two articles turn to older writers. Earl Rovit, "James and Emerson: The Lesson of the Master" (*ASch*, XXXIII, 434-440), contrasts with perhaps some exaggeration James's relatively negative view of Emerson in the 1880's with his high praise in *The American Scene*. Rovit's suggestion that Dencombe, in "The Middle Years," is Emerson's Poet, is engaging, but James's reminiscences of Emerson in *Notes of a Son and Brother* should be read to supplement this article. Roger B. Salomon, "Realism as Disinheritance: Twain, Howells, and James" (*AQ*, XVI, 531-544), shows that, unlike Twain and Howells, James refused to divorce objectivity from memory and a sense of the past.

Robert L. Gale's *The Caught Image: Figurative Language in the Fiction of Henry James* (Chapel Hill, Univ. of N. C. Press) brings together and expands several previous studies of imagery in James. Tabulation of nearly 17,000 images shows that James's use of imagery was conspicuous even in the early work and increased only moderately in "the major phase." Nature imagery was more often than not employed to suggest violence rather than beneficence. In "Imagery in Henry James's Prefaces" (*RLV*, XXX, 431-445), Gale finds that images are twice as frequent in these critical discussions as in the fiction; they are particularly successful in describing the craft of writing. Abigail A. Hamblen, "Henry James and Disease" (*DR*, XLIV, 57-63), notes James's unwillingness to be specific about illnesses in his fiction, but finds in *The Wings of the Dove* emphatic use of illness and death to purify and clarify character. C. F. Burgess's "The Seeds of Art: Henry James's *Donnée*" (*L&P*, XIII, 67-73) examines the images by which James expresses the conscious and non-conscious phases of developing fictional ideas.

Umberto Mariani contrasts James's early romanticism about Italy, his brief resort to realistic detail, and his later use of symbolic impressions to express the quest for beauty and life, in "The Italian Experience of Henry James" (*NCF*, XIX, 237-254). Alberta Fabris, "La Francia di Henry James" (*SA*, IX, 1963, 173-226), emphasizes in a more general way French influences on James's critical views and their utility in modifying his Anglo-American attitudes.

Donald Emerson, in two perceptive articles, draws attention to James's non-fictional prose. In "Henry James on the Role of Imagination in Criticism" (*TWA*, LI, 1962, 287-294), he shows that from 1864 James's criticism became steadily less dogmatic and more emphatic of the role of imagination: James followed Sainte-Beuve rather than the scientifically minded Taine. Morality became more and more a matter of imaginative vision, and James increasingly judged from his own authority, as in "The Art of Fiction." In "Henry James: A Sentimental Tourist and Restless Analyst" (*TWA*, LII, 1963, 17-25), Emerson illustrates how James's observation was supplemented by imagination, memory, and associations.

Five familiar titles of early James criticism were reprinted: Elizabeth Luther Cary's *The Novels of Henry James: A Study* (New York, Haskell House; first published 1905); William C. Brownell's *American Prose Masters*, with its influential chapter on James (Cambridge, Mass., Harvard Univ. Press, Belknap, 1963; first published 1909); Ford Madox Ford's *Henry James: A Critical Study* (New York, Octagon Books; first published 1913); Joseph Warren Beach's *The Method of Henry James* (Philadelphia, Albert Saifer; first published 1918); and C. Hartley Grattan's *The Three Jameses* (New York, New York Univ. Press, 1962; first published 1932). To the Grattan volume Oscar Cargill has contributed a brief note explaining his gradual introduction to James and his first reading of Grattan. Leon Edel, in *Henry James: A Collection of Critical Essays* (Englewood Cliffs, N. J., Prentice-Hall, Inc., 1963), reprints seventeen essays on James ranging from Joseph Conrad to Irving Howe (without duplicating those in F. W. Dupee's *The Question of Henry James*, 1945). Edel's ten-page introduction comments perceptively on the biases and motivations affecting the James revival.

Seven dissertations, chiefly on general topics, were completed. Elsie Gray Minter, "The Image in the Mirror: Henry James and the French Realists" (*DA*, XXIV, 3340-41), studies such problems as knowledge of material, selection, and point of view. Philip L. Greene, "Henry James and George Eliot" (*DA*, XXIV, 4188-89), traces similarities in the theories of realism of these two writers and in their imaginative use of feminine sensibility. Edward Richard Levy, "Henry James and the Pragmatic Assumption: The Conditions of Perception" (*DA*, XXV, 1212), finds that *Roderick Hudson, The Sacred Fount,* and *The Ambassadors* are dramatizations of pragmatic theories. Ralph Arthur Ranald, "Henry James and the Social Question: 'Freedom' and 'Life' in the Social Novels of the 1880's" (*DA*, XXIII, 1963, 2531-32), shows in *The Bostonians, The Princess Casamassima,* and *The Tragic Muse* a center of meaning that clashes with outward form; thus these novels point toward James's later fiction. Sallie Sears Goldstein, "A Critical Study of Henry James's *The Wings of the Dove, The Ambassadors,* and *The Golden Bowl*" (*DA*, XXIV, 5384-85), contends that James's vision is negative rather than tragic. He was both attracted to experience and repelled by it; hence the reality of his situations is more limited than in life, the defiance shown by his characters more intense. Sister Mary C. McGinty, "The Jamesian Parenthesis: Elements of Suspension in the Narrative Sentences of Henry James's Late Style" (*DA*, XXIV, 4193), concludes that James's sentences show every grade of variation and that they are rhetorically effective in their conversational rhythm and frequently poetic effect. Alan B. Donovan's "The Sense of Beauty in the Novels of Henry James" is reported completed at Yale.

iv. Criticism: Individual Novels

J. A. Ward, "James's *The Europeans* and the Structure of Comedy" (*NCF*, XIX, 1-16), considers this early novel "a nearly perfect comic performance." He thus joins Professor Poirier (*The Comic Sense of Henry James*, 1960) in what most readers will consider excessive praise. That the comedy is built on a clash of American responsibility and European opportunism may be true, though these phrases sound too large and ominous; that the comic development of this idea is more than a very minor success is open to question. Eben Bass, "James' *The Europeans*" (*Expl*, XXIII, Item 9), notes a comic mythological reference to Diana when the Baroness is described as "prudent archer."

Two articles attack the traditionally admirable representation of Isabel Archer in *The Portrait of a Lady*. Blair Gates Kenney, "The Two Isabels: A Study in Distortion" (*VN*, No. 25, pp. 15-17), compares James's heroine with Isabel Boncassen, central figure in Trollope's *The Duke's Children*, published in *All the Year Round* just before *The Portrait of a Lady* appeared serially in *Macmillan's*; he finds Isabel Archer more isolated, more eccentric than Trollope's Isabel. A. R. Mills, "*The Portrait of a Lady* and Dr. Leavis" (*EIC*, XIV, 380-387), rejects Leavis' much quoted opinion that the *Portrait* is "one of the two most brilliant novels in the language"; on the contrary, Mills thinks it "blatantly moralistic," lacking in subtlety, and faulty in its values. As for Isabel Archer, "we cannot admire or respect her." The ending of the novel is defended by Thomas F. Smith, "Balance in Henry James's *The Portrait of a Lady*" (*FQ*, XIII, iv, 11-16), on the basis of repeated examples of balance in the general structure of the novel. Paul O. Williams, "James's *The Portrait of a Lady*" (*Expl*, XXII, Item 50), interprets the subtle self-revelation in Osmond's candlestick image (New York Ed., II, 309).

Robert E. Long, "The Society and the Masks: *The Blithedale Romance* and *The Bostonians*" (*NCF*, XIX, 105-122), reinforces Maurice Bewley's essay (reprinted in *The Complex Fate*, 1954) on Hawthorne's romance as an important earlier statement of James's ideas. In Hawthorne's novel James saw "an unconscious allegory of democracy" and in many situations parallels Hawthorne's treatment of this theme. Like most commentators on this story, Long does not take into account the remarkably sympathetic treatment of Miss Birdseye at her death; nor does he consider the possibility of satiric intention with respect to the Southern hero of the novel. In a separate note, "A Source for Dr. Mary Prance in *The Bostonians*" (*NCF*, XIX, 87-88), Long suggests that the name for James's character is a play on the name of Dr. Mary Walker, a well-known supporter of women's rights in James's day.

George Monteiro, "The Campaign of Henry James's Disinherited Princess" (*ES*, XLV, 442-454), sees in *Roderick Hudson* and *The Princess Casamassima* "a strong internal consistency and resilient bravery" in this central figure; Monteiro rejects Edel's characterization of her as a "good-bad heroine." Frederick J. Hoffman, however, in his *The Mortal No: Death and the Modern Imagination* (Princeton, Princeton Univ. Press), finds the second of these two novels "rich, varied, and confused"; the suicide of Hyacinth Robinson seems ambiguous (pp. 41-49).

Robert C. McLean, "The Subjective Adventure of Fleda Vetch" (*AL*, XXXVI, 12-30), suggests a radically new interpretation of *The Spoils of Poynton*. Owen's love for Fleda, he thinks, is only a ruse to get back the spoils of Poynton. Owen, "who appears to be ineffective and morally weak, proves to be the strongest as well as the most humane figure in the book." Arnold L. Goldsmith, however, reinforces the traditional interpretation of Fleda by analyzing the use of the cross which Fleda was to have had as a memento to Poynton ("The Maltese Cross as Sign in *The Spoils of Poynton*," *Ren*, XVI, 73-77). The cross is destroyed in the fire, Goldsmith thinks, because Fleda, like Strether in *The Ambassadors*, was intended "not to have got anything" by her sacrifice.

Eben Bass, "Dramatic Scene and *The Awkward Age*" (*PMLA*, LXXIX, 148-157), shows the novel has a highly schematic structure; the shifting focus on separate characters in individual books is subtly combined with an alternation of "picture" and "scene." Silvana Colognesi, "Apparenza e realta in *The Awkward Age*" (*SA*, IX, 1963, 227-248), studies the use of implication in the novel, the development of "a mere grain of subject matter."

Robert N. Hudspeth, "The Definition of Innocence: James's *The Ambassadors*" (*TSLL*, VI, 354-360), finds that the novel rests on this distinction: "The American innocent cannot conceive of the evil within his own culture but the American initiate can." Epifanio San Juan, Jr., "James's *The Ambassadors*: The Trajectory of the Climax" (*MQ*, V, 295-310), suggests that Strether's acute observation at the end of the novel foreshadows a character of "existential fullness . . . on whom nothing is lost."

Harry Hayden Clark, "Henry James and Science: *The Wings of the Dove*" (*TWA*, LII, 1963, 1-15), presents evidence of Social Darwinism in the imagery of this novel, thus supporting Gale's observation that James's nature imagery is often violent and hostile. Clark emphasizes, however, that James's scientific materialism is counterbalanced by an emphasis on Emersonian self-reliance. R. B. J. Wilson, "An Attempt to Define the Meaning of Henry James's *The Wings of the Dove*" (*AULLA Proceedings*, Canberra, Australian National Univ., 1963, pp. 76-78), states perceptively the changing relationship between Kate Croy and Densher, and the skill with which James prepares and executes the memorable climax of the novel.

A. R. Gard, "Critics of *The Golden Bowl*" (*MCR*, 1963, 102-109), rejects Firebaugh's contention (*EIC*, 1954, pp. 400 ff.) that the Ververs are intended to be villainous, but concedes that James was aware of sinister elements in their characters. Peter Buitenhuis, " 'The Fresh Start and the Broken Link': Henry James's *The Ivory Tower*" (*UTQ*, XXXIII, 355-368), believes that this novel might have been "the artistic correlative" of Veblen's *Theory of the Leisure Class*, and, if completed, would have been James's best novel on American life. Buitenhuis has high praise for James's notes, and he makes illuminating comparisons between *The Ivory Tower* and Dreiser's *The Financier*.

v. Criticism: Short Stories

Krishna Bald Vaid's *Technique in the Tales of Henry James* (Cambridge, Mass., Harvard Univ. Press) treats 22 tales, with incidental reference to some 40 others out of the total 112. The intent is to show that James's skill in first-person narrative and in the omniscient point of view has been unduly neglected. The high praise given to "A Tragedy of Error" (James's first story) and to "Benvolio" and "Fordham Castle" will surprise most readers. Vaid indignantly rejects Wilson's theory of the unreliable narrator as a clue to "The Turn of the Screw."

Nine articles extend the already voluminous discussion of James's famous ghost story. John Lydenburg, "Comment on Mr. Spilka's Paper" (*L&P*, XIV, 6-8, 34), accepts much of Spilka's psychological interpretation (*L&P*, XIII, 1963, 105-111), but does not accept it as final. In a brief rejoinder Mr. Spilka states his position succinctly. Read the story, he says, "as domesticated Gothic, as unresolved dilemma rich with poignant paradox—savior and victims victimized by opposing pulls, savior as forgivably idolatrous. I have already suggested how not to read it: as Christian allegory *a la Faust*, as case study *a la Freud*." Albert E. Stone, "Henry James and Childhood: The Turn of the Screw" (*American Character and Culture*, ed. John A. Hague, Deland, Fla., Everett Edwards Press), emphasizes the importance of class stratification as a factor in the story. He accepts Heilman's Christian interpretation and believes that the story signalizes an end to the tradition of innocent childhood represented by Rousseau and Wordsworth. Above all, James takes childhood seriously and thus points the way to Hemingway, Faulkner, and others who have illuminated the process of moral maturity. Darrel Abel, in *American Literature*, Vol. III: *Masterworks of American Realism* (Great Neck, N. Y., Barron's Ed. Ser., 1963), devotes eighteen pages of his chapter on James to a more than routine examination of "The Turn of the Screw." The ghosts, he thinks, are neither ghosts nor hallucinations, but goblins "ready to lure such victims as are in a condition to perceive their presence." Hans-Joachim Lang, "The Turns in *The Turn of the Screw*" (*JA*, IX, 110-128), associates the story with the Gothic tradition of Poe and Hawthorne; the ghosts "belong" to the house but also to the governess. Lang draws attention to a 1923 comment by F. L. Pattee which anticipates Wilson's theory. George Knox, "Incubi and Succubi in *The Turn of the Screw*" (*WF*, XXII, 1963, 122-123), reminds us of these terms for male and female demons and suggests a rivalry for possession in the ghosts of Peter Quint and Miss Jessel. Muriel West, "The Death of Miles in *The Turn of the Screw*" (*PMLA*, LXXIX, 283-288), rereads the story with close attention to evidence of violence and irrationality in the governess. It is her violence that causes Miles's death—or, perhaps, her dream of how Miles died. Louis D. Rubin, Jr., "One More Turn on the Screw" (*MFS*, IX, 314-328), argues that Douglas, the character in the prologue who produces the governess' story, is in fact Miles. The ambiguity which makes this identification far from obvious, Rubin thinks deliberate and skilful. Eric Solomon, "The Return of the

Screw" (*UR*, XXX, 205-211), contributes an amusing leg-pull designed to end further speculation. On the Sherlock Holmes formula that the least obvious person must be the villain, Solomon deduces that Quint was murdered by Mrs. Grose (the housekeeper) and that the ensuing complications enable her to regain possession of little Flora. Martha Banta, "Henry James and 'The Others,' " (*NEQ*, XXXVII, 171-184), relates James's story to the very considerable interest in spiritualism in the later nineteenth century. In his ghost stories James made serious use of the belief in spirits as a means of "thickening" the human consciousness. Miss Banta finds traces of this process in *The Wings of the Dove* and *The Sense of the Past*, and even in the earlier *The Portrait of a Lady*. "The Turn of the Screw" is enriched by awareness of this continuing interest in "The Others."

Carol Ohmann, *"Daisy Miller*: A Study of Changing Intentions" (*AL*, XXXVI, 1-11), uses James's preface and various revisions to show that James "began by criticising Daisy in certain ways and ended simply by praising her." Michael J. Mendelsohn, " 'Drop a tear . . .': Henry James Dramatizes *Daisy Miller*" (*MD*, VII, 60-64), restates the unfavorable judgment of the play reached by all previous commentators. David H. Hirsch, "William Dean Howells and Daisy Miller" (*ELN*, I, 1963, 123-128), argues that the comment in Howells' *Heroines of Fiction* is unduly defensive and insufficiently appreciative of Daisy's "reality."

Benjamin C. Rountree, "James's *Madame de Mauves* and Madame de La Fayette's *Princesse de Clèves*" (*SSF*, I, 264-271), traces parallels between James's story and the well-known seventeenth-century romance. It is "likely" but not demonstrable that James knew the earlier work. Robert L. Gale, "Pandora and Her President" (*SSF*, I, 222-224), comments on James's knowledge of Hayes, Garfield, and Arthur as the basis of the presidential figure in the story. T. M. Segnitz, "The Actual Genesis of Henry James's 'Paste' " (*AL*, XXXVI, 216-219), suggests that James's statement that the story is based on Maupassant's "La Parure" (Preface, New York Ed., XVI) may be an error. A closer parallel is Maupassant's "Les Bijoux," which James may have confused with "La Parure."

Robert L. Gale, "A Note on Henry James's 'The Real Thing' " (*SSF*, I, 65-66), sees in the artist's rather condescending reference to "black and white" illustrations an allusion to *Black and White*, the periodical in which the story first appeared. Kenneth Bernard, "The Real Thing in 'The Real Thing' " (*BYUS*, V, 1963, 31-32), challenges

the usual interpretation of the story. The Monarchs, he thinks, are
the means by which the artist-narrator discovers that he is in fact a
second-rate artist. His realization that he can transform only unreal-
ity into art is the "permanent harm" which he suffers. Samuel Irving
Bellman, "Henry James's 'The Tree of Knowledge': A Biblical Parallel" (*SSF*, I, 226-228), interprets this story of the incompetent artist
as a parody or inversion of Christ's relation to Peter; the story is
also linked to James's frequent emphasis of artistic failure. Kenneth
Bernard, "Henry James's Unspoken Discourse in 'Mrs. Medwin'"
(*Discourse*, VI, 1963, 310-314), points out rapid shifts of meaning beneath the surface of this satire of English society. Eben Bass, "Lemon-
Colored Volumes and Henry James" (*SSF*, I, 113-122), links the
phrase in *The Ambassadors* to James's contributions to *The Yellow
Book* and to the current association of yellow with artistic idealism.

University of Southern California

7. Faulkner

Richard P. Adams

In 1964 there was a leveling-off of the rapid increase in Faulkner scholarship over the preceding decade. There are 72 items in the *PMLA* list, 8 fewer than for 1963; but the decrease in number is roughly balanced by the fact that 8 of the titles for 1964 represent books, compared to 6 for 1963.[1] Whether this leveling-off is a change in the general trend or merely a temporary breathing spell is anyone's guess; but the presence of 13 dissertations in the 1964 list, against only 6 in the list for 1963, suggests a strong and increasing potential.

i. Bibliography

Except for the current checklists in *PMLA, American Literature,* and *Modern Fiction Studies,* no important contribution to Faulkner bibliography is listed for 1964.

ii. Texts

A new edition of *As I Lay Dying* (not yet listed in *PMLA*) was published in 1964 by Random House. This publisher is making a laudable effort to improve the availability of reliable Faulkner texts. No final judgment can be made, however, on the success of the effort until the various volumes have been reviewed by expert bibliographers.

There is also a new collection of interviews, *Faulkner at West Point* (ed. Joseph L. Fant III and Robert Ashley, New York, Random House), containing a transcribed reading by Faulkner of passages from *The Reivers,* questions and answers recorded during three sessions with cadets and one with representatives of news media, two

1. I have limited this survey, with one exception, to books and articles listed in the *PMLA* supplement dated May, 1965, arbitrarily disregarding the fact that *PMLA* has some items carried over from 1963 and fails to list some that appeared in 1964. If there is any resulting statistical error, it will be ironed out in the long run.

letters from Faulkner to the superintendent of the Academy, and a
reprinting of the Nobel Prize speech of acceptance. There are sixteen
photographs, several of which are excellent portraits of Faulkner.
Although there is nothing very new or startling in what Faulkner
said on the occasion, the book is a welcome and valuable addition
to the body of question-and-answer materials previously collected
by various editors and interviewers.

iii. Biography

One of the books listed in the *PMLA* bibliography, R. N. Raimbault's
Faulkner (Paris, Éditions Universitaires, 1963), is designated
"[Biog.]"; but the hope that it might be the first of the long-awaited
full-length treatments of Faulkner's life is not borne out. Its biographical information is no more complete or reliable than what is
available in some of the recent handbooks. The emphasis is chiefly
on critical discussion of Faulkner's works, and the main purpose is to
introduce those works to French readers. That purpose is well served,
partly because Raimbault has previously translated eleven volumes
of Faulkner into French, seven in collaboration with other translators
and four by himself, and partly because he has done a conscientious
job of gathering together such biographical information as could be
found in print.

A more fundamental piece of biographical research is reported
by Gordon Price-Stephens in "Faulkner and the Royal Air Force"
(*MissQ*, XVII, 123-128). Although he does not provide any information that was not already available somewhere, Price-Stephens does
a helpful job of sorting the more reliable reports from the mass of fictional accounts, for many of which Faulkner himself was partly responsible. Price-Stephens makes what look to be definitive statements on several topics, notably concerning the service Faulkner belonged to (the Royal Air Force, not the Royal Flying Corps); but
other questions, such as that of the nature and extent of injuries
Faulkner suffered during the war, if indeed he suffered any, remain
in doubt.

The accessibility of another body of material with biographical
significance is greatly improved by Bradford Daniel in "William
Faulkner and the Southern Quest for Freedom" (*Black, White and
Gray: Twenty-one Points of View on the Race Question*, ed. Bradford Daniel, New York, Sheed & Ward, pp. 291-308). The article

reprints a series of letters by Faulkner to the Memphis *Commercial Appeal* and his speech to the Southern Historical Association, all written in 1955 and all dealing in various ways with the Supreme Court school desegregation decision of 1954, which Faulkner vigorously and courageously supported. Inasmuch as his views concerning the segregation problem have been insufficiently known and sometimes badly misinterpreted, this propagation of them should help prevent errors in the future.

Some excellent photographs of scenes and people in Faulkner's environment are published by Martin J. Dain in *Faulkner's County: Yoknapatawpha* (New York, Random House), but in order to interpret them one needs to know considerably more about both Yoknapatawpha and Lafayette counties than Dain apparently does. His captions bear little relation either to fact or to Faulkner's fiction.

iv. Criticism

The 1964 bibliography is dominated, as previous ones have been, by criticism, although there is still a great need for other kinds of scholarship. It is probably fair to say, however, that the criticism itself grows better informed and more sophisticated as its quantity accumulates. Several scholarly contributions were made, for example, to the study of Faulkner's literary backgrounds and the sources of influence in his work. Lawrence Edward Bowling, in "Faulkner and the Theme of Isolation" (*GaR*, XVIII, 50-66), mentions that Quentin Compson's fragmentary remark in *The Sound and the Fury*, "*my little sister had no*," is parallel to a passage in the Song of Solomon, "We have a little sister, and she hath no breasts. . . ." Detailed explorations of two European influences are offered by Shirley Parker Callen, in "Bergsonian Dynamism in the Writings of William Faulkner" (*DA*, XXIII, 1963, 2521), and by Jimmie Eugene Tanner, in "The Twentieth Century Impressionistic Novel: Conrad and Faulkner" (*DA*, XXV, 1927-28).[2] Robert M. Slabey's continuing study of the influence of Joyce and Eliot in Faulkner's use of the "mythical method" is pursued in "*Soldiers' Pay*: Faulkner's First Novel" (*RLV*, XXX, 234-243). Donald M. Kartiganer offers related evidence in "The Role of Myth in *Absalom, Absalom!*" (*MFS*, IX, 1963-64, 357-369), pointing out some parallels involving vegetation myths and the Christ story; but he fails

---

2. This item is misnumbered 5235 in the cross-references under Faulkner's name in the *PMLA* list; it should be 5234.

to notice that other myths and stories are used and that various different uses are made of them by the various characters within the novel who help to tell its story.

The Eliot influence and its European backgrounds are emphasized by Mary Jane Dickerson, in "*As I Lay Dying* and *The Waste Land*: Some Relationships" (*MissQ*, XVII, 129-135), and by John Michael Howell, in "The Waste Land Tradition in the Modern Novel" (*DA*, XXIV, 3337). An earlier and more purely American source is indicated in Hans Bungert's "William Faulkner on *Moby-Dick*: An Early Letter" (*SA*, IX, 1963, 371-375). The letter, which Bungert reprints, was written by Faulkner to Fanny Butcher, who published it in her column in the Chicago *Tribune* book section on July 6, 1927; his statement was that *Moby-Dick* was the book he would rather have written than any other, although he also had high praise for *Moll Flanders* and A. A. Milne's *When We Were Very Young*. In "William Faulkners letzter Roman" (*NS*, XII, 1963, 498-506), Bungert reviews *The Reivers*, which he relates to Faulkner's earlier work and, in some detail, to *Huckleberry Finn*. The *Huck Finn* influence is examined in relation to the "Old Man" part of *The Wild Palms* by Nancy Dew Taylor in "The River of Faulkner and Mark Twain" (*MissQ*, XVI, 1963, 191-199). Carl F. Hovde, in "Faulkner's Democratic Rhetoric" (*SAQ*, LXIII, 530-541), observes that Faulkner is "a myth-making democrat in the tradition of Melville, Whitman, and Wolfe," a suggestion that might well be expanded to include a number of other writers in the same tradition. The influence on Faulkner of Sherwood Anderson, which has often been discussed before, is explored again by H. Edward Richardson in "Anderson and Faulkner" (*AL*, XXXVI, 298-314).

Matters of form, technique, and style have received a good deal of attention during the past year. Olga W. Vickery concentrates on this aspect in "William Faulkner and the Figure in the Carpet" (*SAQ*, LXIII, 318-335), arguing that Faulkner's techniques are fashioned for the purpose of developing his presentation of character, and that they result in the creation of coherent, well-unified works of fiction. Her categorization of Faulkner plots is perhaps too abstract, but her departure from the views of George Marion O'Donnell and Malcolm Cowley, who have said that Faulkner's novels are not well-organized, is a healthy corrective, and her general conclusion that the individual works are valuable in themselves, as well as in their contributions to the Yoknapatawpha legend, is thoroughly convincing. Lawrance

Thompson's "A Defense of Difficulties in William Faulkner's Art" (*Carrell*, IV, ii, 1963, 7-19), although it is pitched at an elementary level, offers sound justification for the complexities of Faulkner's narrative methods, particularly in *Absalom, Absalom!* and *Go Down, Moses*. Mario Materassi, in "Le immagini in *Soldiers' Pay*" (*SA*, IX, 1963, 353-370), analyzes the use of imagery to characterize Cecily Saunders, and shows how that imagery foreshadows the more effective techniques of Faulkner's later fiction. Functions of humor are explored by Otis B. Wheeler in "Some Uses of Folk Humor by Faulkner" (*MissQ*, XVII, 107-122).

The question whether Faulkner's increasingly frequent practice of making a novel partly or wholly out of materials previously formulated as independent short stories is successful or not is discussed, in passing, by Vickery. It is the topic of more specialized analysis in Jane Millgate's "Short Story into Novel: Faulkner's Reworking of 'Gold is not Always'" (*ES*, XLV, 310-317) and in Robert M. Slabey's "Quentin Compson's 'Lost Childhood'" (*SSF*, I, 173-183). Millgate supports the view, which is also supported by Vickery, but which other critics have not always agreed to, that on at least some occasions Faulkner uses such material in his novels to good effect. Slabey concentrates on the technical use of Quentin's point of view in "That Evening Sun." His further suggestion that the matter of Damuddy's death may have been a short story before being incorporated into Benjy's section of *The Sound and the Fury* is conjectural, and its inconclusiveness points up the need for study of manuscripts and other literary remains so that we may know more than we do about when Faulkner wrote what, especially in the early periods of his activity.

An interesting parallel is drawn by Carolyn Wynne in "Aspects of Space: John Marin and William Faulkner" (*AQ*, XVI, 59-71). She argues that both artists practiced what Bergson called the spatialization of time, and that both rendered motion by means of rhythmic forms. There have been enough other hints of this kind to suggest that it might be profitable for someone to make a systematic study of Faulkner's relations with techniques of modern painting and with the philosophical concepts on which some of those techniques have been based.

Ever since Conrad Aiken's essay in 1939, stylistic analyses have afforded one of the most successful approaches to Faulkner criticism, although their number has been comparatively small. On the 1964 list there are two, both good: Carl F. Hovde's article mentioned above and Irena Kałuża's "William Faulkner's Subjective Style" (*KN*, XI, 13-29). Kałuża, approaching the subject from a more purely linguistic direction than most other critics have done, offers convincing support for the argument generally advanced by Aiken, Karl E. Zink, Walter J. Slatoff, and others that Faulkner's style, rhetoric, and grammar are functional in his effort to present his fiction in a concretely moving way.

The most cultivated and least fertile field of Faulkner criticism deals with the contents, meanings, and themes of his work. The only book-length critical study on the 1964 list, Monique Nathan's *Faulkner par lui-même* (Paris, Éditions du Seuil, 1963), is focused mainly on the metaphysical implications of Faulkner's fiction and on his handling of historical themes and family relationships. It is a useful addition to the series in which it appears, partly because it has some good photographs of Mississippi scenes and people, very different from anything to be seen in France, and a descriptive account of Oxford and Lafayette County, evidently based on the author's personal experience. However, Faulkner's speaking for himself is sometimes rendered in excessively free translations, as when his remark about Quentin Compson, "Who loved not the idea of the incest which he would not commit, but some presbyterian concept of its eternal punishment," becomes, "Quentin, qui aimait non l'idée de l'inceste qu'il n'aurait jamais voulu commettre, mais quelque conception presbytérienne du châtiment éternel par lequel cet inceste eût été châtié." It is even more misleading when Nathan attributes ideas expressed by fictional characters to Faulkner himself, and when she describes Southern society before the Civil War in sentimentally idyllic terms which the bulk of Faulkner's work explicitly shows to be false.

Articles on thematic topics take a wide variety of approaches. Bowling, in "Faulkner and the Theme of Isolation," mentioned above, advances once more the often discussed formula that "*The Sound and the Fury* is the portrait of the break-up of a culture, the death of a civilization which has lost its ideals and its moral perspective." He pursues a similar formula in "William Faulkner: The Importance of Love" (*DR*, XLIII, 1963, 474-482). His comments are intelligent, but the key-words unlock very little that has not been brought to light before. A more novel and suggestive theory is proposed by Nicholas Michael Rinaldi in "Game-Consciousness and Game-Metaphor in the Work of William Faulkner" (*DA*, XXIV, 4196-97) and "Game Imagery and Game-Consciousness in Faulkner's Fiction" (*TCL*, X,

108-118), namely that "game-consciousness" is a dehumanizing factor in Faulkner's view, that when his characters enter into contests with one another they play to destroy their opponents, and that they are themselves defeated because they cut themselves off from the eternal verities of the heart by means of which man is to endure and prevail. Another original observation is made by Ralph Haven Wolfe and Edgar F. Daniels in "Beneath the Dust of 'Dry September'" (*SSF*, I, 158-159). They suggest that Hawkshaw, the presumably good-intentioned barber, unconsciously wants to have Will Mayes lynched, and that his actions contribute to bring about that result. The same hypothesis might well be tested with relation to other Faulkner works, such as *Sanctuary* or *Pylon*, where meddlers with ostensibly high motives are much more clearly shown to bring disaster on characters whom they are supposed to be helping.

The moral dimension in Faulkner's work, a complex and difficult subject, is studied by Pamela Anne Ulrey in "Faulkner's *Sanctuary* and *Requiem for a Nun*: Songs of Innocence and Experience" (*DA*, XXIV, 1963, 2043-44). Her thesis is sound, and her conclusions, based on Faulkner's hierarchy of three kinds of men (one who is appalled by evil and commits suicide, a second who hates evil but endures it, and a third who defies evil and does something about it), are sensible. Michel Gresset approaches from a more abstract angle in "Temps et destin chez Faulkner" (*Preuves*, No. 155, pp. 44-49), building on André Malraux's thesis concerning "l'irrémédiable" in Faulkner. Gresset, however, takes a concrete direction by analyzing the use of such words as "outrage" and "astonishment," and by showing the working relations between concepts of time and of space, so that his final result is a considerable modification of Malraux's views. J. Robert Barth remains abstract in "Faulkner and the Calvinist Tradition" (*Thought*, XXXIX, 100-120), identifying Faulkner's "doom" with predestination in a way that the Faulkner text will hardly support; but he issues a proper warning when he points out that Faulkner's interest in Puritanism is less moral than imaginative.

There seems to have been a falling-off in the study of individual Faulkner characters, for which the quality of the studies is perhaps a sufficient explanation. Arthur F. Kinney tries a defense of Ike McCaslin in "'Delta Autumn': William Faulkner's Answer for David H. Stewart" (*PMASAL*, XLIX, 541-549), but in the face of Faulkner's statement that Ike represents the second of his three men the defense remains unconvincing. Maurice Bassan, in "Benjy at the Monument"

(*ELN*, II, 46-50), advances the ingenious hypothesis that the court-house square is a symbolic clock-face, on which Benjy moves counter-clockwise because he is not in time, and that when the surrey turns left, putting him into time, he is horrified. One hesitates to say that anything is too complex for Faulkner to have in mind, but for this particular matter there are simpler explanations that seem to work about as well.

Existentialist approaches are still being tried, specifically by Vernon Theodore Hornback, Jr., in "William Faulkner and the Terror of History: Myth, History and Moral Freedom in the Yoknapatawpha Cycle" (*DA*, XXV, 476), and William J. Sowder, in "Christmas as Existentialist Hero" (*UR*, XXX, 279-284); but the effect, at least on me, is only to emphasize what was clear enough already, that the existentialist patterns do not fit.

A welcome contribution is made by two articles in which hitherto obscure comments on Faulkner are rendered currently available. James B. Meriwether, in "Early Notices of Faulkner by Phil Stone and Louis Cochran" (*MissQ*, XVII, 136-164), publishes a letter from Stone to Cochran dated December 28, 1931, an article by Cochran in the Memphis *Commercial Appeal* for November 6, 1932, and a long article by Stone in the *Oxford Magazine* for April, June, and November, 1934. O. B. Emerson's "Prophet Next Door" (*Reality and Myth*, pp. 237-274) quotes liberally from early reviews to show that Southern readers were among the first to recognize and describe the qualities in Faulkner that have since made him world famous.

Criticism of Faulkner is surveyed with a different result by T. B. Tomlinson in "Faulkner and American Sophistication" (*MCR*, No. 7, pp. 92-103). Tomlinson contends that the naïveté of American readers, who fail to recognize Faulkner "for the sentimentalist he really is," is exceeded only by the naïveté of Faulkner himself, who "constantly shows a tendency towards glib sophistication and empty philosophizing which his remarkable fluency only exacerbates." Since Faulkner is a writer of fiction rather than philosophy, the only naïveté that Tomlinson really succeeds in demonstrating is his own.

The market for guides and handbooks to Faulkner now seems well saturated; three more appeared in 1964, in addition to the two published in 1963. Harry Runyan's *A Faulkner Glossary* (New York, Citadel Press) contains a reasonably complete alphabetical listing of characters, place names, and titles of Faulkner works, and seven appendixes: a biographical sketch, lists of Faulkner's poems, non-fiction prose pieces, and fictional works, histories of his fictional families, a discussion of Yoknapatawpha geography, and an analytical listing and discussion of "documents" (i.e., Faulkner works) relating to various persons, families, classes of people, and activities. *Crowell's Handbook of Faulkner*, by Dorothy Tuck (New York, Thomas Y. Crowell Co.), contains a history of Yoknapatawpha County, a note on Faulkner's style, chronologically listed discussions of the Yokna-patawpha novels and of Faulkner's other novels, an alphabetical list-ing and discussion of the short stories, a short list of the more im-portant characters, a biographical sketch of Faulkner, a brief selected bibliography, and an index. The Introduction to this handbook, writ-ten by Lewis Leary, is one of the best short general essays on Faulk-ner in print. *A Reader's Guide to William Faulkner*, by Edmond L. Volpe (New York, Noonday Press), does not have the customary list of characters. After an introduction, consisting of a biographical sketch of Faulkner and discussions of his character types and themes, narrative structure and techniques, and style, the main part of the book is devoted to unusually long and detailed critical discussions of the novels, after which an appendix provides chronologies of scenes, paraphrases of scene fragments put in chronological order, and guides to scene shifts in the first two sections of *The Sound and the Fury* and chronologies of events in *As I Lay Dying, Sanctuary, Go Down, Moses, A Fable*, and the Snopes trilogy. This is followed by notes, a fairly large selected bibliography, and an index. These guides are most likely to be useful to beginning students or casual readers of Faulkner. All three contain errors and doubtful interpretations. Kirk and Klotz's *Faulkner's People* still has a few more names of char-acters than any other index, and its apparatus, by providing page citations to specified texts, makes it the most useful reference work for systematic Faulkner scholars.

Tulane University

8. Hemingway and Fitzgerald

Frederick J. Hoffman

i. Bibliographies and Texts

Aside from translations into foreign languages, the most newsworthy event in 1964-1965 was the appearance of *The Apprentice Fiction of F. Scott Fitzgerald* (New Brunswick, Rutgers Univ. Press, 1965). The editor, John Kuehl, cites the basic sources of his selection, from the "two small red-bound scrapbooks" of the Princeton Library's Fitzgerald Papers. There are some twelve stories or sketches, with an appendix offset of the holograph of Fitzgerald's sketch, "The Death of My Father." The book thus serves much the same purpose for Fitzgerald as Carvel Collins' editing of the *New Orleans Sketches* and especially the *Early Prose and Poetry* does for William Faulkner; that is, it makes juvenilia available to those advanced enough in biographical scholarship to use them. Intrinsic values are scarcely to the point in any case. As Jackson Bryer has suggested (*FN*, No. 28), Kuehl should have gone far beyond the present selection if he wished maximum effectiveness. The pieces published are from magazines published at Fitzgerald's schools, the Saint Paul Academy, the Newman School, and Princeton University. But as to the third of these, there is not enough to make a genuine association with the beginnings of Fitzgerald's mature career.

There has been much discussion of corrupt texts and the need for newly edited ones. As for Fitzgerald, the best source of information in this regard (as well as in other matters) is Matthew J. Bruccoli's *Fitzgerald Newsletter*. James B. Meriwether, in what he modestly calls "the first attempt to examine any of the larger problems of the Hemingway text in the light of present-day bibliographical scholarship" (*PBSA*, CVII, 1963, p. 404),[1] proceeds to examine the state of Hemingway bibliography, cites Louis Henry Cohn's bibliography as

---

1. This 1963 publication was published too late for acknowledgment in *ALS*, *1963*. Items other than those published in 1964 will be considered here in such circumstances as these: when an item appears that has not been noticed before and—in the case of 1965 publication—when it is very important. In any case, this review of scholarship and criticism should be considered selective, not complete.

superb "of its kind," and calls for the kind of attention to Hemingway that Bruccoli has already given to Fitzgerald, Herbert Cahoon to Joyce, and Bruce Harkness to Conrad. Among other situations Mr. Meriwether deplores is the genuinely deplorable misfortune of Hemingway's having forbidden the publication of his letters. Carlos Baker, in the forthcoming authorized biography, will apparently have to paraphrase in places where for good effect he should quote. Nothing of consequence has occurred in the area of correcting texts; in any case, the activity of Meriwether, Bruccoli, and others helps us to see any seriously damaging errors, no matter whose responsibility they may be.

ii. Memoirs, Biography, and Criticism

There was little published biography of either Hemingway or Fitzgerald in 1964. Despite Arthur Mizener's *The Far Side of Paradise* (1951), written without the full advantage of papers and therefore liable to interesting exercises of the author's imagination, and Andrew Turnbull's *F. Scott Fitzgerald* (1962), discussed in last year's annual review, Fitzgerald's life seems to yield new insights, details, and facts steadily. Of course, the papers in the Princeton Library are rich in resources; John Kuehl (in his edition of the *Apprentice Fiction*, discussed above) offers interesting details of the years before *This Side of Paradise* (1920), but these are incidental to the main purpose, which is to distribute quite rare and little known texts.

In the biography and criticism of Fitzgerald, by all odds the most important recent event is the publication of Henry Dan Piper's long awaited *F. Scott Fitzgerald: A Critical Biography* (New York, Holt, Rinehart, and Winston, 1965). This book has been in the making for many years and was announced for publication in the 1950's. The only genuine criticism one can have of it now is that much of the information it contains has been given out piecemeal since Piper began plans for publication. But the book is not merely a repetition of what has been said before; it is, in fact, a major contribution to the understanding of both Fitzgerald's life and his work. Unlike Mizener's, Piper's study does not yield to the temptation to cast illumination upon the work simply from the point of its having relevance to an exciting personality or to a "symptomatic" twentieth-century figure. Piper's aims are modest, but they have the kind of important limit that precision and knowledgeability help to endow with value. He wants, he says in his Preface, "to separate myth from fact and to tell the story of Fitzgerald's life as a writer more fully than it has ever been told before" (p. viii). Despite the work's being exhaustively annotated (there are twenty-four pages of "Notes" in fine print), the respect for verification in no way impedes the quality of the writing, which is in every way admirable. Piper's book should certainly stand up and stand out for many years as the fullest and the most reliable study of Fitzgerald.

Ultimately, of course, there will be the "grand play" in the cases of both Fitzgerald and Hemingway. Carlos Baker may do it for Hemingway, but one somehow doubts that even in his work the record will be complete. As Philip Young has said ("Our Hemingway Man," *KR*, XXVI, 676-707), the real biography of Hemingway, if it is to be what it ought to be, will have to "hurt"; and the hovering presence of an alert widow may well produce, "in the name of Good Taste, a freshly washed, shaved, combed Hemingway" (pp. 687, 688). It is only fair to say that, in the basic work so far done in Fitzgerald's and Hemingway's cases, the standards have been high, the errors remarkably few, and the critical intelligence gratifyingly available.

This does not mean that there have not been downright blunders, even acts of total immodesty and incaution. One of the virtues of Young's essay is its having, from the point of view of a person jealously guarding his own pre-emptive right to critical intelligence, pointed out the absurdities of recent Hemingway criticism. These have been in the areas of the spot biography (often rushed to the printer almost before the body was cold) and of the "Case Book." As for the latter, it is a much maligned phrase and the range from good to bad in works of its kind is great. Young cites for his especial "approval" [this comes under the heading "Comic Books (But No Pictures)"] an anonymously published student's "aid": *A Farewell to Arms: Notes* (Lincoln, Neb., Cliff's Notes). To judge from the samples given, this book achieves a low in style and generally in intelligence in an area where lows are very difficult to "bottom" (see pp. 696-697).

Young's essay is notable in many ways. It is quite possible that no one should have dared to undertake the regimen that writing it demanded. He describes himself as the grand "academic slob" (p. 676) who, having gathered about him all of the books published on Hemingway since his own (1952), proceeds to stuff himself to the ears with good, bad, and indifferent texts. The results are wondrous to behold. There is a native intelligence in the critic which allows him to prevail through many trials and tribulations. The essay is written in the style of the "notes while preparing to write" ploy, and the results are nervous, conversational, sometimes quite brilliant, frequently quite subjectively moved. One of its most noticeable characteristics is the 1952 author hunting for critics who (a) imitated him, (b) lifted from him without acknowledgment, and (c) attended to him as person-critic. Perhaps the extreme example of absurdity which this kind of hypersensitivity to self as author can cause occurs in his discussion of Baker's novel, *The Land of Rumbelow* (1963): ". . . Hemingway had middle name (Miller) he didn't use. So has Kemp [the author on whom Dan Sherwood is working, whose biography he finally decides to postpone writing] but (Baker and Miller being a little too close?) the middle name is Young. Well now: Prof. Sherwood went to Amherst, is short, was boxer. (Prof. Baker went to Dartmouth, is tall, athletic prowess not known.) Who went to Amherst, is short, and (for brief but deplorable period) was wrestler (not boxer)? Damned if *Young* didn't (isn't, didn't)" (Young, p. 688).

There is much more of the same. The essay continuously threatens to become a steamy *"bain de moi,"* and its effectiveness is therefore not so much diminished as blocked (that is, one has to reach *around* Young to get close to his genuinely intelligent judgments).

Eventually we may have as many published memories of Fitzgerald and Hemingway as there were persons who knew them. For some reason—perhaps because, despite the talk of impersonality, the 1920's were a decade in which both the personality and the creative act counted equally—memoirs of the age are accumulating. The rough edges of one of these (Jed Kiley, *Hemingway: An Old Friend Remembers*, New York, Hawthorne Books, 1965) are presented *sui generis* and without polishing. Kiley first published the book in a series of *Playboy* sketches, 1956-1957; there are differences between that version and the present, for which information I credit Mr. Meriwether's nervously proud concern. (There *are* texts, it does appear to me, that it is a gratuitous act to refine.)

The friend of Hemingway seems to have been a combination of journalist and bartender ("You might say I was literary in the daytime and mercenary at night," p. 21), a mixture Hemingway would of course have considered most happily conceived. The memoir is interesting for its emphasis on Hemingway, the "tough guy," the

sportsman, the man of unlimited endurance and hardiness. As for
Hemingway's writings, Kiley rarely liked any of them; he seems—or
claims—to have been all the more interesting because he was openly
opinionated about the writing. Kiley's book is ephemeral, amusing
only to the person to whom Hemingway is not genuine as an artist.
Otherwise, it is conversation of the "I knew him when" sort, naïve and
wide-eyed in its evaluation of the artist-as-personality. ("You had to
give the guy credit for one thing. He was always himself. Natural
like"—p. 46.)

Criticism of Fitzgerald has alternated between being thoroughly
biographical and pretending to be neoformalistic. Despite the great
difficulty of maintaining the latter stance (to say nothing of its being
absurdly unnecessary in mature criticism), it is still proposed at least
as the point of view from which a writer can most precisely be seen.
In Sergio Perosa's *The Art of F. Scott Fitzgerald* (Ann Arbor, Univ.
of Mich. Press, 1965), translated from the Italian in which it appeared
in 1961 (Rome), which proposes to examine Fitzgerald's works "as a
whole . . . the stress falls on the interdependent links that exist among
them. . . ." In this "strictly literary" study, attention is paid Fitzgerald's
life in an honorific first chapter, but the author is hard put to it to
keep the man out of his work after that. One of many examples of the
embarrassment caused by a position neither wanted nor gracefully
demonstrated occurs when he quotes one of Fitzgerald's bad poems
("The Pope at Confession") as "an imagistic achievement" and follows the quotation with this naïve remark: "It is not for nothing that
the young student had marked in his anthology of English poetry the
poems of T. S. Eliot and Pound, at that time hardly known. . . ." (pp.
14-15).

In fact, Perosa's book is all too literary; the associations made with
Fitzgerald's contemporaries and with contemporary culture, while
sometimes worthy, are scarcely ever without false literary adhesions.
Amory Blaine reminds him of Melville's Pierre; at the end of *This Side
of Paradise*, Amory has to "shore up his fragments against the ruin";
the short story, "Bernice Bobs Her Hair," suggests Pope's *The Rape
of the Lock*, and "The Cut-Glass Bowl" reminds him of Henry James's
The Golden Bowl. The list is long of such catchpenny resemblances.
Beyond them there is the imprecision of such interpretations as this
(of *The Beautiful and Damned*): it is "a parable on the deceptive-
ness of dreams, on the impossibility of evading reality through illusions, and on the painful destructiveness of time" (p. 41).

Signor Perosa's study distinguishes itself as the first book-length examination in Italian. As such, it points to a growing European interest in modern American literature. While the center has not altogether shifted (there are surely more theses, in the aggregate, on Shakespeare and Shelley), the European interest is nevertheless on the increase. The consequences of this phenomenon are odd, if not a bit ironic. While Americans seem now to be taken over by an increasingly myopic concern with the eye of the needle, Europeans are seeing every variety and color of thread. The time of aberrant impressions has not entirely disappeared, but there is always the very real and menacing danger that some son of Fredson Bowers will insist that our authors had actually meant "sullied" rather than "solid." In the work of foreign critics writing on American literature, these concerns over precision seem not as yet to have prevailed. The results are interesting speculations, though none of them is likely to become definitive. There is much concern, for example, over Hemingway and religion, Hemingway and death; but these were, at least in their general outlines, advanced some years ago by American critics.

There are interesting variants of originality, however. Jean Malaquais, in "Hemingway, ou le champion et la mort" (*Preuves*, No. 147, 1963, pp. 32-41), offers this interesting paradox: "Pour le personnage hémingwayen, la mort est ce qu'il vit, la vie est ce qu'il meurt" (p. 34). Generally, the French have carried on the "classic" existentialist interpretation discovered in Camus and Sartre fifteen or so years before. This remark, from Françoise Gaston-Chérau's "Ernest Hemingway et le 'catholicisme sceptique'" (*Esprit*, No. 228, 1953, p. 1133), is echoed in recent studies: "Totale ou partielle, la mort met l'homme en demeure de montrer ce qu'il est."

iii. Conclusion

The philosophic paradox is not a monopoly of any group of critics. The recent history of critical perspectives contains many attempts to place twentieth-century writers within a tradition of religious or philosophical speculation. The results are not exclusively damaging, but they often substitute the skeleton for the flesh. One of the most confused of these forays into the magic world of *Weltanschauungen* is Julanne Isabelle's book, *Hemingway's Religious Experience* (New York, Vantage Press). "I have probed into the soul of a man," she says in the brief Introduction, "and found beauty and courage dedicated to God." Unfortunately, the quality of the book itself scarcely reaches the level of so wholesome a remark.

In fact, Mrs. Isabelle dominates the subject until it permits her own effusions regarding the destiny of man and the paradoxes of modern culture. Such a summary of Hemingway as the following can only be put down to an enthusiasm incidentally related to the subject that originally was alleged to have sponsored it. ". . . Hemingway was a religiously oriented man whose tempered faith was forged within the framework of an American Protestant tradition, hardened by the disillusionment of war and the 1920's, and annealed within the framework of a broad, ancient Catholic tradition, constantly being tested for its tenacity and possessing the properties essential to a universal belief" (p. 17).

It is enough to conclude that 1964 has not been a good vintage year for criticism and scholarship, if we consider the fates of Hemingway and Fitzgerald and their literary reputations. Only a few basic events have redeemed it: Matthew Bruccoli's unceasing attention to the "facts that may, if one is pressed, be proved"; Piper's book, which, while published in 1965, belongs to any year since 1955[2]; and the growing and substantial interest in both artists as representative American literary heroes. As for the third of these, Roger Asselineau's editing of *The Literary Reputation of Hemingway in Europe* (Paris, Minard, 1965) is a testimony of a maturing respect for American literature. The individual essays are in themselves good enough speculations upon national predispositions and weaknesses to merit publication; beyond this merit, they have a contribution to make to scholarly witnesses that—except for the curiously unenlightening Introduction by Heinrich Straumann (who has been known to perform much more skilfully)—is gratifying and encouraging. As between Philip Young's strangely personal debates over Hemingway criticism and James Meriwether's educated horror over corrupt texts, I should like to suggest a perdurably lively critical intelligence, as well as a cluster of expectations about future work.

University of Wisconsin, Milwaukee

---

2. As recently as 1962, I received permission to print a chapter of the original MS in *The Great Gatsby: A Study*; at that time publication seemed imminent; it was not.

Part II

9. Literature to 1800

Richard Beale Davis

Again, as in the survey for 1963, bibliographies employed as a basis for this chapter attest that the term "literature" is here employed more broadly, as applied to books and authors and movements, than is usually the case for later periods and individual writers. Travel and geographical observation, science, religion, and politics are as frequently the subjects of our writers as verse is, and more frequently than drama and the familiar essay, though all are represented. Biography here is concerned primarily with men who are remembered for their sermons, diaries, scientific inventions and theories, and political activities, though again there are belletristic exceptions. Colonial libraries and publishing history are also included, for they do as much to explain the present and future state of letters as do criticism and literary history.

i. Bibliography, Libraries, and Publishing History

Although publications concerning printing, books, and bibliography were perhaps fewer in quantity than during the preceding year, several interesting and useful studies appeared. There remains the crying need for adequate bibliographies of colonial sermons, political pamphlets, essays of many kinds, and verse (this last especially for the middle and Southern regions). One significant list not previously mentioned but begun in 1963 did continue to completion in its third and fourth installments, Gaylord P. Albaugh's "American Presbyterian Periodicals and Newspaper Publications, 1752-1830, with Library Locations" (*JPH*, XLII, Pt. 3, 54-67; Pt. 4, 124-144).

Richard F. Hixon, in "A New Jersey Printer's 'Pocket Memorandum' for 1795" (*JRUL*, XXVII, 1963, 24-27), has presented from one pocket almanac a record of business activity in Isaac Collins' Trenton shop. From the February to December entries one may reconstruct a good sample of the printing trade in the middle states at the close of the eighteenth century. From Bibles and religious tracts to spelling books and state laws, Collins totaled nearly three thousand volumes.

An account of the publishing history of one significant book appears in Elaine F. Crane's "Publius in the Provinces: Where Was *The Federalist* Reprinted outside New York City?" (*WMQ*, XXI, 589-592). Based on a survey of all existing issues of eighty-nine newspapers and three magazines printed between October 27, 1787, and August 31, 1788, it reveals that only sixteen newspapers—four each in Massachusetts, New York, and Virginia, two in Pennsylvania, and one each in New Hampshire and Rhode Island—and one magazine outside New York City reprinted numbers of *The Federalist*. The essay offers a good bibliography for any student of the great political series.

"The First Wesley Hymn Book" (*BNYPL*, LXVIII, 225-238), by Martha W. England, tells of the "first in-gathering of [Wesley's] Catholic spirit," *A Collection of Psalms and Hymns*, first published in Charleston, South Carolina, in 1737. David C. Skaggs, in "Editorial Policies of the *Maryland Gazette*, 1765-1783" (*MDHM*, LIX, 341-349), demonstrates Jonas Green's practice of allowing for or even encouraging divergent points of view on politics, religion, and trade, though he occasionally rejected as "too personal" an article, even by an Anglican rector "reasoning" with his recalcitrant vestry. Richard L. Merritt's "The Colonists Discover America: Attention Patterns in the Colonial Press, 1735-1775" (*WMQ*, XXI, 270-287) considers the question of how "integrated" a community America was on the eve of the Revolution by charting and weighing significantly American symbols and news in the years mentioned. The author draws convincing conclusions as to the trend toward America's interest in herself. Paul S. Boyer, in "Borrowed Rhetoric: The Massachusetts Excise Controversy of 1754" (*WMQ*, XXI, 328-351), looks at certain Boston newspapers within a narrower compass than Merritt's, for he is concerned only with the origin of the Controversy pamphlets of 1754 and finds that they were influenced strongly by Boston awareness of the British precedent of 1733 for this American protest. He even discovers that the New Englanders employed terms straight from their English predecessors.

Two writers have been especially concerned with editing. Rollo G. Silver's "Mathew Carey's Proofreaders" (*SB*, XVII, 123-133) lists the principal men who read for the Philadelphia publisher, the prices paid, and the names of the books they "proofed," such as Weems's *Washington*, Blair's *Lectures*, and Crèvecoeur's *Letters from an*

American Farmer. Alan Margolies, "The Editing and Publication of *The Journal of Madam Knight*" (*PBSA*, LVIII, 25-32), discusses the three nineteenth-century editions of this work and their possible relation to the now-lost manuscript.

Adrian H. Jaffe, in "French Literature in American Periodicals of the Eighteenth Century" (*RLC*, XXXVIII, 51-60), finds in American magazines considerable interest in French science, politics, and such authors as Voltaire, Fontenelle, Scarron, and Diderot. Knowledge of France certainly was not thorough, but these journals indicate what concept America actually had of that country. For the late seventeenth and early eighteenth centuries Jules P. Seigel, in "Puritan Light Reading" (*NEQ*, XXXVII, 185-199), examines invoices of two firms of New England to discover what they imported. He finds that Puritan tastes much resembled middle-class British tastes in popular and didactic fiction, romances and tales of chivalry, and the literature of roguery—in other words, almost all fiction from *Pilgrim's Progress* to *The English Rogue.*

The history of one more book should be noted. J. B. Nolan, in "Peter Williamson in America, a Colonial Odyssey" (*PH*, XXI, 23-29), traces the history of a captivity-narrative pamphlet concerning the adventures of a Scot held by Indians. It went through ten editions, at least one in America, and included woodcuts of the narrator in Indian dress and of the horrors practiced by the red men.

ii. Texts

A number of newly edited or translated texts, in some instances printed for the first time, appeared in 1964, including several diaries or journals. Perhaps the most imposing is the Yale-American Philosophical Society text of *The Autobiography of Benjamin Franklin* (New Haven, Yale Univ. Press), ed. Leonard W. Labaree, *et al.*, a handsome volume including in its introduction discussions of the work's literary and historical qualities, its influence, and its principal critics. The history of the manuscript is traced and strong arguments advanced for the editors' use of the original manuscripts. The editors' arguments may appear to some at least as debatable as Max Farrand's were for a different basic text for his 1949 version. The introduction might have profited by the sensitive appraisals of the *Autobiography* published by Sayre and Ward in 1963 (cf. *ALS, 1963*, p. 105), though perhaps these appeared too late for consideration. As it is, the reader may be somewhat disappointed in what will probably long remain the standard edition.

Clara S. Bostelmann has translated from the French Michel-Guillaume St. Jean de Crèvecoeur's *Journey into Northern Pennsylvania and the State of New York* (Ann Arbor, Univ. of Mich. Press), the first complete English translation of a work first published in 1801. This is a usually faithful but sometimes infelicitous translation of the work, which is a long and frequently tedious mixture of charming description and acute observation padded with an enormous proportion of direct borrowings from others. It should be compared with Percy G. Adams' 1961 translation, Crèvecoeur's *Eighteenth Century Travels in Pennsylvania and New York* (Lexington, Univ. of Ky. Press), a selected text of almost all the original material with a most perspicacious Introduction.

Although Joel Barlow translated J. P. Brissot de Warville's *New Travels in the United States of America 1788* (original French ed., 1791; this ed., Cambridge, Mass., Harvard Univ. Press, Belknap) the year after the original appeared, he gave only an incomplete and inaccurate selection of about 55 per cent of the whole. Now Mara S. Vamos and Durand Echeverria have translated and edited the entire book and written a discerning introduction. The editor-translators emphasize the partisan quality of the writing, representing only one portion of the United States, and the fact that the author was "not an original thinker."

The student of New England Puritanism will find most useful William R. Manierre II's edition of the newly discovered *Diary of Cotton Mather, D.D., F.R.S., for the Year 1712* (Charlottesville, Univ. Press of Va.), for it offers many new details of the character, writing, and ideas of the great preacher. The introduction includes an analysis of the paradoxes of Mather's nature as they are revealed in this and other of his diaries (see section iv below). Donald E. Stanford, editor of the standard edition of Taylor's *Poems*, has printed in full for the first time "Edward Taylor's 'Spiritual Relation'" (*AL*, XXXV, 467-475) from the copy in the Westfield Athenaeum. This prose essay-sermon, delivered in 1679, reaffirms Stanford's belief (see also section iv below) that Taylor was "an orthodox New England Congregationalist in full agreement with the Calvinistic dogma defined by the Westminster Assembly."

Perhaps also should be mentioned, since it has received little attention, Stanford's edition of *A Transcript of Edward Taylor's Metri-*

cal History of Christianity (Cleveland, Bell and Howell, 1962), a microphoto offset reproduction (from a typed copy) of the more than 21,000 lines of this recently discovered poem. Surely by Edward Taylor though the manuscript does not bear his name, it is a rhymed history of the martyrs (based on two books known to have been in Taylor's library) interspersed with lyrics on "Patience," "The Shine of Divine Truth," and other subjects. Varied in meter but in its narrative portions tedious and clumsily phrased, it is a text which everyone interested in Taylor's poetry and theology must see. One might guess that it is the Puritan's practice work for his now better-known and certainly greater verse, which the same editor has prepared in letterpress.

Though so far available only in *DA* (XXV, 1195-96) in summary and in full on film, Daniel Marder's study and collection of "The Best of Brackenridge" gathers the scattered work of the author of *Modern Chivalry* into a neat package and places it in the three major divisions of his writing and thinking. It includes materials from his earliest magazine writing to his period of reflection and recollection after 1800. A like valuable service to scholars of the first Federal period has been performed by Lawrence H. Leder, who has edited, with an introduction, "Robert Hunter's *Androboros*" (*BNYPL*, LXVIII, 153-190), the first play written and printed in America (1714). The text of the rare first edition is here printed. This play by a governor of New York was directed against his political enemies in the Assembly and against the Anglican clergy.

Two Southern texts of the late eighteenth or early nineteenth centuries are of some interest. O. I. A. Roche has edited (with an Introduction by Henry Wilder Foote and a Foreword by Donald S. Harrington) *The Jefferson Bible: With the Annotated Commentaries on Religion of Thomas Jefferson* (New York, Clarkson N. Potter). This is a gathering of scriptural passages, collected over a considerable period and completed by 1819, which Jefferson himself called "The Morals of Jesus of Nazareth." It was first printed in 1904. Here in handsome format, with photographic reproductions of Jefferson's clipped printed-text in four languages, his commentaries upon it, and quotations from other of his writings, together with a dispassionate introduction, is what should remain the standard text of this facet of the Virginian's mind—until Julian Boyd re-evaluates and prints it in his Jefferson *Papers*. Another side of the Virginia intellect and interest is exhibited in Curtis C. Davis' "'A National Property': Richard Claiborne's Tobacco Treatise for Poland" (*WMQ*, XXI, 93-117). This is a translation, with comprehensive introductory remarks, of Claiborne's "Method of Tobacco Cultivation in Virginia," which the editor unearthed in its Polish form and translated from one of the two versions he discovered. This treatise, one of a number written by Virginians on the subject during the later eighteenth century for European *philosophes*, is an excellent example of the American part in the dissemination of knowledge of agricultural methods which was a significant phase of the Enlightenment.

Journals or diaries kept by relatively obscure figures supply details of life and thought. J. C. Lobdell's edition of "The Revolutionary War Journal of Sergeant Thomas McCarty, August 23, 1776—February 16, 1777" (*NJHSP*, LXXXII, 29-46) is primarily of historical value. Thomas E. Andrews' "The Diary of Elizabeth (Porter) Phelps" (*NEHGR*, CXVIII, 3-30; 108-126; 217-236; 297-308) is a fascinating story of social and cultural life in a typical New England town from about 1770. Francis G. Walett has continued his edition of "The Diary of Ebenezer Parkman 1749-1750" (*PAAS*, LXXIV, Pt. 1, 37-203) and included more material on reading, preaching, and introspection. Considerably different impressions of life were recorded by Henrietta Liston, wife of the British minister to the United States from 1796, whose travel account is quoted and paraphrased in Irene J. Murray, "Henrietta Liston in America" (*VC*, XIV, 28-33). An early picture of the deep South appears in George F. Jones's translation of "Pastor Boltzius' Letter of June 1737 to a Friend in Berlin" (*GaR*, XVIII, 457-467), in which the chief pastor of the Salzburgers of Georgia describes conditions after three years in the colony.

iii. Biography

Seven biographies of major and minor figures and a number of shorter sketches add significantly to our knowledge of colonial individuals and their work. A number of major figures are surveyed at full-length, and the materials of lesser length and nature are often of considerable value.

At least four of the biographies are major contributions. Ola Elizabeth Winslow, who has already written of at least three other New Englanders, devotes her *Samuel Sewall of Boston* (New York, Macmillan) to a serious study of the life of the diarist as representative of the second and third generations in Boston. As in her previous works, she devotes more time to the man than to his writing, and in this case her subject was particularly suitable for such treatment. But she does devote considerable attention to two of his pamphlets as well as to his *Diary*, to the last as "a chapter in New England living." Few readers will know beforehand as much about another New Englander drawn at full-length, but Charles W. Akers, in *Called Unto Liberty: A Life of Jonathan Mayhew* (Cambridge, Mass., Harvard Univ. Press), has given us a beautifully organized and well-written book centering on a late eighteenth-century liberal in religion and politics. His life and writing do much to explain the transfer from Puritanism to Unitarianism, which recently published lives like that of Ezra Stiles do not. As a survey of the mind of New England Whiggery, as it expressed itself in sermon and tract from 1747 to 1766, it offers fresh and clarifying materials.

Philip L. Barbour's *The Three Worlds of Captain John Smith* (Boston, Houghton Mifflin) is perhaps even more significant than the lives of Sewall and Mayhew, for its new materials settle once and for all several qualities and episodes in the life of the controversial Virginia governor. Barbour, a linguist-biographer-historian with a wide knowledge of middle-European languages and literatures, has in several previous essays indicated the direction this study would take. Within the past decade Bradford Smith's and Laura P. Striker's studies of the same man indicated from authentic sources that Smith's own account of his Hungarian experiences, though challenged long ago by Charles Deane and Henry Adams, are indeed accurate. In a sense Barbour has taken up where Bradford Smith and Mrs. Striker left off. For he follows the Captain through his other European and American experiences, checking events and places in a variety of languages and literatures. Moderate, modest, well written, Barbour's account concludes with the comment that there now exists no single shred of evidence that Smith ever lied. It is our best book on a man who was a founder of American literature as well as of the American nation.

The fourth biography of real importance concerns a scientific figure, Brooke Hindle's *David Rittenhouse* (Philadelphia, Univ. of Pa. Press), a major and perhaps definitive study by a scholar who knows a great deal about the milieu in which his subject worked as well as about Rittenhouse's mechanical and theoretical achievement.

This is the story of a born scientist working against odds, but it is also a critical survey of his recorded writings on his favorite subjects of science and politics.

A fifth biography of a major worthy, Robert G. Raymer's *John Winthrop, Governor of the Company of Massachusetts Bay in New England* (New York, Vantage, 1963), is based almost entirely on much-used sources and adds nothing to our knowledge of its subject. It may be fairly interesting reading for the undergraduate concerned with Puritans and Puritanism. Much more useful to the scholar of the earlier period is J. A. Leo Lemay's *Ebenezer Kinnersley, Franklin's Friend* (Philadelphia, Univ. of Pa. Press), a brief biographical and critical study of the relationship of the scientific ideas of the two men mentioned in the title. Lemay also, in "Franklin's 'Dr. Spence': the Reverend Archibald Spencer (1698?-1760) M.D." (*MdHM*, LIX, 199-216), pieces together the story of the activities and writing of the man Franklin once claimed had introduced him to the study of electricity. Important though brief is Alfred O. Aldridge's *Jonathan Edwards* (New York, Washington Square Press), a little book about one-third biography and two-thirds a succinct and somewhat unorthodox account of the great Puritan's significance. Aldridge places Edwards in the main stream of English philosophical thinkers, almost totally devoid of continental influences, the culmination of systematic presentation of Calvinism in Anglo-Saxon countries. Clarity and originality render this short study worthy of comparison with the work on Edwards by Perry Miller and his school.

In a sense Darline Shapiro's "Ethan Allen, Philosopher-Theologian to a Generation of American Revolutionaries" (*WMQ*, XXI, 236-255) continues the study of eighteenth-century New England religious liberalism recorded in Akers' life of Mayhew. But Allen is shown as a Vermonter far removed from the Boston neighborhood, an Arminian who attacked Calvinism directly in a book published in 1784 and other earlier writings, a political Whig deriving his ideas largely from Locke. His *Reason the Only Oracle of Man*, known as "Ethan Allen's Bible," reflects the kind of rationalism which might be found in the mountain country.

Brief but useful biographical material appears in Edmund and Dorothy S. Berkeley's "John Clayton, Scientist" (*VC*, XIII, 36-42), a condensed version of their book on Clayton discussed in *ALS, 1963*, p. 101. David L. Jacobson attempts to identify an anonymous political writer of July, 1768, in "The Puzzle of 'Pacificus'" (*PH*, XXI, 406-

418), by a comparison of two pamphlets. John B. Shipley supplies interesting notes on Franklin's quondam partner in "James Ralph's
Place and Date of Birth" (*AL*, XXXVI, 343-346). Finally a great
amount of detail of literary interest is included in the sketches of
physicians in Joseph I. Waring's *A History of Medicine in South Carolina, 1670-1825* (Columbia, S.C., Bryan), for the verse and belletristic
essays as well as scientific writing of these gentlemen is frequently
considered in some detail.

iv. Criticism and Literary and Cultural History

Naturally the editions of texts, the essays on publishing, and the
biography discussed above present a certain amount of critical analysis and literary and cultural milieu. Therefore additional consideration of items already mentioned will be confined to only a few
especially representative of the subject of this section. During 1964
Edwards, Franklin, Mather, Smith, and Taylor continued to receive
attention in books and essays; a dozen or more lesser writers and
movements were presented; and several general cultural or literary
historical studies, a few quite distinguished, appeared.

Alfred O. Aldridge's stimulating terse study of Jonathan Edwards noted above deserves attention from several points of view.
The New England theologian also received three briefer treatments.
Wallace E. Anderson, in "Immaterialism in Jonathan Edwards' Early
Philosophical Notes" (*JHI*, XXV, 181-200), concludes that Edwards'
idealism derives not from Berkeley or anyone else but was arrived at
independently, a conclusion with which Aldridge might, with quali-
fications and reservations, agree. Emily S. Watts, "Jonathan Edwards
and the Cambridge Platonists" (*DA*, XXIV, 4180-81), argues that the
source of the theologian's idealism is probably in Cudworth, Smith,
Gale, and More, pointing out the influence of these philosophers at
Yale in Edwards' time and the pervasiveness of their thought in his
later investigations. Robert H. Woodward, in "Jonathan Edwards and
the Sweet Life" (*Fellowship in Prayer*, XV, No. 4, 11-13), emphasizes, by a study of Edwards' use of the word "sweet" and its derivatives, his awareness of the nature of divinity.

Benjamin Franklin received the most extensive and varied attention among all colonial literary figures during the period, for
three books other than the edition of the *Autobiography* already mentioned were entirely or largely concerned with him, and five essays

presented features of his life or thinking. Bruce I. Granger, in *Benja-min Franklin, An American Man of Letters* (Ithaca, Cornell Univ. Press), published the first book on this subject since McMaster's in 1883, the new study made imperative by the enlarged Franklin bibli-ography and the *Papers* now appearing. Granger presents Franklin's literary background, his periodical essay, the *Almanac*, his various forms of letters and bagatelles, and his *Autobiography* in a series of nine chapters which are concise, comprehensive, and intelligently critical. It is a useful and welcome book. A more specialized study outside the realm of pure belles-lettres, William S. Hanna's *Benjamin Franklin and Pennsylvania Politics* (Palo Alto, Stanford Univ. Press) nevertheless presents the developing politician in part through his newspaper and periodical essays, which aid us in seeing the gradual changes in his thinking and actually in his character. The third book, by Robert F. Sayre, *The Examined Self: Benjamin Franklin, Henry Adams, Henry James* (Princeton, Princeton Univ. Press), a delight-ful and incisive study of the autobiographies of the three men as rep-resentative of the American mind, begins with an excellent analysis of the organization of the *Autobiography*, the circumstances of time and composition, and the divergent roles played by the author in his text. Sayre's section on Franklin might well be adapted as an enlight-ening introduction to that work.

David Levin, in "*The Autobiography of Benjamin Franklin*: The Puritan Experimenter in Life and Art" (*YR*, LIII, 258-275), stresses the author's characterization of himself, the varying contents of the different parts, and the philosophy of practical virtue which under-lies it. This essay should be compared with Sayre's, for both are il-luminating and perceptive.

Alfred O. Aldridge's "A Religious Hoax by Benjamin Franklin" (*AL*, XXXVI, 204-209) finds from internal evidence that two essays in the *Pennsylvania Gazette* of 1734 may be added to the Franklin canon. These are meditations, one apparently serious, the other bur-lesque. Ralph Ketcham, in "Benjamin Franklin and William Smith: New Light on an Old Philadelphia Quarrel" (*PMHB*, LXXXVIII, 142-163), gives a reappraisal with some new evidence of a long friendship-enmity: its causes, nature, and significance. Max Savelle, "Benjamin Franklin and American Liberalism" (*WHR*, XVIII, 197-209), concludes that Franklin was "a practicing liberal in every aspect of his life during the period under discussion" (p. 200). In religion, education, freedom of the press, he championed liberalism so that he actually conditioned his society. This interpretation may well be contrasted with Hanna's in the book noted above. Finally, one of these liberal attitudes is discussed in Daniel Walden's "Benjamin Franklin's Deism: A Phase" (*Historian*, XXVI, 350-361). Walden sees his subject as an early and practical deist who sought authenticity for his beliefs throughout his life. The *Dissertation on Liberty and Necessity, Pleasure and Pain* (1725) is discussed as the author's first recorded step in his search. In the end Franklin remained "a practical . . . , constructive deist . . . , an eighteenth century American existentialist."

One of Franklin's confessed models in his early writing, Cotton Mather, is represented this year by William R. Manierre II's useful edition of the newly discovered *Diary . . . 1712* mentioned above. Also Manierre continued his "Notes from Cotton Mather's 'Missing' Diary of 1712" (*AN&Q*, II, 68-70, 84-85; see *ALS*, *1963*, p. 100), with running commentaries on such things as the way this text elucidates Sewall's *Diary* and proves Kittredge wrong in asserting that Mather did not propose himself as a member of the Royal Society. Austin Warren, in "Grandfather Mather and His Wonder Book" (*SR*, LXXII, 96-116), in this critic's usual inimitable prose writes of the *Magnalia* as that "almost masterpiece" which, because of its infinite variety of fact and fable, of life and baroque style, will continue to delight the sophisticated reader.

Philip L. Barbour not only published the biography of Captain John Smith noted above but buttressed his arguments with two essays containing new materials on individual portions of Smith's writings. "Fact and Fiction in Captain John Smith's *True Travels*" (*BNYPL*, LXVII, 1963, 517-528) is a study of Smith's spelling of place names from ear-knowledge and of his use of "quotations" from others. An overwhelming amount of detail is verifiable, Barbour finds here as he did in his biography. In "A French Account of Captain John Smith's Adventures in the Azores, 1615" (*VMHB*, LXXII, 293-303), Smith's account and a contemporary French one are reproduced in parallel columns to demonstrate again the reliability of the Virginia adventurer.

The Puritan poet Edward Taylor is represented by five brief studies of individual works, theories, or groups of poems. John Clendenning, "Piety and Imagery in Edward Taylor's 'The Reflexion'" (*AQ*, XVI, 203-210), explicates the poem as an example of the poet's orthodoxy, with the Eucharist as his symbol of Grace, and points out

Taylor's four basic, "brilliantly controlled" images. Stephen Fender, "Edward Taylor and 'The Application of Redemption' " (*MLR*, LIX, 331-334), poses again the question of the degree of indebtedness of *God's Determinations* to Ignatian meditation. Fender believes that Taylor owed more to the meditative scheme of Thomas Hooker's *The Application of Redemption* as a principal source than to the sort of Ignatian meditation suggested by Martz. Norman S. Grabo, in "Edward Taylor's Spiritual Huswifery" (*PMLA*, LXXIX, 554-560), delves more deeply than have previous critics into the ultimate meaning of one poem, which he feels is to be understood only in the context of the full body of Taylor's prose and poetry. He concludes that "Huswifery" must be accepted as a poem about the author's preparation for the Sacrament.

Donald A. Junkins, "An Analytical Study of Edward Taylor's *Preparatory Meditations*" (*DA*, XXIV, 2013-14), declares the purpose of his dissertation is to substantiate Taylor's Puritanism through analysis of the poems named in his title. This abstract suggests that Junkins has composed a well-reasoned support for an attitude now frequently held. Charles W. Mignon, Jr., "The American Puritan and Private Qualities of Edward Taylor the Poet" (*DA*, XXIV, 4679-80), argues that it is the "private quality" of Taylor's verse, not unorthodoxy, that explains the author's injunction that it not be published. In other words, Mignon feels that Taylor wrote his poems for himself as *personal* preparation for the Sacrament.

Short studies of colonial New England writing range in time from the first settlement to the threshold of the Revolution. Thomas B. Adams' "Of Plimoth Plantation" (*PMHS*, LXXV, 3-9) is a general appreciative essay which discusses other early worthies as well as Bradford and his book. Ken Akiyama continued from Japan his studies of colonial America in "William Bradford and Cotton Mather: A Stylistic Analysis of the New England Mind" (*SELit*, XLI, 59-71; Japanese with English abstract). Akiyama sees evidence of an interesting change in the psychology of early New England in the fifty years between Bradford's work and Mather's *Magnalia*. It seems demonstrated in the development from a Biblical, symmetrical, and simple style in Bradford to the heavy complex "belated Baroque prose" of Mather, the latter indicative of its author's feeling that New England had changed from a geographical reality to "a state of mind like Heaven and Hell."

Robert O. Stephens' "The Odyssey of Sarah Kemble Knight"

(*CLAJ*, VII, 247-255) holds that the schoolmistress' journey was an odyssey of Old World experience in the New, with indications that she saw many parallels between the incidents of her travels and the wanderings of Ulysses. Norman Farmer, Jr., in "The Literary Borrowings of Philip Pain" (*N&Q*, CCIX, 465-467), stresses his subject's indebtedness to Francis Quarles as more significant than what he owed to George Herbert. Winthrop S. Hudson, "John Locke—Preparing the Way for the Revolution" (*JPH*, XLII, 19-38), once more discovers Locke among the roots of America's developing liberalism, this time in works of Roger Williams such as *The Hireling Ministry*. "New England's Tom Paine: John Allen and the Spirit of Liberty" (*WMQ*, XXI, 561-570), by John M. Bumsted and Charles E. Clark, centers on one phase or segment of Massachusetts liberalism on the threshold of the Revolution. Certain pamphlets now identified and analyzed were the work of John Allen, a Baptist minister preaching and writing in Boston in the early 1770's. And in "*The History of New-Hampshire*: Jeremy Belknap as Literary Craftsman" (*WMQ*, XXI, 18-39), Sidney Kaplan describes the three-volume work of 1784-1792 as "a milestone in American historiography" in its patterns of presentation and its two prose styles.

Richard M. Gummere, in "Byrd and Sewall: Two Colonial Classicists" (*TCSM*, XLII, 156-173), contrasts the use made of the classics by the Virginia and New England diarists as somewhat representative of their respective cultures. The political and moral writing of one other Virginian receives far more detailed scrutiny than ever before in Charles Crowe's "Bishop James Madison and the Republic of Virtue" (*JSH*, XXX, 58-70). In pamphlets, petitions, sermons, and letters the president of William and Mary, between 1772 and 1800, showed his concept of the new nation as "a Republic of Virtue, the home of liberty and equality, free enquiry and social action." These and a number of other qualities Madison came, in his final years, to doubt the possibility of America's actually ever fully attaining. This is an enlightening study of the Southern revolutionary liberal intellectual, which the New England-centered scholar sometimes ignores.

Another revolutionary-age figure outside the New England periphery who received some attention is Crèvecoeur, the new translation of whose *Journey* is discussed in section ii above. Norman A. Plotkin, in "Saint-John de Crèvecoeur Rediscovered: Critic or Panegyrist?" (*FHS*, III, 390-404), contributes a much-needed analysis and evaluation of the agrarian-philosopher's actual attitudes toward

America, American life, and American individuals. Plotkin sees
Crèvecoeur as neither an unquenchable optimist nor a secret cynic,
but as a man who illustrated his theories from what he saw of American conditions. Alfred O. Aldridge, in "*The Rights of Man* de Thomas
Paine, symbole du siècle des lumières et leur influence en France"
(*Utopie et institutions au XVIIIᵉ siècle: Le pragmatisme des lumières*,
ed. Pierre Francastel, Paris, Mouton, 1963, pp. 277-287), sees in
Paine's bridge and his theories of governmental organization parallel
projections of the principle held by the *philosophes* that all knowledge sprang from observations of the laws of nature. Paine in all his
work established a parallel between the natural universe and social
structure, particularly in *The Rights of Man* as a reply to Burke's *Reflections*. Aldridge continues with a detailed description of the situation when *The Rights of Man* was published, the readers for whom
it was intended, and its curious (to us) reception in France.

In " 'The Captain's Wife': a Native Short Story before Irving"
(*SSF*, I, 103-106) by Jack B. Moore, we have identification as American for a tale printed in the *Gentleman and Ladies Town and Country Magazine* in 1789 by the unknown "Ruricolla." It is thoroughly
New England in theme and mood, with something of fantasy and
magic, and materials from folklore and fact, blended in a strong
matter-of-fact tone. Future historians and anthologists of our short
fiction should remember it.

More general studies in literary and cultural history are in several
instances significant and in at least one distinguished. Distinguished
in style, novelty of approach, and intellectual grasp is Howard Mumford Jones's *O Strange New World: American Culture, The Formative
Years* (New York, Viking), the first of a projected two-volume discussion of the paradox which formed the American mind and American creativity, this volume covering the period from pre-Columbian
days roughly to the 1840's. Taking its title from Lowell's line, "O
strange New World, thet yit wast never young," it combines in astonishing and admirable synthesis materials from literature sometimes
familiar, but more frequently not, into the story of the interplay of
the two great sets of forces—the Old World and the New—which have
made the Western Hemisphere what it is. Scores of questions are
asked directly or merely suggested, and their possible answers indicated. What did the Renaissance mean to the New World? How did
the Spanish-Portuguese idea of racial fusion and the Anglo-Saxon
one of separation prepare for the differences in the politics and cul-

ture of the northern and southern portions of the double-continent today? Jones ranges with surety of understanding and detail back and forth in literatures about and produced by the American peoples. He suggests cogent reasons for the enduring American repulsion-attraction to-from Europe. He suggests what the traveler, the settler, the frontiersman held within his perspective as he recorded. Behind it all is his amazingly comprehensive knowledge of what early Europe and America thought and did about the New World. The book is one of the great imaginative explanations of why we are what we are.

George Sensabaugh's *Milton in Early America* (Princeton, Princeton Univ. Press) is the kind of book which should be done for a dozen English and continental authors in early America. Anyone who has read in eighteenth-century verse knows that Milton is pervasive, and Leon Howard years ago pointed out some of the manners and matters in which this is true. But here, in a consideration which carries us from colonial sermons and poems to the *North American Review*, we are shown the English Puritan's place in the thought of liberals like Mayhew among the clergy, in Trumbull's satire, in Jefferson's political notes and pamphlets, and in the early Fourth of July orations. Yet there is conspicuously lacking the abundant evidence of Milton's influence in the as-yet-uncollected or reprinted essays and poetry which appeared in the colonial gazettes. At least another book could be written to show Milton in the forming of ideas, meter, and imagery, of freedom of press and government, as they are entombed in the files of the Pennsylvania, Maryland, Virginia, and South Carolina gazettes. This volume is a fine beginning. From it some enterprising student of colonial culture should work backward. He will find rich material.

Only a decade of our period is considered in Richard Beale Davis' *Intellectual Life in Jefferson's Virginia 1790-1830* (Chapel Hill, Univ. of N. C. Press), a study designed partially to demonstrate the invalidity of Henry Adams' generalization that Virginians of 1800 were interested only in law and politics, and only in those areas achieved anything. Chapters on education, reading, general and agricultural science, law and oratory, politics and economics, the fine arts, and belletristic writing assemble a multitude of facts in evidence. The chapter on theatrical history and the playwright and the one on the early verse, essay, letter, and novel (which runs more than one hundred pages) contain a considerable amount of literary and cultural history for the decade of the 1790's and much more for the new century.

Darrel Abel's *American Literature*: Vol. I, *Colonial and National Writing* (Great Neck, N.Y., Barron's Educ. Ser., 1963) is hardly a literary history, for it simply goes through a number of major authors and works and summarizes them, with little critical interpretation. Its bibliography and internal evidence of source materials for this early period are sadly out of date. The material on Captain John Smith is a case in point. Worst of all, it is written in the old-fashioned New England-oriented fashion in which most Southern and middle-states figures of equal importance with those considered are not even mentioned. One gets the idea that *The Federalist* is essentially Hamilton's, while most modern scholarship would indicate that in that work Madison's ideas and reasoning are the more original and influential as well as the better written. Among colonial preachers the sermons of James Blair and Samuel Davies are not mentioned, though the latter's at least are as good and perhaps far more significant than those of some New Englanders discussed. In other words, it is sad that a paperback designed for popular use follows, and in too much detail, the "New England Way," largely ignoring the early contributions of the middle and Southern colonies to our writing and thinking.

Not all the fault for the above is Mr. Abel's. There are simply too few monographs and books as yet on west-and-south-of-the-Hudson writing. One useful and enlightening little monograph which is one of those beginning to fill the lacunae, however, is René J. Le Gardeur, Jr.'s *The First New Orleans Theatre 1792-1803* (New Orleans, Leeward Books), a study from original manuscript letters and records of the theater and the plays introduced to Louisiana by Frenchmen inmigrating from the former French colony of Saint-Dominique. Buildings, organization, actors, and plays, even amounts invested, are included in this account of the beginnings of the histrionic art in one of our provincial cities where it has been most enduring. Another contribution to dramatic history is Charles R. Lown's "The Businessman in Early American Drama" (*ETJ*, XV, 1963, 47-54), an essay on the role of the native merchant in plays by Americans from 1787-1788 to 1810, including his place in works by Samuel Low, William Dunlap, J. Robinson, and John Minshull, among others.

"Puritan Poetry" (*Criticism*, VI, 291-312), by Hyatt H. Waggoner, is a critical survey of the qualities of New England verse from Philip

Pain and Bradstreet to Barlow. This clear, fresh essay is well worth reading. A. W. Plumstead's "Puritanism and Nineteenth Century American Literature" (*QQ*, LXX, 1963, 209-222) elaborates the author's belief that in metaphorical style, in its peculiar interpretation of the American dream, in its diaries, sermons, and letters, Puritanism had much to do with the stimulation and shaping of later writing in America. This rather superficial study is unfortunately flawed by its total failure to consider the contributions of other sections to our literary forms and ideas in the same era. Metaphor or sermon are by no means peculiar to New England, and dialect, the tall tale, the mock-heroic, and the Calvinistic were at least as much a part of the Franklin and Jefferson as of the Emerson and Hawthorne country.

Oral S. Coad, who has long been interested in the materials and themes of our literature, has, in "Pine Barrens and Robber Barons" (*NJHSP*, LXXXII, 185-199), gone into the history and nature of the eighteenth-century outlaws who became favorite subjects in American fiction from 1835 to the end of the nineteenth century. M. Ray Adams' "Della Cruscanism in America" (*PMLA*, LXXIX 259-265) shows how verse of the school had reached America by 1790; appeared in the work of such writers as Sarah Wentworth Morton and Robert Treat Paine; was reacted against by Royall Tyler in certain satires; but was still strong after 1800 in the epistolary-verse exchanges of John Davis and Lucas George in the *South Carolina Gazette*. Rudolf Glanz's "Jewish Names in Early American Humor" (*For Max Weinreich on His Seventieth Birthday: Studies in Jewish Languages, Literature, and Society*, The Hague, Mouton, pp. 63-71) explores briefly the relationship of two significant, though sometimes forgotten, elements in our early culture.

Of more general cultural than literary interest are four essays which nevertheless deserve the attention of students of our mind and its expression. Edmund S. Morgan's "Perry Miller and the Historians" (*PAAS*, LXXIV, Pt. 1, 11-18) asserts that "The career of Perry Miller rebukes us all" and goes on to show how the Harvard scholar worked from a conviction "that the narrative of the Bay Colony's early history can be strung on the thread of an idea." What Miller saw in Puritan theology as "a vast apparatus for describing reality" and other aspects of his unconventional intellectual-historical "method" should be pondered by all who have read or will read Miller's volumes. Morgan's summing up (p. 17) of what we now know "because of him" is a masterly tribute from one distinguished scholar to a departed brother.

The literary student also should be concerned with Henry F. May's "The Recovery of American Religious History" (*AHR*, LXX, 79-92), for it offers suggestions as to what is happening in an area to which he must always turn.

Neither exhaustive nor profound, Shunsuke Kamei's "Cultural Clubs in Colonial America, 1720-1750" (*SELit*, Eng. No., pp. 37-70) is yet a useful and suggestive account of real and "newspaper" clubs along the Atlantic coast from Boston to Savannah. Their potential significance in the development of a creative and critical conscious- ness is occasionally specifically demonstrated. The suggestions of possibilities for further research as to what these clubs actually pro- duced and were is implied throughout this essay, though the author has apparently had access to little more than secondary sources. The extrapolation or broadening and deepening of studies such as this might give us that so badly needed comprehensive understanding of the *whole* great area of the colonies in which belletristic writings and other forms of intellectual expression were major activities of at least certain groups and individuals. For neither Mark Twain nor the Puritan theologian is the only begetter of our literature. There were dozens of other ancestors before 1800 who have left identifiable traits in our living creative expression.

University of Tennessee

10. Nineteenth-Century Fiction

Louis J. Budd

The over-all shape of scholarship for 1964 shows more functional changes than, at least, the annual miracles from the assembly lines in Detroit. With the centennial about over, the bulge in Civil War themes is subsiding. With more scholars publishing in a growing market, the minor figures are getting wider attention. In a more basic trend, Washington Irving is attracting fuller study from both the interior analysts and the long-arching theorists of American fiction who need a firm starting point. Far beyond the stage of rediscovery, native humor continues to solidify its gains, partly at the expense of local color. But the rise of realism is surely being rediscovered, to the special benefit of the work of Harold Frederic and Frank Norris. Stephen Crane, climactically, has just about—so far as scholarly proportion and emphasis go—become a major figure discussed often in terms of world literature rather than his native contemporaries.

i. Popular Writers

As taste keeps changing and once-popular writers seem less and less inviting, the tendency is to defend them on extraliterary grounds, most often those of social and intellectual history. Still, John H. Kemble's two-volume edition of Richard Henry Dana's *Two Years before the Mast* (Los Angeles, Ward Ritchie Press) shows unqualified respect in the commentary, lavish format, full appendixes, and restoration of all omitted or altered passages. Ignoring aesthetic questions, Helene G. Baer, *The Heart Is like Heaven: The Life of Lydia Maria Child* (Philadelphia, Univ. of Pa. Press), memorializes the human warmth and political courage of one of our first "scribbling women." Similarly ignoring aesthetics for the historical backgrounds, Donald A. Koch's eighty-page introduction to a facsimile of the 1854 edition

---

1. This essay excludes four major figures: Hawthorne, Melville, Twain, and James.

of Timothy Shay Arthur, *Ten Nights in a Bar-Room* (Cambridge, Mass., Harvard Univ. Press, Belknap), throws much light on the temperance movement, about which our best writers said surprisingly little. A much broader approach guides Helen S. Smith's brilliant introductory essay for Elizabeth Stuart Phelps, *The Gates Ajar* (Cambridge, Mass., Harvard Univ. Press, Belknap); she analyzes that blob of post-bellum piety from several major perspectives, including its technical devices for striking the tastes of the artless reader.

Less scintillating but capable essays come from Walter L. Fertig, whose "Maurice Thompson as a Spokesman for the New South" (*IMH*, LX, 323-330) covers two fairly popular novels keyed on sectional reconciliation; from Henry M. Littlefield, in "The Wizard of Oz: Parable on Populism" (*AQ*, XVI, 47-58), who shows that *The Wonderful Wizard of Oz* was a "gentle and friendly" critique of the Populist movement; and from Maxwell Bloomfield, in "Dixon's *The Leopard's Spots*: A Study in Popular Racism" (*AQ*, XVI, 387-401), who draws linkages between the Progressive rationale and Dixon's racist classic. David Bleich, "Eros and Bellamy" (*AQ*, XVI, 445-459), provocatively examines *Looking Backward* in the light of socio-Freudian theories to find a profound forecast of mankind's victory over the stultifying principles of repression and dominance. No trace of such adventuring in social psychology disturbs John Pilkington's *Francis Marion Crawford* (TUSAS); written smoothly after carefully patient research, this critical biography admires Crawford at every turn without exploring the hidden or darker sides of his vast audience. In another contrast, two essays on fiction as an index to common ideas reach different levels of insight while surveying a period of time instead of a single figure. Elmer F. Suderman, "Criticisms of the Protestant Church in the American Novel: 1870-1900" (*MASJ*, V, 17-23), unexpectedly finds a disapproval of institutional religion in even the mass-cult writers of the later nineteenth century. By searching out all the relevant fiction, Joyce Appleby, "Reconciliation and the Northern Novelist, 1865-1880" (*CWH*, X, 117-129), succeeds in disproving some clichés in our literary histories, but she goes on to question the use of major writers as representative spokesmen and even the reliability of novels as a guide to general attitudes.

Horatio Alger, Jr., used less as a spokesman than as a tag for a syndrome, has also yielded sudden difficulties. In a breezily contemptuous biography (*From Rags to Riches*, New York, Macmillan, 1963), John Tebbel thought he was fashioning the valedictory on a childish hack and psychopath. But Gilbert K. Westgard II has reverently collected "all of Alger's known poetry" in *Alger Street* (Boston, J. S. Canner), which holds no hidden treasure. Just as reverent, Ralph D. Gardner, *Horatio Alger, or the American Hero Era* (Mendota, Ill., Wayside Press), supplies a meticulous bibliography of the welter of novels; he also intuits Alger's inner life with far more propriety than Tebbel. More persuasively, Fred Schroeder, "America's First Literary Realist" (*WHR*, XVII, 1963, 129-137), defends Alger's early novels as dispensing not a naïve myth of success but antisentimental, sensible advice for lads who wanted to get oriented in the big city and rise in a laissez-faire world. Still more convincing, Robert Falk, "Notes on the 'Higher Criticism' of Horatio Alger, Jr." (*ArQ*, XIX, 1963, 151-167), points out that the religious vein of his mind ran deep, that he "reintroduced into the dream of success a strain of the older idealism which the prudential wisdom of Franklin had largely discarded," that the now derided stroke of Providence in his plots was doctrine rather than ineptness. Even the Alger novels, then, can be misread by those who handle popular literature facilely.

ii. Irving, Cooper, and Contemporaries

Concern with the beginnings of serious American fiction keeps filling in the record. Ralph M. Aderman, "James Kirke Paulding's Contributions to American Magazines" (*SB*, XVII, 141-151), establishes a base-list arranged by periodicals in which the material appeared. With a brief yet helpful introduction by John D. Seelye, *Rachel Dyer* (1828) (Gainesville, Fla., Scholars' Facsimiles & Reprints) is now better available to prove that John Neal had some talent for characterization and provincial dialogue. Randall C. Randall's *James Hall: Spokesman of the New West* (Columbus, Ohio State Univ. Press), the fruit of many years labor, is one of those few books that actually will not be done again, at least so far as biography goes, though others will extend its cautious literary judgments. But the busiest filling of lacunae centers on Washington Irving. To help the definitive edition in progress, H. L. Kleinfield has made an annotated census of the journals, notebooks, manuscripts, and letters in "A Census of Washington Irving Manuscripts" (*BNYPL*, LXVIII, 13-32). As a separate venture, Edgeley W. Todd has meticulously edited *Astoria* (Norman, Univ. of Okla. Press) and insists that Irving sifted his sources responsibly to become an effective historian of the Far West.

Still, Irving's fiction will remain his chief claim on posterity. John Clendenning, "Irving and the Gothic Tradition" (*BuR*, XII, ii, 90-98), deftly analyzes how he played on the nocturnal and supernatural with masterly variations, from parody and "sportive" renderings to original uses of the Gothic as a distorted view of experience or as a losing resistance toward the pressure of American realities. Allying one tale to a much older tradition, Marjorie W. Bruner, in " 'The Legend of Sleepy Hollow': A Mythological Parody" (*CE*, XXV, 274-283), argues too ingeniously that "The Legend of Sleepy Hollow" is a "rollicking parody of ancient Greek myths and rites of Greek fertility." An appreciative essay on his most famous tale, "Characterization in 'Rip Van Winkle' " by Marvin E. Mengeling (*EJ*, LIII, 643-646), ends with the idea that Rip Van Winkle's wife symbolized the American qualities from which Irving had fled to England. Broadening and deepening this lately active approach, Allen Guttmann, "Washington Irving and the Conservative Imagination" (*AL*, XXXVI, 165-173), delineates an ambivalence between harking back to an "ordered and agrarian society" like Bracebridge Hall and an "implicit celebration" of New World democrats like Brom Bones.

Probably the most important new essay on James Fenimore Cooper, David W. Noble's "Cooper, Leatherstocking and the Death of the American Adam" (*AQ*, XVI, 419-431) contends that if, ignoring the order of composition, we take the five romances in the sequence of Natty Bumppo's life—a very vulnerable step—it turns out that they are destroying instead of affirming the myth of the American child of nature. Except for perhaps allowing Cooper too much disciplined craft, Thomas Philbrick, "Cooper's *The Pioneers*: Origins and Structure" (*PMLA*, LXXIX, 579-593), more persuasively holds that the first Leatherstocking book integrates its three main elements into a compelling image of New World landscape, society, and history. Kenneth Wayne Kuiper, "James Fenimore Cooper's *The Oak Openings, or The Bee Hunter*: An Interpretation and Evaluation" (*DA*, XXV, 452), declares a little-read, late novel to be underestimated. The most promising of the recent dissertations, Morton Lee Ross, "The Rhetoric of Manners: The Art of James Fenimore Cooper's Social Criticism" (*DA*, XXV, 1198-99), traces how social commentary is welded with art through a penetrating concept of manners. In the area of simple fact, Philbrick, in "The Sources of Cooper's Knowledge of Fort William Henry" (*AL*, XXXVI, 209-214), pins down some historical sources for *The Last of the Mohicans*. But the richest substantive additions are, of course, James Franklin Beard's third and fourth volumes of *The Letters and Journals of James Fenimore Cooper* (Cambridge, Mass., Harvard Univ. Press), which cover the period from 1833 to 1844, continue to print many unknown items, and achieve fresh biography in the background essays.

The revival of William Gilmore Simms, sometimes praised as Cooper's peer, is still more promise than reality. Joseph V. Ridgely has done a thoughtful introduction for *The Yemassee* (New York, Twayne), and L. Moffitt Cecil, in "Symbolic Pattern in *The Yemassee*" (*AL*, XXXV, 510-514), explicates an "integrated symbolic pattern" in it. Yet the socio-historical approach seems the most cogent, as in Austin J. Shelton, "African Realistic Commentary on Culture Hierarchy and Racistic Sentimentalism in *The Yamassee*" (*Phylon*, XXV, 72-78), which retails the judgments of some "senior students" at the University of Nigeria. In "The Romantic Mind," a chapter in *The Mind of the Old South* (Baton Rouge, La. State Univ. Press), Clement Eaton, an accomplished historian, evaluates Simms's upbringing and books with results fairly close to W. P. Trent's often-deplored biography.

iii. Mid-Century and Post-Bellum Writers

The stature of native humor is taken for granted in Willard Thorp's graceful, affectionate *American Humorists* (UMPAW, No. 42, Minneapolis, Univ. of Minn. Press); shunning intricate theory, Thorp radiates an informed gusto for all schools past and present. However, since one school now overshadows the rest, it is especially useful to have James C. Austin's *Artemus Ward* (TUSAS). While too charitable on some counts, Austin separates Ward from the Charles F. Browne who created him, insists on the differences between Ward the letter-writer and the platform wit, and effectively argues his influence. By chance, this study is nicely complemented by a facsimile of the 1862 edition of *Artemus Ward, His Book* (Santa Barbara, Calif., Wallace Hebberd), which includes the period-piece illustrations. Austin's "Petroleum V. Nasby to Gen Ulissis S. Grant" (*YULG*, XXXIX, 46-50) prints a manuscript item which reveals that David R. Locke, one of those who learned from Ward's letters, could do much more revising than legend allows.

Proof of the solidified position of the southern school lies in *Humor of the Old Southwest* (ed. Hennig Cohen and William B. Dillingham,

Boston, Houghton Mifflin), which knowledgeably pushes on to new writers. Further proof is a special issue of the *MissQ* (XVII, Spring) with five admiring essays. One of these, by John Q. Anderson, reviews past commentary mainly in terms of its assumptions, theorizes about origins of content and form, and points up fresh subjects; another, by John K. Bettersworth, follows the changing patterns of this humor up to the present day. "The Southern Yeoman: The Humorists' View," another chapter in Eaton's *The Mind of the Old South*, praises the ante-bellum school for limning the inarticulate small farmers and poor-whites, whom historians have tended to overlook. The creator of Sut Lovingood has escaped all danger of being overlooked himself. M. Thomas Inge, "George Washington Harris and Southern Poetry and Music" (*MissQ*, XVII, 36-44), runs down a minor point exhaustively. A fresh batch of uncollected pieces and news on work in progress fills up *The Lovingood Papers, 1964* (Knoxville, Univ. of Tenn. Press), edited by Ben Harris McClary. A definitive biography and collected tales are seemingly sure to come.

Harris and his predecessors have distracted interest from the local colorists, for whom they had helped to clear the road. Of that sprawling and once acclaimed school, Sarah Orne Jewett may end up as one of the few to be read at all, partly because she almost transcended it. She occupies an entire number of the *CLQ* (Ser. VI, June): a bibliography by John E. Frost shows the substantial amount of writing on her since 1949; Robin Magowan, "The Outer Island Sequence in *Pointed Firs*," convincingly displays her subtlety and (as in an earlier essay) her skill in adapting the pastoral mode; Richard Cary, "Jewett on Writing Short Stories," edits a sequence of letters that cast light on her working tastes and tactics. Trying to breast the tide of scholarly interest, W. Powell Jones, "Matt Crim: Forgotten Georgia Writer" (*EUQ*, XX, 149-159), asserts that *In Beaver Cove and Elsewhere* (1892), a volume of local color stories about North Georgia mountaineers, deserves better than neglect. He is perhaps right, but this rediscovery—and, one suspects, others on the way—will have to wait until tastes change again.

On the other hand, the tides of taste are moving back toward Ambrose Bierce, as a serious fabulist instead of a bad-boy wit. At the very outset, Robert A. Wiggins, *Ambrose Bierce* (UMPAW, No. 37, Minneapolis, Univ. of Minn. Press), claims Bierce for the modern revival of the Gothic-grotesque and makes a stimulating case, all the more because it is willing to concede that Bierce tends to disintegrate into his neuroses. Such balance of judgment goes so far in Stuart C. Woodruff, *The Short Stories of Ambrose Bierce: A Study in Polarity* (Pittsburgh, Univ. of Pittsburgh Press), that we are likely to conclude that the subject is not worth so much space; more particularly, he defends only the Civil War stories, explicating them capably in light of Bierce's contempt for illusion or self-delusion and his respect for the surrealistic workings of the imagination. Eric Solomon, "The Bitterness of Battle" (*MQ*, V, 147-165), extols the war stories even more highly for radically fresh insights springing from Bierce's affinity for the nightmares of combat, his love of irony, and his commitment to the short story over the novel. All facets of the other leading exotic in Bierce's day are defended in Beongcheon Yu's vigorous *An Ape of Gods: The Art and Thought of Lafcadio Hearn* (Detroit, Wayne State Univ. Press). Still, with full competence on both Hearn's occidental and oriental phases, it argues that he synthesized them best as a literary critic and traveler. Yu has naturally leaned on the long-running, multifarious researches of Albert Mordell—now summed up in his *Discoveries: Essays on Lafcadio Hearn* (Tokyo, Orient-West)—which go far toward establishing the Hearn canon.

iv. The Realists

No matter how assiduously some recent schemata of the novel ignore William Dean Howells, his massive body of work is immovably there, illuminated by a faithful circle of scholars. Two dissertations have taken a single volume for intensive work—Marilyn Austin Baldwin's on *My Mark Twain* (*DA*, XXIV, 4172) and Eugene Hamilton Pattison's on *The Leatherwood God* (*DA*, XXIV, 1963, 2039). With too broad a title, Thomas W. Ford, "Howells and the American Negro" (*TSLL*, V, 530-537), spells out the racial attitudes behind the minor novel *An Imperative Duty*. Robert W. Walts, in "Howells's Plans for Two Travel Books" (*PBSA*, LVII, 453-459), gathers details on the preparation for two late Howells travel books dealing with England. On a more active question, David H. Hirsch, "William Dean Howells and Daisy Miller" (*ELN*, I, 1963, 123-128), tries to unravel the tangle of Howells' feelings toward Henry James's controversial heroine. Robert Earl Mitchell, "Aesthetic Values as Depicted in the Fiction of William Dean Howells" (*Essays and Studies*, pp. 207-218), opens up a promising line of inquiry into his handling of American taste in the fine arts. But the most revealing word on Howells comes in Roger

B. Salomon, "Realism as Disinheritance: Twain, Howells and James" (*AQ*, XVI, 531-544), which masterfully pursues the interplay of realism and senses of the past or historical tradition.

Howells had few allies of consequence, though he was eager to welcome John W. DeForest and Edgar Watson Howe. Still curiously underestimated, DeForest at least gets a sympathetic reading for one of his lesser novels from Leo B. Levy, "Naturalism in the Making: DeForest's *Honest John Vane*" (*NEQ*, XXXVII, 89-98), who too firmly sees it as moving toward a mechanistic and biological view of character. Brom Weber's attempt, in an introduction for *The Story of a Country Town* (New York, Holt, Rinehart and Winston), to dissociate Howe from the rise of realism threatens what importance he has. Critical support for Howells came from H. H. Boyesen, who— Marc Ratner, "The Iron Madonna: H. H. Boyesen's American Girl" (*JA*, IX, 166-172)—pleaded for a "reciprocal action" in which the realist would free the genteel lady from her "romantic prison" while she in turn would free him from her constricting taboos. Hamlin Garland, who yearned for shattering success, may be helped tardily by *Centennial Tributes and a Checklist of the Hamlin Garland Papers in the University of Southern California Library* (ed. Lloyd A. Arvidson, Los Angeles, Univ. of So. Calif. Lib., 1962), a thorough index to a first-class collection. But soon after his early triumphs, he felt unhappy enough with his reviews to try new modes, as pointed out in James B. Stronks, "A Realist Experiments with Impressionism: Hamlin Garland's Chicago Studies" (*AL*, XXXVI, 38-52); Stronks expands on some interesting, unknown sketches and sharpens the lines of theory that Garland was developing. However, he had fatal limitations, exemplified in Robert Mane's "Une rencontre littéraire: Hamlin Garland et Stephen Crane" (*EA*, XVII, 30-46), which shows that he never understood Crane's personality or goals.

Lately, Harold Frederic has emerged as possibly a worthier contemporary of Howells and Crane. His socio-economic ideas in *The Lawton Girl* are solemnly weighed by Heinz Wüstenhagen ("Harold Frederics *The Lawton Girl*," ZAA, XII, 32-53). Richard VanDerBeets, in "The Ending of *The Damnation of Theron Ware*" (*AL*, XXXVI, 358-359), cites some working notes to suggest that the "restrainedly optimistic" ending of *The Damnation of Theron Ware* may have resulted from his compromise with a publisher's wishes. However, making him out a dark realist is opposed in two dissertations aimed at broad reappraisal: Austin Eugene Briggs, Jr., in "The Novels of Harold Frederic" (*DA*, XXIV, 3332-33), identifies his main theme as the comic gap "between what men aspire to and what they achieve," while Stanton Berry Garner, in "Harold Frederic: The Major Works" (*DA*, XXIV, 3747-48), concludes that he was, at his creative peak, a "writer of romance." A core of consensus on Frederic still lies ahead.

In the case of Frank Norris, critical skirmishing has led to a desire for more hard facts. After warning that we have no authoritative study on the dates of writing and publication of his novels, John S. Hill, in "The Writing and Publication of the Novels of Frank Norris" (*AN&Q*, II, 151-152), offers a firm outline, and James Childs tries to redate Norris' first novel in "The First Draft of *McTeague*: 1893" (*AN&Q*, III, 37-38). Donald Pizer continues his fine amplifications, both with "The Masculine-Feminine Ethic in Frank Norris' Popular Novels" (*TSLL*, VI, 84-91) and *The Literary Criticism of Frank Norris* (Austin, Univ. of Texas Press), which for the first time gathers all of Norris' significant essays and compiles a definitive bibliography. Uncovering the range of his ideas as well as their unappreciated coherence, the headnotes for this collection go beneath and beyond the easy label of "naturalism." Also provocative is the contention by Gilbert A. Schloss, in "Frank Norris, Form and Development" (*DA*, XXIV, 1963, 2486), that Norris' "ideological base and major thematic source" was Joseph LeConte, the eminent Western evolutionist.

v. Stephen Crane

The only mark of academic prestige now lacking for Crane is a newsletter. Under the editing of Robert N. Hudspeth, the second installment for an annual bibliography of Crane scholarship (*Thoth*, V, 85-87) has appeared. A leader in the search for rare items, Robert W. Stallman has printed three interesting sketches as "New Short Fiction by Stephen Crane" (*SSF*, I, 1-7, 147-152); biographical commentary on one of these sketches, by Lillian B. Gilkes, "Stephen Crane's 'Dan Emmonds': A Pig in a Storm" (*SSF*, II, 66-71), elicited a stinging rejoinder by Stallman ("Was Crane's Sketch of the Fleet off Crete a Journalistic Hoax?" *SSF*, II, 72-76) and a softer reply ("No Hoax: A Reply to Mr. Stallman," *SSF*, II, 77-83). With E. R. Hagemann, Stallman has also edited *The War Dispatches of Stephen Crane* (New York, New York Univ. Press), which brings together scarce and unknown items and fresh background materials, mostly to his clear credit as both a human being and a writer. Bernard O'Donnell, "An Analysis of Prose Style to Determine Authorship: *The*

O'Ruddy, A Novel by Stephen Crane and Robert Barr" (*DA*, XXIV, 2894), turns to statistical techniques to indicate what parts of a posthumous novel were his. In a more crucial area of editing, Maurice Bassan, "A Bibliographical Study of Stephen Crane's Poem, 'In the Night'" (*PBSA*, LVIII, 173-179), proves that the texts of his poems have been handled far too casually for the complexities of manuscripts and early printings.

The most direct contribution to biography, Eric Solomon's *Stephen Crane in England* (Columbus, Ohio State Univ. Press), grapples with the question of why Crane was so fully accepted in literary circles when he went abroad in 1897; it provides some satisfying answers by following up his relations with H. G. Wells, F. M. Ford, Henry James, and especially Joseph Conrad; it also sees a "steady growth" in his craft up to the end. His death was hastened by his heroics in Cuba, with no compensating gain, according to Frederic Griswold Hyde, "American Literature and the Spanish-American War: A Study of the Work of Crane, Norris, Fox, and R. H. Davis" (*DA*, XXIV, 1963, 2478-79). As for over-all views of his personality, Stanley Wertheim, "Stephen Crane" (*LitR*, VII, 499-508) eloquently restates the theory that he was fleeing from his father's religiosity while learning to trust self-reliant awareness as his only escape from nihilism.

Wertheim's dissertation on the sources, reputation, imagery, and structure of *The Red Badge of Courage* (*DA*, XXIV, 3734-35) decides that its central device is "ironic paradox" and that self-knowledge emerges as the ideal, which is never fully attainable. Though competition will keep active, Frederick C. Crews's edition of *The Red Badge* (Indianapolis, Bobbs-Merrill) will stand as the best, both in the introduction and sensitive notes, for some years at least. Another perspective has been added already by Warren D. Anderson, in "Homer and Stephen Crane" (*NCF*, XIX, 77-86); working mainly from internal evidence, he argues that the *Iliad* and the *Odyssey* strongly influenced both the character development and rhetorical patterns in *The Red Badge*. With respect so high for its craft, Cecil D. Eby, Jr., "Stephen Crane's 'Fierce Red Wafer'" (*ELN*, I, 1963, 128-130), will persuade few that its most debated simile is merely a "neutral, descriptive phrase deriving from his fund of visual images." On another controversial point, Edward Stone, "Crane and Zola" (*ELN*, I, 1963, 46-47), traces verbal parallels between a passage in *L'Assommoir* and Jim Conklin's death scene.

The sources and quality of Crane's realism are even more controversial for the Bowery prose. David Fitelson, "Stephen Crane's *Maggie* and Darwinism" (*AQ*, XVI, 182-194), rigorously insists that his first novel reduces conduct to the tropisms of animal behavior, with violence for the sake of survival as the guiding value. Citing figurative patterns, Maurice Kramer, in "Crane's *Maggie: A Girl of the Streets*" (*Expl*, XXII, Item 49), takes the opposite stand that the "dominant mode" of *Maggie* is irony rather than naturalism or, for that matter, impressionism. Its immediate context as a corrective to sentimental fiction about the slums is filled in by Maurice Bassan, "Crane, Townsend and Realism of a Good Kind" (*NJHSP*, LXXXII, 128-135). Bassan's note on "An Experiment in Misery," in "The Design of Stephen Crane's Bowery 'Experiment'" (*SSF*, I, 129-132), centers on the imagery, proclaiming it "patterned and tightly welded to the structure." Few authors have generated as much concern with both their matter and method as Crane.

"The Blue Hotel" still holds its challenge as one of his most cross-grained stories. Neal J. Osborn, "Crane's 'The Monster' and 'The Blue Hotel'" (*Expl*, XXIII, Item 10), searches for vital puns in the names of his characters. Just as intriguing, William B. Dillingham's "'The Blue Hotel' and the Gentle Reader" (*SSF*, I, 224-226) suggests that Crane intends for us finally to feel abashed over sharing antagonism toward the Swede, to feel that we also failed in sympathy. Donald B. Gibson, "'The Blue Hotel' and the Ideal of Human Courage" (*TSLL*, VI, 388-397), likewise spurning a nihilistic reading, finds a brief for brotherhood as well as courage tempered by perceptivity. The larger theme of courage, through which man overcomes his demoralizing and dehumanizing fears, controls Gibson's "The Fiction of Stephen Crane" (*DA*, XXIII, 1963, 2525).

As yet, explication of Crane has kept to the same few items, even though many more are now easily available. The looming question is whether the bulk of his work deserves or can endure intensive treatment. This question is much more threatening for Cooper, Simms, Norris, and others who are being explicated—rather than explained—for the first time. Irving's best tales, it turns out, can stand the test. But, taken as a whole, the scholarship and commentary of 1964 still leave in doubt whether nineteenth-century fiction can meet the standards of modern criticism or whether, aside from the obvious alternative of accepting it on its own grounds, most of it must end up as mainly a tool of cultural and intellectual history.

Duke University

11. Nineteenth-Century Poetry

J. Albert Robbins

Though one's individual interests are the real factor in determining what scholarship one reads, it might be helpful here to indicate what books and articles are, by virtue of subject and treatment, most noteworthy. Clearly Clark Griffith's new book on Emily Dickinson as a tragic poet is the most significant of the year; and, though one does not read concordances, scholars will find S. P. Rosenbaum's concordance of Dickinson indispensable. The broadest and most generally useful essay is by Bernard Duffey on the Protestant imagination as basic in achieving "romantic coherence." That we should not consider such writers as Holmes and Whittier closed subjects, Howard Mumford Jones shows in writing on the former and Perry Miller on the latter. Finally, the detailed and interesting article by J. O. Bailey on the vampire motif in "The Fall of the House of Usher" is a model of this form of scholarship and a contribution that may well be central in understanding intention and meaning in that tale.

i. Edgar Allan Poe

The most substantial book on Poe this year comes from a series of lectures on Poe as critic, given at Mercer University. Edd Winfield Parks has expanded and annotated these lectures in *Edgar Allan Poe as Literary Critic* (Athens, Univ. of Ga. Press). Under the topics Poe as magazine critic and Poe on fiction and on poetry, Parks has usefully noted the critical works which Poe knew, the authors and literary forms he admired or disliked, his contributions to our thinking on the purposes and means of fiction and poetry, shifts in his critical thinking, and finally aspects of his strength and weakness. For all his limitations, Poe sought a broader, less provincial criticism, set an example of close textual analysis, tried to fashion a more flexible theory of metrics, and believed that meaning should be woven artfully into the very texture of literature. And, Parks contends, much of what he did in his own writing and much of what he advocated in his criticism can be related to his evolving aesthetics for a magazine literature.

a. **Poetry.** Of the small yield of articles on the poems, the longest and most ambitious is James M. Kiehl's "The Valley of Unrest: A Major Metaphor in the Poetry of Edgar Allan Poe" (*Thoth,* V, 42-52), an essay marred by a contrapuntal playing of his main theme against a sometimes opaque explication of five other poems. In doing the latter task, one feels, every fact, allusion, and hunch is thrown in, that nothing in his mind, or sheaf of notes, may be wasted. In "The Valley of Unrest," he notes, the metaphor is clearly stated: "*Once,*" in a more innocent time, the valley was happy; "*Now,*" the valley is a place of unrest, disquiet. Seeing man's mortal life as a time of torment, Poe uses the valley of unrest as a metaphor for "the anguish of sensual life, whose crisis is mortality." Considering "Poe's Revisions of 'Lenore'" (*AL,* XXXV, 504-510), John C. Broderick feels that the intermediate (1843) version of the poem does not deserve the rather general preference for it. There are two basic versions, "'A Paean,' which is a dramatic monologue of the bereaved lover, and 'Lenore,' which is a dramatic dialogue between the bereaved lover and the false friends." The intermediate version is not superior and "is important chiefly for its evidence that Poe is moving from a somewhat strained lyrical subjectivity to the firmness of dramatic dialogue." An examination of structure and diction shows a steady improvement in concept and execution. As a result, there is "a spiral movement from hypo-critical grief to a consolatory acquiescence, the customary destination of elegiac poems."

In "'The City in the Sea': A Reexamination" (*CE,* XXV, 436-439), T. Frederick Keefer feels that many a critic has wrongly viewed Poe's city as submerged in the sea. Rather, it is "in"—surrounded by— the sea. The poem is a tour de force in achieving effect by a tension of unnatural and unrelieved immobility, emphasized all the more by the slight movement in the final twelve lines. There is no moral meaning, for Poe has sought only to present a succession of images. Concerning the famous refrain of his most famous poem, Edwin Fussell rejects as "demonstrably spurious" the author's account of it all in "The Philosophy of Composition" ("Poe's 'Raven'; or, How to Concoct a Popular Poem from Almost Nothing at All," *ELN,* II, 36-39). He believes that Poe found the key word in John Webster's *Duchess of Malfi* (V, iii), where Eccho says, "Never see her more." We know that Poe was aware of the play from his early days as a poet, and "The Raven" may have been "in the works" in his mind longer than we think and longer than Poe admitted.

David A. Randall, bibliophile and present Lilly Librarian, has written *The J. K. Lilly Collection of Edgar Allan Poe, An Account of its Formation* (Bloomington, Ind., Lilly Library), a chapter in the history of an era of book collecting that is not likely to be repeated. Of more interest to the Poe scholar is a final section on " L'Affaire 'Musiad.' " It concerns an eight-page pamphlet published in Baltimore in 1830 "by Diabolus." Only one copy, in the Harris Collection at Brown, can be located, but it is the apparently imperfect eight-page copy that Sarah Helen Whitman saw. She thought that the prose preface was in Poe's style and sent John Neal some excerpts and other relevant facts for his opinion. Neal replied that, though he knew nothing of the pamphlet, the excerpts "were written by Poe himself." Thomas O. Mabbott thinks it is not Poe's, but if not, it is the earliest poetical reference to Poe—for there are four lines on Poe, including these: "Now strain'd a license, and now crack'd a string, / But sang as older children dare not sing." The *Musiad* pamphlet is photographically reproduced.

As a doctoral dissertation, Harry C. Snider has attempted "An Edition of the Poems in Poe's Last Collection Based Largely on His Own Critical Principles" (*DA*, XXIV, 3344). Concentrating upon twenty-seven short poems, he has tried to apply Poe's own critical theory and practice in establishing a text.

b. **Fiction.**   The basic premise of an article last year by Lyle H. Kendall, Jr. (see *ALS*, 1963, p. 122) was interesting, but not fully convincing; meanwhile another scholar has been at work on the same topic, the vampire motif in "Usher." The longer and more detailed study by J. O. Bailey is very persuasive by its treatment in depth, with attention to details of description, characterization, narrative, and allusion ("What Happens in 'The Fall of the House of Usher'?" *AL*, XXXV, 445-466). What does happen is deliberately obscured and concealed by Poe, who, Bailey believes, took a precise body of vampire lore and to heighten terror refined the disgusting details into "the strange and mystical" to produce a powerful story whose purpose is elusive and puzzling. Bailey is able to cite actual parallels in vampire lore for all the details of the tale (and what a resource is Montague Summers, that authority on the black arts). Only a sampling of Bailey's evidence is possible here, but these are among the more central: the House itself may be vampiric; Madeline shows many symptons of the vampire victim; several of Roderick's actions (his painting of a *lighted* vault, his reading the actual book of medieval ritual, *Vigilæ Mortuorum*) suggest attempts at exorcism; when he imprisoned Madeline in the vault, Roderick may well have known her to be undead in the vampiric sense—just as he knew that the House itself might succeed in freeing her (in evil houses, doors can be thrown open supernaturally). Presumably, too, Roderick knows his vampire lore well enough to realize that if he dies before Madeline sucks his blood, the House and Madeline must also die in agonies. The narrator, who is of the natural world and who tends to reject the supernatural, is, as Roderick says near the close, a madman—as he is in the context of this evil realm of which Roderick seems to be so knowledgeable. Though it is another dimension of the story altogether and beyond the main concern of this study, Bailey believes that an area of the tale may have autobiographical import—that of the degenerative strain (for example, Poe's sister Rosalie was not mentally normal). The story can still represent Poe's search for identity. Another attack upon meaning in the story (Joseph Gold, "Reconstructing the 'House of Usher,'" *ESQ*, No. 37, 74-76) more conventionally seeks an explanation in the premature-burial theme. Mr. Gold believes that it is not death that Usher fears but survival-in-death. Madeline is symptomatic of this fear, "a fear which he tries to 'bury' in the dark depths and recesses of both his house and mind." But Madeline is a part of Usher and burying her is burying a part of himself.

An article by Charles T. Samuels, "Usher's Fall; Poe's Rise" (*GaR*, XVIII, 208-216), is, oddly enough, really about "Ligeia." The experts cannot agree on the meaning of "Usher," a tale in which "no important question is answered, no character comes clear, no event yields its significance." On the other hand, "Ligeia" is clear and powerful, and its theme—the soul's quest for perfection, for spiritual purity or oneness—is basically American, found from Jonathan Edwards down. "Ligeia," Mr. Samuels ventures, is "the only time in fiction or poetry when Poe came clear." Muriel West also seeks Poe's intention in the tale and arrives at an answer by a rather devious route. In "Poe's 'Ligeia' and Isaac D'Israeli" (*CL*, XVI, 19-28), she recalls Poe's letter to P. P. Cooke (Ostrom, 82) in which he said that no one had seen his intention better than D'Israeli. No such letter from D'Israeli exists, but, undiscouraged, Miss West goes to his romance, *Mejnoun and Leila,* to infer how he might have read Poe's story. To make a long inference short, Miss West believes that the despised Rowena "symbolizes whatever it was that Poe tried to do when he gave up writing poetry because it did not pay." Ligeia, then, is the "Ideal Presence" or muse who performs the miracle of discovery that the loathed and inferior tale can become a prose poem of great beauty.

Joseph P. Roppolo considers "Meaning and 'The Masque of the Red Death'" (*TSE*, XIII, 1963, 59-69), after a look at earlier criticism, and reminds us of the early statement in the tale that "Blood was its Avatar and its seal" and of the fact that "not once does Poe say that the figure is the Red Death." Blood is symbolic of the life force, as well as a reminder of death. "The intruder is not the plague, not death itself, but man's creation, his self-aroused and self-developed fear of his own mistaken concept of death."

Everyone is aware that the cause of the revenge in "The Cask of Amontillado" is completely unspecified, and some would be happier if Poe had told us. Why he did not, and should not, have told us is suggested by John H. Randall III in "Poe's 'The Cask of Amontillado' and the Code of the Duello" (*SGG*, V, 1963, 175-184) "The story is about an extreme version of the gentleman's code" associated with the specific, formalized code of the duello. Such a code presupposes pure aristocracy, the personal honor of such a gentleman as an absolute value, the right and need of retribution for any affront to that honor, and the pseudogentleman as beneath contempt (but not beneath revenge). Montresor "does not even consider Fortunato a member of the human family," and by the end of the tale he has "reduced his foe to an animal level, the ultimate in degradation." Such a code as this can be seen in more recent fiction—Robert Penn Warren's *World Enough and Time*, Faulkner's *Absalom, Absalom!* and in Jake Barnes's contempt for Robert Cohn in *The Sun Also Rises*.

The differing guesses as to where Poe found the name, C. Auguste Dupin, in "The Murders in the Rue Morgue" are wrong, W. T. Bandy believes ("Who Was Monsieur Dupin?" *PMLA*, LXXIX, 509-510). In a letter written to Poe, September, 1840—when Poe was probably writing the tale—the correspondent, S. Maupin, speaks of a French teacher, C. Auguste Dubouchet. By combining two syllables of the surnames, *voilà*, we have Dupin.

Obsession, the demonic, and anguish as we find them in Poe derive from American circumstances and make him an ally of Hawthorne, Melville, and Dickinson, Marisa Bulgheroni affirms ("Poe e il demone americano," *SA*, IX, 1963, 69-82). Unlike the other three Americans, however, Poe did not construct a system of moral values since to him art was sufficient. The detachment, lucidity, and coldness of his analyses are "more apparent than real, the fruit of a passionate esthetic discipline." There is attention to four stories ("The Imp of the Perverse," "The Angel of the Odd," "The Tell-Tale Heart," and "The Black Cat") by way of documenting the origin and nature of the dark forces that concerned Poe and the other three writers.

A dissertation by Donald B. Stauffer examines the "Prose Style in the Fiction of Edgar A. Poe" (*DA*, XXIV, 2912). Following a look at Poe's awareness of style in his criticism and his reputation as a prose stylist with an examination of his characteristic sentence structure and diction, Mr. Stauffer observes five recognizable categories of style: the plausible or verisimilar, the critical or analytical, the hyperbolic, the parabolic, and the arabesque. "Whether controlled and coldly analytic, or loosely constructed and highly emotional, Poe's style almost always reflects this tension between the intuitive and the ratiocinative."

"The Literary Uses of Astronomy in the Writings of Edgar Allan Poe" get a thorough treatment by Elva B. Kremenliev (*DA*, XXIV, 4176). She finds that interest in astronomy, largely speculative and theoretical, turns up in every form of composition from poetry to miscellaneous prose fillers; that Poe saw "*Eureka* as a final synthesis of his own conflicting loyalties to the mathematical reason and the poetical imagination"; and finally that "the critical theory not only preceded the cosmological theory but actually shaped it."

c. **Miscellaneous.** The first actual French translation of Poe was "Le Scarabee d'or" (1845), and, since Poe was specified as the author, this is the first reference to him in print outside English-speaking countries. W. T. Bandy has now identified this pseudonymous first translator ("Poe's Secret Translator: Amédée Pichot," *MLN*, LXXIX, 277-280).

Poe's reception and influence in Hungarian literature is given close scrutiny by Béla Korponay in "Edgar Allan Poe in Hungary" (*HSE*, I, 1963, 43-62). It began with a biography and two translated stories in 1856, and soon Poe the poet was important to Hungarian poets as a symbolist. About the turn of the century there was a decadent interest in Poe's world of death, "voluptuous melancholy and over-ripe masterful musicality." The leading Hungarian poet of the period "consciously regarded Poe as an ancestor," and later poets considered him their intellectual predecessor. By 1949 Poe was well regarded for political rather than literary reasons—for his "passionate protest against the wildly competitive spirit of his age."

ii. Bryant, Longfellow, Lowell, Holmes, Whittier, Carleton, Clarke

There has been no substantial book on Bryant for thirteen years. Now there is one, *William Cullen Bryant,* by Albert F. McLean, Jr. (TUSAS), which in the space of a six-chapter volume gives some sense of the man's intellectual growth but, more importantly, assesses thirty key poems. Mr. McLean gives attention to the anthology favorites ("Thanatopsis" has the better part of a chapter) and also suggests the worth to a thoughtful reader of such poems as "Monument Mountain," "The Fountain," and "The Painted Cup." Though Bryant struck off several of his best poems at a very precocious age, his thought and his art never matured in a significant way. His gift was concentric, not linear. He was caught between two ages, McLean suggests: he could not forego the formalism of the reasoned discourse of an earlier age, nor could he embrace the visionary aestheticism of the newer one. In some instances his theory could propose possibilities beyond his practice, and "while the rhetoric of eloquence could provide him with a stable center for his creative activity, it could also leave his expression vaporous, void of content, and out of touch with his listeners."

Bryant as the literary patriarch in his own day has been succeeded by Bryant the pre-Romantic, but, Vito Amoruso believes, he can be viewed, at least in part, as an inheritor of the eighteenth-century continental tradition of grace in expression and formality in structure ("La poesie di Bryant," *SA,* IX, 1963, 39-67). The artist in him made him seek beauty of form; the bourgeois in him forced the inclusion of moral teaching. Bryant was the conscious poet in his verse, much different from Bryant the man. As poet he "was more interested in the *way* of expressing things than in the things themselves." The artist's unique way of seeing, of feeling, his formal way of expressing himself bespeak an earlier literary tradition that is European.

Last year we had Newton Arvin's book on Longfellow (see *ALS,* 1963, p. 124) and, this year, we have another book and a pamphlet.

It is coincidental and does not signify a Longfellow renaissance. Arvin made a manly attempt to refurbish Longfellow, yet felt that we should, "once and for all," confess him to be a minor writer. Cecil B. Williams, in *Henry Wadsworth Longfellow* (TUSAS), cannot make the confession, nor can he elevate him above that rank. His book is half biography and half running commentary and resumé—short on the commentary and long on the resumé. It has its reference uses, but one will find little useful criticism. Occasionally there is a smile to be had ("Evangeline is nothing if not persistent") and occasionally a useful, if apparent, admission ("Longfellow developed an extraordinary faculty for phrasing neatly what his contemporaries already believed"). One wishes that the writer would more often run the risk of obvious, yet helpful, generalizations. For example, it is clear —from the published works and from unrealized plans to write pieces on La Rochefoucauld, Alfieri, Bach, Machiavelli, Mazarin, and Swift's Stella and Vanessa—that Longfellow was often the victim of his erudition, but the point is nowhere clearly made. The shorter study, with the same bare title, by Edward Hirsh (UMPAW, No. 35), is a forty-page summary of essential facts handy for the undergraduate in a hurry who may want a sense of the life, the career, the variety of poetic types and prose, and the shifting reputation. It has the antiseptic quality of the encyclopedia article, with here and there a thought-provoking insight.

In a substantial article, Marston LaFrance ("Longfellow's Critical Preferences," *CLQ*, Ser. VI, pp. 398-402) notes the early influence of Alison's associationist theory, but believes that the crises in Longfellow's life between 1835 and 1843 required a "more strenuous doctrine" to sustain him. He found it in a close study of Goethe, which helped him "to turn from a mere idyllic and romantic contemplation of life to sterner issues." This is seen earliest in *Hyperion* and at its best in the later *Michael Angelo*. John T. Krumpelmann has uncovered documentary evidence that Longfellow was enrolled, in the winter semester of 1835-1836, in two courses at Heidelberg—aesthetic readings in Schiller and in Shakespeare. The writer uses this occasion to review other evidence of Longfellow's early interest in Shakespeare ("Longfellow's Shakespeare Studies in Heidelberg," *NS*, XIII, 405-413). In "Longfellow's 'Chaucer,'" Nancy L. Tenfelde (*Expl*, XXII, Item 55) notes that the opening lines of the sonnet echo Chaucer's description of his chamber in *The Book of the Duchess*.

A doctoral dissertation by a Hispanic specialist, Lawrence H.

Klibbe, is now in print: *James Russell Lowell's Residence in Spain*
(*1877-1880*) (Newark, N. J., Washington Irving Pub. Co.). It brings
together published letters and references to the subject and adds for
the first time, so far as I am aware, a sampling of Lowell's diplo-
matic dispatches. Much of Lowell's residence in Spain is ridiculous,
in a comic-opera way. Though he had taught Spanish at Harvard,
Lowell had trouble speaking the language. Though he had admired
Spain at a distance, he was homesick. His wife suffered an illness and
Lowell had an attack of gout. Though Lowell had keen insight into
the personalities and forces that kept the country unprogressive, he
could do nothing. In his period of service, nothing momentous hap-
pened, so that his dispatches are idle communiqués from a dead
front. So well equipped to respond creatively to Spanish character
and culture, Lowell wrote nothing of any importance—apparently
suffering from the national malaise of mañana. The writer is hard put
to justify the enterprise and in trying to do so can forget his own evidence. On page 107 he says that Lowell must have been familiar to
the local reading public because the king quoted some of his verses
when Lowell presented his credentials. But back on page 43, the
writer has quoted Lowell's honest diagnosis: "He had been crammed,
of course, beforehand."

An unpublished letter of 1871 records Lowell's repugnance for
Mrs. Browning's "pushing expression to an unpleasant *physical* ex-
cess" in *Aurora Leigh* (Charles J. Rooney, Jr., "A New Letter by
Lowell," *AL*, XXXVI, 214-215) and states that he has never read
Swinburne's "Laus Veneris." Thus Lowell did not, as some have
thought, write the review of Swinburne's poem in the *North American Review*.

With his usual clarity and illumination, Howard Mumford Jones
writes on "Oliver Wendell Holmes (1809-1894)." Written as an address given at Miami University five years ago, it is now included in
a collection with eight other pieces (revisions of articles separately
published as far back as 1944) called *History and the Contemporary:
Essays in Nineteenth-Century Literature* (Madison, Univ. of Wis.
Press).[1] Jones describes both the breadth and narrowness of the
man and speculates on reasons, some of them valid, why Holmes

1. The reprinted essays are "History and the Contemporary," "The Greatness
of the Nineteenth Century," "The Generation of 1830," "Prose and Pictures:
James Fenimore Cooper," "Arnold, Aristocracy, and America," "Thoreau as
Moralist," "Poe, 'The Raven,' and the Anonymous Young Man," and "Whittier
Reconsidered."

is now so seldom in our minds. He was of an age and a culture which was self-contained—intelligent without being seminal, parochial and self-satisfied. The final third of the piece considers "the most 'modern' theme in the twelve volumes of Holmes' complete works . . . the nature of consciousness in its relation to personality." In both prose and poetry Holmes revealed his thought on the development of personality, the relation of personality and freedom, and the meaning of consciousness, thinking which shows modernity but stops short of its full implications. "He hovered on the edge of philosophical determinism," for example, "but his urbanity rebuked his pessimism, and, child of a hopeful era, he thought that God and science would ever move from more to more."

In a memorial issue of the *Harvard Review* dedicated to Perry Miller, we have the text of a lecture on Whittier which Miller delivered at Swarthmore College in 1957 ("John Greenleaf Whittier: The Conscience in Poetry," II, ii, 8-24). It is fresh and superbly thoughtful, and it cuts through the conventional "image" of the dear, upright poet. "Whittier," says Miller, "is a more complicated figure, both as man and as writer, than he appears in the conventional view. . . . He possessed a fair amount of guile, which he employed most systematically in building up the legend of his guileless simplicity." In so presenting his nature to the public, Whittier doomed himself when the modern revolution of taste and fashion turned against the image he had created. A revealing bit of evidence is, just prior to his joining Garrison, his coveting a nomination for congressman and inventing a conniving political scheme to try to swing it. As a writer, Whittier, we all know, owed much to Burns, but, Miller contends, his early works were Scott-ish efforts to give his region a legendary past—and he even succumbed to the Byron-disease. There are other eye-openers in the article to indicate that we should reconsider this gentle Quaker.

A summary of representative criticism of Whittier is collected and analyzed by Lewis E. Weeks, Jr., in "Whittier Criticism over the Years" (*EIHC*, C, 159-182). Contemporary reviewers noted his freshness, simplicity, earnestness, and sincerity; and clearly the poet was beloved. As the years passed, Whittier's didacticism came under increasing censure. British critics were generous but tended to overrate the elements most interesting to them—the poems about Indians and purely native themes. The commentators of our century have a larger perspective, but few have taken note of his prose, though the

Southern Literary Messenger considered him, next to Hawthorne, our most polished writer of prose. Altogether the qualities most often cited were Whittier's sense of justice, and his love of humanity and sincerity. The poetry itself revealed simplicity, directness, clarity, vigor, manliness, tenderness, and melody.

Whittier's mixed feelings about a serious split in the American Anti-Slavery Society are the subject of a letter of 1840, here printed in complete text for the first time (John B. Pickard, "John Greenleaf Whittier and the Abolitionist Schism of 1840," *NEQ*, XXXVII, 250-254). The heavy-handed tactics of Garrison caused a convention walkout of the leadership because Garrison opposed a positive policy of political action. Whittier, who was not present, told his sister that the two groups *"could not* work together on any terms. . . . I am sick of their folly."

John L. O'Sullivan, editor of the *Democratic Review*, reprinted some Whittier items in one of his newspapers, the New York *Weekly News* (G. Thomas Tanselle, "Some Reprinted Whittier Items," *AN&Q*, II, 99-100). The 1903 sale catalog of manuscripts and books in Whittier's personal library is photographically reproduced in *ESQ*, No. 34.

The author of the famous *Farm Ballads* (1882) was "a kind of Midwest Whittier in a minor key." Maurice Bassan's article, "The Poetaster and the Horse-Doctors" (*MASJ*, V, i, 56-59), recounts the hassle over admitting Will Carleton to the Authors' Club in New York. Some wanted him admitted; others opposed it, and both sides wrote Mark Twain for proxy support. Twain may have left the club as a result of the ridiculous controversy.

C. Carroll Hollis, in "The 'Mad Poet' McDonald Clarke" (*Essays and Studies, DSPS*, V, 176-206), narrates the life of a man whose mild, mad eccentricities made him a living legend and the butt of heartless hoaxes, though he was also treated gently by many a famous New Yorker of the day. As Mr. Hollis' quotations show, his able verse deteriorated over the years with his mind until 1842, when he died in the madhouse—by water, as his parents had died before him.

iii. Emily Dickinson

There are three books on Dickinson (four, if we include a 1963 study by an Italian critic), and they are of substantial quality. We now have a badly needed concordance based upon the variorum text, another collection of reprinted criticism, and a perceptive study of Dickinson as a tragic poet.

The first American in the series of Cornell concordances to be computerized is Emily Dickinson. The massive *Concordance to the Poems of Emily Dickinson*, edited by S. P. Rosenbaum (Ithaca, N. Y., Cornell Univ. Press), is a reliable and comprehensive index to over 100,000 of Dickinson's words, giving the context of the line where each word occurs, the opening words of the first line of the poem (by which poems are likely to be indexed or remembered), the number of the poem in Johnson's text, and the line number of the poem. Variants are noted and cross-references supplied. Expendable words such as *and, the,* and *a* are dropped, but common words especially important to Dickinson are included: *like, as, be* (though other forms of *to be* are excluded), *I* (her most used word—it occurs 1,682 times), and other relevant personal pronouns. If you are interested in the poet's preoccupation with death, you will find her using that word 141 times and that word with variants of *to die*, 344 times—and using *life* 156 times and that word with variants of *to live*, 250 times. The possibilities of comprehensive quantitative and qualitative studies of her imagery and similes, for example, are now fully open and, since the Johnson text attempts to establish chronology, developments in her use of language can be traced over the years.

The editorial methods are outlined by Rosenbaum, if I may be allowed to look forward to his article prepared but not published before the concordance, in "Emily Dickinson and the Machine" (*SB*, XVIII, 1965, 207-227). Necessarily there is some duplication with matter in the preface of the concordance, but additionally there is a description of how such a work is fitted to the capacities of the modern computer. Once the editor has examined Johnson's variorum text and anticipated all problems, each line of poetry is punched on an IBM card. A second operator, presiding at a "verifier," covers the same ground to detect errors. Following this checking, a machine-printed text is proofread against the original text, a procedure which detected a mere six errors. What would have taken years by manual methods now can be done faster, and more accurately, in months. Finally, since Cornell is preserving the magnetic tape used for this volume, future scholars can ask the machine to search it for special data. The machine age is fully, and beneficially, upon us.

There was last year a sampling of recent Dickinson criticism edited by Richard B. Sewall in the Prentice-Hall "Twentieth Century

Views" series (see *ALS, 1963*, pp. 126-127). This year there is a broader-based volume edited by Caesar R. Blake and Carlton F. Wells, *The Recognition of Emily Dickinson, Selected Criticism since 1890* (Ann Arbor, Univ. of Mich. Press). The former provides sixteen reprinted essays from 1924 to 1961; the latter, forty-five reprinted essays and reviews from 1890 to 1960—and with only four duplications. The former aims to sample critically valid essays, while the latter undertakes more fully to document the general as well as the critical reception. With as little overlapping as there is, each volume has its usefulness, though if one had a choice, he might prefer to have the Blake-Wells collection as more versatile and comprehensive.

The opening lines of a familiar poem ("Presentiment—is that long Shadow—on the Lawn— / Indicative that Suns go down—") provide Clark Griffith with the title for a new study, *The Long Shadow: Emily Dickinson's Tragic Poetry* (Princeton, N. J., Princeton Univ. Press), a fine, perceptive, and selective bio-critical study of Dickinson's central themes. She is tragic, of course, not in the classic but in the modern sense—"tragic by her sense of the discrepancy between man's potential glory and the actual horror that contains him." Griffith has concentrated upon what he sees as the informing theses in virtually all her mature poetry: "dread of change; the wish to avoid commitments which magnify the fact of change; the sense that no event can be enjoyed because, in another moment, it may cease to be; the countering realization that commitments are inescapable and events must be borne." The method employed is thematic, with spare reference to the biography and with a close analysis of some fifty relevant poems. To strip Griffith's assertions and inferences down to their barest form, the chief of them are these: Dickinson starts with the Emersonian position (a need to believe in some overlying plan; correspondence between natural and supernatural, etc.), but by the force of her later time and inner needs and by her incapacity for Emersonian generalization, she moves toward the modern position in thought (life is more bleak than rewarding) and in method (reliance upon a new and intense form of symbolism); her metaphysical view of the cosmos and her type of personal despair are remarkably similar to Melville's for, to both, nature is "treacherous and unpredictable," the universe "contaminated to the core"; her central concern is with dread and fear, involving time as a betrayer, change as a threat to security and stability, death as the ultimate mystery (and paradoxically both fearful and to be wished); irony is the natural weapon for mockery and defense; she analyzes the self with forthright, almost clinical, precision in its threefold aspects—the physical, the mental, and the spiritual. Griffith considers the love poems, when cosmic, to be fine, but when personal or social, he says, they tend to be weak. He refuses to play the old game of Find-the-lover and instead examines "Emily and *Him*"—Dickinson's psychosexual suspicion of the world of the masculine; her sense of deprivation as a female; ways in which her father, her brother, and God the Father failed her; her "dread of generalized masculinity," so vital and obsessive in her poetry. Finally, all these concerns are summarized as three dominant forces and images—the clock, the father, and the child. Altogether this is a book of persuasive insights and illuminating explications—well-written and sound, even in the daring trapezework of pure speculation.

The Italian study of Dickinson (*Emily Dickinson, Prospettive Critiche*, Firenze, Le Monnier, 1963) is less unified than Clark Griffith's book, for in it Biancamaria Tedeschini Lalli considers differing types of issues. She explores Dickinson's cultural bases and sense of poetic vocation; the significance of her reclusive nature (Griffith and others have more useful insights on this matter); those of her poems that involve anxiety (her "sentimental, existential, and even religious anxiety" forms the psychological base of her poetry); her poetry "in a minor key" (treating modest, intimate things in her daily life—a poetry of "small things," which at times indicates a decadent sensibility); her great themes of love, death, and eternity; and finally her "surrealism"—poems concerned with the obsessive, dream states, horror, and silence, for example—which relate her to Baudelaire, Mallarmé, and "pure poetry," and even with paintings by the decadents and surrealists.

Ways in which Dickinson anticipated modern poetry are examined by Suzanne M. Wilson. In "Emily Dickinson and Twentieth-Century Poetry of Sensibility" (*AL*, XXXVI, 349-358), the writer notes that, although Dickinson uses a rigid, rational, sermonic structure in much of her poetry, she did achieve complex techniques that have become important in contemporary poetry—techniques which demand much of a reader's intuition and involve varying degrees of multiple-meaning or suggestion. In three poems Miss Wilson discusses examples and, in conclusion, notes ways in which Pound, Eliot, and the American Imagists developed these methods. "It is in her use of suggestion, both free and limited," she says, "as well as in her use of sharp, extended images that Emily Dickinson most resembles twentieth-century poets who developed their techniques after the pattern of the French Symbolists and Japanese poets."

In writing on "Emily Dickinson" (*NHQ*, V, No. 15, 181-186), Robert Goffin, a Belgian poet and literary historian, makes similar observations. "Everything she did unconsciously and mysteriously at the command of her tormented nature," he says, "was to become systematic with French poets from Mallarmé to Saint-John Pearse." The "breath-taking complexity" of her poetry "will be understood better if one is aware that, before Mallarmé, she unconsciously put into practice the principle of describing not the object but the emotion it evokes." Beyond her precocious modernity, M. Goffin (whose remarks on Dickinson come from his recently published volume on world poetry) undertakes a reading of several poems to emphasize sexuality in her work and the results of embittered and disappointed love. "Mine by the Right of White Election" is not so much on spiritual love as it is her use of "biblical or religious language to suggest sensual trance by superposing associations which sometimes expand to the point of eroticism," and in "My Life Had Stood a Loaded Gun" she could "hardly have found a more expressive symbol to show the fullness of her carnal fire."

The importance of color to Dickinson is treated by Rebecca Patterson in "Emily Dickinson's Palette" (*MQ*, V, 271-292; VI, 97-117). The increasing attention to color, along with other aspects of the poetic art, derives from Dickinson's favorite models, Emerson, the Brownings, Keats, Shakespeare, Milton, and the Book of Revelation. As emotional intensity increases in the poetry, so does the use of color up to the peak year, 1862, with a diminishing—as well as a dulling—of the palette after 1865. Dickinson was unusually responsive to colors and to shadings of those colors and, indeed, saw "her world in the emotional tone of its colors." Miss Patterson samples the varied uses of color, noting by way of generalization that green is the color of the grave and hence of death and that blue is one of her favorite personal colors, largely representing warmth and freedom. "Red," she says, "is Emily Dickinson's color. Outwardly she may wear the white of martyred renunciation, but inwardly she is red . . . , whether in ecstatic happiness or in the violence of loss and suffering"—until after 1865 when her vitality declines and the white gains upon the red and pales it to pink. The author provides a frequency table and, as well, a statistical comparison with Dickinson's favorite poet-models.

Four poems come under explicatory scrutiny. Paul O. Williams gives a line-by-line reading of "One Day Is There of the Series" (*Expl*, XXIII, Item 28), a poem whose obscurity comes from puzzling metaphors and syntactical elision. Thanksgiving Day, Dickinson says, is not completely a day of thanks because of bereavements in the past year. Mario L. D'Avanzo ("'Came a Wind Like a Bugle': Dickinson's Poetic Apocalypse," *Ren*, XVII, 29-31) considers the imagery in that poem "not one of private conjuration" but Biblical in source (the early chapters of Revelation). The "ominous and apparently personal revelation of the nature of things presented in the poem parallels the vision which St. John is given on Judgment Day." In "Dickinson's 'I Had Not Minded Walls'" (*Expl*, XXIII, Item 25), Robert Merideth considers "vail" a key—what is unveiled and to whom. This and other aspects of the religious, the chivalric, and the "hesitantly erotic" help to illuminate her meaning. Regarding "One Dignity Delays for All" (*Expl*, XXIII, Item 16), Erhardt H. Essig disagrees with Charles R. Anderson's reading of "our meek escutscheon" as a tombstone and says that, more logically, it is "man's mortality, his essential humanity, which is the only condition for his admission to the rank in question."

Paola Guidetti traces the rising reputation of Dickinson in her country in "La fortuna di Emily Dickinson in Italia (1933-1962)" (*SA*, IX, 1963, 121-172). Dickinson was first introduced to Italians with the translation of five poems in 1933. The first critic to treat her was Emilio Cecchi in an article in 1936 and a critical volume in 1939. Since then, her poetry has gained so much acclaim in Italy that one might term her a popular poet. It is the modern spirit in her poems—concern with insecurity and estrangement, for example—that makes her relevant today. Italian critics, Guidetti believes, have rather quickly responded to the essence in Dickinson's poetry—its "tragic color," complexity, affinity with modern symbolist poetry, and creation of a new poetic language in America; most Italian observers have fortunately avoided the pseudopsychoanalytic that fascinates Americans. There is a list of published translations and critical works.

Three hundred and one poems written from 1850 to 1861 form the basis for David T. Porter's look at "The Art of Emily Dickinson's Early Poetry" (*DA*, XXV, 1921-22). Among these, there are twenty-

nine superior poems. He believes that perhaps her greatest achievement "was her ability to dissociate the emotion in her poetry from any
specific causal experience."

iv. Timrod, Chivers, Hayne, Lanier, Harris, Weeden

Southern poets have come in for a fairer share of attention this year,
the most important of these studies being a TUSAS volume by Edd
Winfield Parks on *Henry Timrod*. Because of the unreliable nature of
much published material, Mr. Parks has felt a need to stress biography and to annotate rather fully. His thirty-five pages on the life are
doubtless the most reliable short study in print. In the four critical
chapters on the work and career of this frail and short-lived Caro-
linian, we gain a sense of Timrod's range and the nature of his failures
and successes. As a critic, Parks says, Timrod was fundamentally
ethical and he saw the local condition of literature with clarity. He
knew that "before the South could have a great literature, the intellectual climate had to be changed and vivified"—but what a lost
cause that was! The South's leading citizens refused to support its
literary magazines, for example, but when Timrod's thumping, chau-
vinistic poem "Ethnogenesis" was read at a dinner party of distinguished South Carolinians, these delighted leaders made up a "handsome purse of gold" to bestow—in an abominably unique gesture of
largesse—upon the poet. The name "Timrod" has never, for me, con-
jured up a very sharp image of a man's nature and personality and, I
must confess, not much emerges in this careful study. The failure, I
am sure, is not Mr. Parks's but is inherent in his subject.

"The Letters of Thomas Holley Chivers" John Olin Eidson (*GaR*,
XVIII, 143-149) uses to summon up the lively, contradictory personality of this contemporary of Timrod. The correspondence is
unusually revealing, and we see his great ego, self-dramatization, fascination with defeat and death, "fine" writing, attraction to Transcendentalism, and wild literary enthusiasms. To Simms he was a
"wild Mazeppa" of literature and to Stedman, "a sort of Poe-run-
mad."

John Archer Carter deals with an uncollected poem of Hayne in
"Paul Hayne's Sonnet 'To the New South'" (*GaHQ*, XLVIII, 193-
195). Not written until 1881 at the earliest, it opens with a quatrain
of praise to the "New South" but then enjoins respect for the beauty

and grandness of the Old. One cannot be sure of Hayne's postwar attitudes, for they seem to be ambivalent.

A nostalgia for the Old South of his youth and a distrust of the implications of Negro freedom and industrialization in the New South give Sidney Lanier a "bifold," but consistent and almost predictable, attitude toward his beloved Georgia and the South. After a sampling of Lanier's chief pieces, Kenneth England ("Sidney Lanier in C Major," *Reality and Myth*, pp. 60-70) concludes that Lanier could never outgrow his ante-bellum convictions, that his later poetry is still in this C-Major key, and that these and other factors "prevented him from being a truly good poet." Another scholar treats an early segment of Lanier's life—the two and one-half years he spent in Alabama after the Civil War—and does it thoroughly and readably (Cecil Abernethy, "Lanier in Alabama," *AlaR*, XVII, 5-21). The young man went there to visit an uncle and try to recover his health and spirits. He held a desk clerk's job for a time in a Montgomery hotel, was principal of a small-town school, had various affairs of the heart, completed work on *Tiger Lilies*, and, as a just-published novelist, married. The years were a time of self-searching that largely settled the matter of literature as a life's work. A dissertation by Jack Angelo DeBellis ("Sidney Lanier and the Morality of Feeling," *DA*, XXV, 1907) examines the poetry critically and observes "the shaping power of a philosophical tradition that held emotion to be man's primary faculty." Heart and love are, for Lanier, "the symbols for the South."

George Washington Harris, the creator of Sut Lovingood, is not renowned for poetry, but M. Thomas Inge ("George Washington Harris and Southern Poetry and Music," *MissQ*, XVII, 36-44) has found a fragment of doggerel that appeared in a Knoxville newspaper in 1868 and a conventionally sentimental poem, "The Coat of Faded Grey," that was printed in a Nashville newspaper in 1866 and set to music the same year.

Technically, a volume published in 1962 should go unnoticed here, but one does appear in the 1964 *PMLA* bibliography that deserves to be known as a useful work about a little-known poet. Frances C. Roberts and Sarah Huff Fisk have reprinted, under the title of Miss Howard Weeden's first (1898) volume, the poetic works of this Alabama poet, have reprinted the Introduction by Joel Chandler Harris to her second volume (*Bandanna Ballads*, 1899), and have prepared a twenty-four page biographical memoir (*Shadows on the Wall: The Life and Works of Howard Weeden*, Northport, Ala., Colonial Press). It is an attractive volume, with the merit of reproducing Miss Weeden's skilful portraits of Negroes that originally accompanied her Negro-dialect poems. They are undistinguished verse, but the verse and the art record an age which, even then, Harris knew had largely passed. The tender Negro character here depicted would now earn the derisive epithet of "Uncle Tom"—all the more reason for reminding ourselves of the historical past in this virtually forgotten literary document.

v. General

Whether one agrees totally with the premise of his essay or not, Bernard Duffey's carefully reasoned ideas on "Romantic Coherence and Romantic Incoherence in American Poetry" (*CRAS*, VII, 1963, 219-236; VIII, 453-464) will have to be reckoned with. The substance of romantic coherence is "a particular feeling for religious reality." "The poets of our romantic coherence," he believes, "were only secondarily poets of nature or self or America. These were data, matter for poetry, but by the same token were not determining marks. The Protestant imagination was their illuminating principle and nature or self only the objects of potential illuminations." In *The Continuity of American Poetry* Roy Harvey Pearce views Bryant and Emerson as antithetical, but Duffey thinks that they must be grouped together "as spokesmen for the Protestant spirit, for the coherence of American romanticism." Bryant "is the celebrant of a holy communion and its blessings: his is the rhetoric of thanksgiving and praise," while Emerson as a poet "is mainly the preacher of divine providence"; but they "share a community of imagination, a view of nature as lying in the arms of encompassing spirit and as constituting the means for man's participation in spirit." Incoherence entered with Whitman, for "to make the human spirit depend on sex or any other bodily function was, simply, to deny spirit and so destroy the essence of romantic coherence." Melville's lyrics introduce "the cultivation of obscurity as a stylistic means" and bring us to the threshold of a recognizably "modern" poetry. We can see romantic coherence losing its power at "the point at which homily or hymn pass over to epigram, as in Stephen Crane, or anecdote as in Robinson or Frost, or subjective lyric as in Cummings or Millay, or dramatic lyric as in Pound or Eliot, into dialectic as in Stevens or Tate or Ransom, or the plain declaration of William Carlos Williams."

To end on a lighter tone, we might note the curious versifier, "A Poetic Precursor of Bellamy's 'Looking Backward,'" unearthed and reprinted by Ben W. Fuson (*Extrapolation*, V, 31-36). These twenty-one stanzas called "A Century Hence" appeared in the early pages of *A Century Hence and Other Poems* (Kansas City, Mo., 1880), the work of a Platte City, Mo., lawyer. Well before Bellamy, William M. Paxton foresaw remarkable personal wealth (though somehow there are servants about), climate control, one-man aircraft capable of circling the globe, color photography, lighting by sky reflectors, meals by telephone, and a new source of power ("a motor, much stronger than steam, had appeared, / Yet cheap, economic and mild"). The nation stretches from Panama to the north pole, with St. Louis the capital of a billion people—a land made morally perfect by wealth ("So people were able to add to their store, / And be generous, noble and true"), though in much of the rest of the world "ignorance, vice and oppression held sway."

Indiana University

12. Fiction: 1900 to the 1930's

C. Hugh Holman

The fiction writers who dominated the first third of the twentieth century were, with few exceptions,[1] concerned with the relationship of the novel to the society whose accurate portrayal they saw as one of their primary objectives or were fascinated by the magnitude of the vast audience which the mass-circulation magazines gave them. These novelists, frequently possessed of great talent, through their pursuit of one or the other of these objectives relegated their work, as we see it today, however astigmatically, to the second order of artistic achievement. The ideals and the methods of such writers are generally little valued by contemporary critics hot in the pursuit of symbols or eager for existential studies of the search for personal identity. To see such writers in perspective requires that they be examined in their historical context and in terms of the literary traditions within which they worked. For the writers of the first third of this century neither of these basic scholarly tasks has been adequately performed, but in 1964 approaches to these tasks were seriously undertaken in several general studies and in several relatively brief books examining the works and lives of a number of minor figures.

i. General Studies

Walter Allen, in *The Modern Novel in Britain and the United States* (New York, Dutton), brought his rich knowledge of the history of the novel to bear upon modern writers and produced a study which, although it makes relatively few fresh or original judgments about individual novelists, places them in a historical context so that some sense of the flow of literary history may be gained from his graceful record. This history is, in terms of general usefulness, probably the

---

1. These exceptions are, I believe, Thomas Wolfe, who is discussed in this essay, and Ernest Hemingway, William Faulkner, and to a certain extent F. Scott Fitzgerald, who are treated in other essays in this volume.

most valuable single work produced in 1964 about the writers who are the subject of this essay.

Other book-length studies tended toward the definition of the novel in its relation to society. The most sophisticated of these was Arthur Mizener's *The Sense of Life in the Modern Novel* (Boston, Houghton Mifflin), a serious treatment of the realistic novel—essentially the novel of manners—with emphasis on British and American writers, notably Trollope, Fitzgerald, Hemingway, Faulkner, and Anthony Powell. Mr. Mizener sees the central problem of American fiction as the conflict between personal and public life. He is excellent in his treatment of James Gould Cozzens and good on Dos Passos, Dreiser, and Marquand, and he sees Allen Tate's *The Fathers* as an almost ideal social novel. Mr. Mizener believes that our ideas of what the novel is as a form are confused and that our critics need a firmer concentration on the nature of fiction, a position with which few who have examined any sizable amount of contemporary criticism would disagree.

Some of this concentration is present, however, in several special studies. Michael Millgate, in *American Social Fiction: James to Cozzens* (Edinburgh, Oliver and Boyd; New York, Barnes and Noble), makes an historical and critical examination of American novelists "who set out deliberately to create an image of the society in which their characters live." He examines Howells, Norris, Wharton, Dreiser, Anderson, Lewis, Dos Passos, and Marquand—usually cursorily, except in their relation to this image of society. Mr. Millgate, a British critic, accepts the view expressed a number of years ago by Lionel Trilling in his essay "Manners, Morals, and the Novel," a view which has tended to dominate critical treatments of realism in recent years. In this country Mr. Trilling's major assumptions have produced such offspring as Richard Chase, Leslie Fiedler, and Marius Bewley. In "Reality, Manners, and Mr. Trilling" (*SR*, LXXII, 420-432), a brilliant and thoughtful analysis of that essay, David H. Hirsch concludes that Trilling's view of reality rests upon a too narrowly based conception of society and of the novel's relation to it.

Efforts at broadening the awareness of society in the novel were made by E. Digby Baltzell, in *The Protestant Establishment: Aristocracy and Caste in America* (New York, Random House), who makes a sociological analysis of the Protestant upper class as representing a conservative elite group in our society and examines the use of this

group by Fitzgerald, Marquand, O'Hara, and others. W. Tasker
Witham, in *The Adolescent in the American Novel: 1920-1960* (New
York, Ungar), analyzes in terms of specialized subject matter over
five hundred novels dealing with the numerous and not always exciting problems of adolescence. Frederick Feied's *No Pie in the Sky:
The Hobo As American Cultural Hero* (New York, Citadel) surveys
the initial appearance of the hobo in American fiction during the last
quarter of the nineteenth century and examines in detail Jack London's *The Road*, Dos Passos's *U.S.A.*, and Jack Kerouac's *On the Road*
and *The Dharma Bums*. This brief book is an excellent treatment of
a minor theme that is significant in the fictional portrayal of social
deprivation in the twentieth-century novel, although its omission of
Jim Tully is strange. In a symposium, assembled by Louis D. Rubin,
Jr., on "Three Modes of Fiction" (*GaR*, XVIII, 298-324), Walter Sullivan examines the use of regionalism; Robert M. Figg III, the way in
which naturalism imposes a special form on the novel; and C. Hugh
Holman, the way in which the epistemology of the realist needs to be
recognized in the understanding of realistic fiction. Wendell V.
Harris, in "Style and the Twentieth-Century Novel" (*WHR*, XVIII,
127-140), attacks the abandonment in this century of the ideal of lucidity in style and concludes unhappily that writers farthest from
clarity are frequently most admired as stylists today.

ii. Major Writers

In any twelve-month period the quantity of work done on writers
such as those being reviewed in this essay varies greatly and constitutes no firm index to the standing which such writers have in the critical mind. The following writers will be treated as major ones for this
period despite the great variation quantitatively in the comment
which they received in 1964: Jack London, Ellen Glasgow, Edith
Wharton, Willa Cather, Sherwood Anderson, Sinclair Lewis, John
Dos Passos, John Steinbeck, James Gould Cozzens, and Thomas
Wolfe.

Jack London, after Thomas Wolfe, was the subject of the greatest
amount of work during 1964. Richard O'Connor's *Jack London, A
Biography* (Boston, Little, Brown) is a long, thorough, and systematically documented record of his life and, perhaps, as definitive a
treatment as we shall have in this generation, although it contains
relatively little on London as a novelist. It called forth reviews

which attempted to evaluate his work. As William Ward said in his review (*Nation*, CC, Jan. 4, 1965, 14), "to study London is to study the floor plan of the twentieth century American novel"; and Maxwell Geismar, in a review article, "Jack London Today" (*NR*, CLI, Nov. 14, 29-31), concluded that "London was the first genuine proletarian talent in our literature." Although London's personal life was most unattractive, Geismar felt that his paradoxes drove him away from the world of men and made him most genuinely at home in the animal world. London had been represented late in 1963 by the publication of a short novel, *The Assassination Bureau, Ltd.* (New York, McGraw-Hill, 1963), based on a plot that London purchased from Sinclair Lewis and which he abandoned after writing 40,000 words. The present edition was completed by the detective novelist Robert L. Fish. It increases the corpus of London's work without adding to its quality. Robert Woodward reprinted Jack London's lost poem, "The Sea Sprite and the Shooting Star" (*MTJ*, XII, iii, 6-8). Its recovery is interesting but of little value. Under the general editorship of Arthur Calder-Marshall, the publication of *The Bodley Head Jack London* (London, Bodley Head), a handsomely bound and well-printed standard set of London's works, with excellent introductions by the editor, began appearing in 1963 with Volume I, containing *The Call of the Wild* and 17 short stories. Volume II, which appeared in 1964, contained *John Barleycorn, The Cruise of the Dazzler*, and *The Road*. Early in 1965 Volume III, containing *Martin Eden*, appeared. When the Bodley Head edition is completed, it will make London one of the few twentieth-century American authors with a well-designed edition of his works. Significantly, it is being done in England; the great appreciation of London has always been in Europe rather than in America, a fact borne out in part by Renate Schubert's "Eine Jack London Auswahlbibliographie" (*ZAA*, XII, 94-108), a detailed listing of the many German translations of London's work. A brief article by Alfred S. Shivers, "Jack London's Mate-Women" (*ABC*, XV, ii, 17-21), examines London's heroines and finds them, like his heroes, reflections of an "Anglo-Saxon racist orientation."

Ellen Glasgow was treated handsomely by William W. Kelly in *Ellen Glasgow, A Bibliography* (Charlottesville, Univ. Press of Va.). This excellent listing of her writings, of writing about her, and of manuscripts and letters is an invaluable tool for those interested in the early history of realism in this century. Louis Auchincloss, in *Ellen*

Glasgow (UMPAW, No. 33, Minneapolis, Univ. of Minn. Press),
a "University of Minnesota Pamphlet on American Writers," gave an
urbane and appreciative criticism of Miss Glasgow's novels, emphasizing their quality as novels of manners and giving refreshingly
minor emphasis to her qualities as a Southern writer. Auchincloss,
himself a distinguished novelist of manners, can write with quiet authority on Miss Glasgow. She would almost certainly have been
pleased with his essay. Nancy Minter McCollum, in "Glasgow's and
Cabell's Comedies of Virginia" (*GaR*, XVIII, 236-241), produced an
essay comparing the treatments of their Virginia heritage by these
two writers. The essay is of more value for what it says on Cabell than
what it says on Miss Glasgow, perhaps because the Cabell material
is less familiar. John R. Welsh, in "Egdon Heath Revisited: Ellen
Glasgow's *Barren Ground*" (*Reality and Myth,* pp. 71-79), sees
analogies of character, symbol, theme, and circumstance between
The Return of the Native and *Barren Ground* and considers both
novels to be "studies of life in traditional societies" and "tributes to
the courage sometimes found in the human spirit." This sound essay
appears in a book of very uneven studies of American writers.

   Theodore Dreiser was the subject of an appreciative effort to
sketch the outlines of his life and the contents, themes, and ideas
of his novels by Philip L. Gerber in *Theodore Dreiser* (TUSAS). Mr.
Gerber's study tends to overpraise Dreiser, but not offensively so.
It has a bibliography which is particularly useful. The running dialogue between those who value Dreiser highly and those who, following Lionel Trilling, deplore his work continued in 1964. Irving
Howe, in "Dreiser and the Tragedy" (*NR*, CLI, July 25, 19-21), sees
An American Tragedy as a powerful national expression of the "collective smallness" of Americans and, deploring the disdain which
many modern critics have for Dreiser, argues that his novels have
created an authentic fictional world and display an exceptional sense
of American institutions. On the opposite side, Charles T. Samuels,
in "Mr. Trilling, Mr. Warren, and *An American Tragedy*" (*YR*, LIII,
629-640), attacked an article by Robert Penn Warren on Dreiser's
An American Tragedy published in the *Yale Review* of Autumn,
1962, declaring that Warren was advocating trashy work in espous-
ing Dreiser's methods. Philip Williams, in the "Chapter Titles of
Sister Carrie" (*AL*, XXXVI, 359-365), saw them as an attempt to add
symbolic force to the book. Yoshinobu Hakutani examined the rela-

tionship of Dreiser to French realism ("Dreiser and French Realism," *TSLL*, VI, 200-212); Griffith Dudding looked briefly at Dreiser's beliefs ("A Note Concerning Theodore Dreiser's Philosophy," *LC*, XXX, 36-37); and Robert E. Long found similarities between *Sister Carrie* and F. Scott Fitzgerald's novels ("*Sister Carrie* and the Rhythm of Failure in Fitzgerald," *FN*, No. 25, Spring, pp. 2-4).

Edith Wharton, who received a substantial amount of attention in 1963 and about whom much work has been announced for 1965, went almost unnoticed in 1964. Alexander M. Buchan, in "Edith Wharton and 'The Elusive Bright-Winged Thing' " (*NEQ*, XXXVII, 343-362), examined *Hudson River Bracketed* as an attempt to present through its protagonist, Vance Weston, a theory of artistic creation; and Patricia R. Plante, in "Edith Wharton and the Invading Goths" (*MASJ*, V, ii, 18-23), studied the war books, *The Marne* and *A Son at the Front*.

Willa Cather was the subject of a critical study by Dorothy Van Ghent (*Willa Cather*, UMPAW, No. 36, Minneapolis, Univ. of Minn. Press). Using psychological and mythological methods, Miss Van Ghent surveys and evaluates Miss Cather's fiction in a biographical context. Contrary to the customary view, she prefers the late works which search for the past to the early works which define a region. Holding that Miss Cather has "no world-view," she regards her as essentially a novelist of the five senses. Robert Strozier, in "Willa Cather, Story Teller" (*Descant*, VIII, Winter, 41-48), finds her values to reside, on the other hand, in her brilliant narrative ability. Sister Colette Toler, in "Willa Cather's Vision of the Artist" (*Person*, XLV, 503-523), sees her greatest significance in her view of the creative artist's struggle against a Philistine world; while Grace Pleasant Well-born, in "Willa Cather and the Southwest" (*ForumH*, IV, Winter, 1963, 38-41), sees the relatively late works, *Death Comes for the Archbishop* and *The Professor's House*, as contributions to southwestern literature and an assertion of the pioneer's way of life. Richard Giannone, on the other hand, sees music, used essentially as a metaphor, as a controlling device in *My Ántonia* ("Music in *My Ántonia*," *PrS*, XXXVIII, 346-361), although his argument would have been strengthened by a statement of what he meant by "music." *The Prairie Schooner* reprinted four short critical pieces which Miss Cather had written in 1894-1895 as "Willa Cather on Shakespeare" (*PrS*, XXXVIII, 65-74) and also reprinted her early short story, "The

Treasurer of Far Island," originally published in 1902, and two of her reviews of musical programs written in 1894 and 1897 (*PrS*, XXXVIII, 323-345).

Two book-length critical works were published on Sherwood Anderson. Brom Weber, in *Sherwood Anderson* (UMPAW, No. 43, Minneapolis, Univ. of Minn. Press), presented a biographical-critical sketch to 1925. After 1925, Mr. Weber's work is largely an insistence that Anderson's later work be studied rather than a study of Anderson's later work. Weber sees Anderson's principle virtues as being in *Winesburg, Ohio* and in his short stories, particularly those which emphasize the autobiographical element in his work. Rex Burbank's *Sherwood Anderson* (TUSAS) creates what is virtually a handbook to Anderson's sources, the nature of his talent, and his social, psychological, and moral themes, concentrating on Anderson's better-known works. The result is a useful, judicious, and thoughtful book. August Derleth, the "Sac Prairie Saga" novelist and man of letters, presents his recollections of Anderson, Sinclair Lewis, and Edgar Lee Masters in *Three Literary Men* (New York, Candlelight Press,[2] 1963), a curious but interesting little book. It deals in certain respects more with Derleth himself than with the three literary men, and it becomes a defense of regionalism and a denial that the "Revolt from the Village" really occurred. H. Edward Richardson, in "Anderson and Faulkner" (*AL*, XXXVI, 298-314), examines the early relationship of these two writers and concludes that Anderson's principal influence on his greater contemporary was to convince Faulkner that his proper task was the evaluation of the society of the South.

Sinclair Lewis, after occupying a substantial amount of the critics' time and energies in 1962 and 1963, was treated only casually in 1964. William Couch, Jr., saw him as an advocate and example of the American dream ("Sinclair Lewis: Crisis in the American Dream," *CLAJ*, VII, 224-234). Martin Light saw the women in Lewis' fiction as reflections of his personal attitude toward the female sex ("Lewis' Finicky Girls and Faithful Workers," *UR*, XXX, 1963, 151-159). D. Bruce Lockerbie identifies the William H. Ridgway mentioned in *Babbitt* as the industrialist who wrote for the *Sunday School Times* ("Sinclair Lewis and William Ridgway," *AL*, XXXVI, 68-72); and G. Thomas Tanselle, comparing Lewis and Floyd Dell, questioned the judgment that these two writers were engaged in a "Revolt from

2. The address of the Candlelight Press is 115 East 86 Street, New York—a piece of information not easily arrived at.

the Village" but saw *Main Street* and *Moon-Calf* as being both rebel-
lions and defenses ("Sinclair Lewis and Floyd Dell: Two Views of
the Midwest," *TCL*, IX, 175-184).

John Dos Passos was interviewed by David Sanders ("Interview
with John Dos Passos," *ClareQ*, XI, iii, 89-100), was examined in
terms of his relationship to painting by George Knox ("Dos Passos
and Painting," *TSLL*, VI, 22-38), and the influence of his conservative father upon him in his early political development was examined
by Melvin Landsberg ("John R. Dos Passos: His Influence on the
Novelist's Early Political Development," *AQ*, XVI, 473-486). An important article about Dos Passos was Gene W. Ruoff's "Social Mobil-
ity and the Artist in *Manhattan Transfer* and the *Music of Time*"
(*WSCL*, V, 64-76), in which Ruoff sees Dos Passos and Anthony
Powell as being alike in their concern for society in flux and for the
artist's reaction to a social order that is constantly breaking apart
and realigning as well as in their use of "empirically arrested spatial
cross-sections" to reveal the nature of society. The value of each novelist, Mr. Ruoff feels, rests on his empirical analysis of the relation
between individual and social forces.

John Steinbeck, who elicited extensive comment in 1963 as a
result of his recent Nobel Prize, received scant attention in 1964. Margaret C. Roane saw "John Steinbeck as a Spokesman for the Mentally
Retarded" (*WSCL*, V, 127-132) because she found five such characters in his fiction. Orland Sawey took "Another Look at *East of
Eden*" (*Appalachian State Teachers College Faculty Publications*,
1964, pp. 54-58) and decided that the novel was successful, affirma-
tive, and unified. James Woodress, in "John Steinbeck: Hostage to
Fortune" (*SAQ*, LXIII, 385-398), examined the literary consequences of Steinbeck's social attitudes and concluded that there was
an inverse relationship between Steinbeck's popularity and monetary
success and his artistic worth as a social critic and that his popularity
in the past two decades sent him into an artistic decline, as a result
of which he ceased to be an artist and "became a public property."

D. E. S. Maxwell, in *Cozzens* (Edinburgh, Oliver and Boyd, the
Scottish "Writers and Critics" series), studies James Gould Cozzens as a successful and realistic portrayer of the complexity and ambiguity of man's place in society. Maxwell, whose *American Fiction*
(1963) emphasized the relationship of the novel to society, is sympathetic to Cozzens' conservatism, praises his "stern, wakeful grasp
of the nature of things," finds his theme important and his form an

imaginative use of the "traditional novel" for new situations, and believes him to utter "an uncompromisingly stoic view of life" in a flexible and original style. This brief work is an excellent, sympathetic
study of an important novelist. The article by Chester E. Eisinger,
"The Voice of Aggressive Aristocracy" (*Midway* [Chicago], No. 18,
pp. 100-128), is a reprinting of his very good chapter on Cozzens from
his *Fiction of the 1940's* (1963). When Arthur Mizener's treatment in
The Sense of Life in the Modern Novel (see section i above) is
added, justice seems at last to be being done to Cozzens.

William Braswell and Leslie A. Field edited the speech which
Thomas Wolfe made at Purdue University on May 19, 1938, from
manuscripts in large part at the University of North Carolina and
from portions of manuscripts at Harvard, and published it as *Thomas
Wolfe's Purdue Speech, "Writing and Living"* (Lafayette, Ind., Purdue Univ. Stud.). The result is a painstakingly careful, thorough, and
commendable job of editing a significant unpublished Thomas Wolfe
document. The inclusion of revisions of the sections of the speech
which Wolfe made in manuscript for *You Can't Go Home Again* increases the value of the document for Wolfe scholars and raises
questions about the common notion that Wolfe never revised but
simply rewrote. B. R. McElderry, Jr., published a thorough, careful,
no-nonsense examination of Wolfe's life and works as *Thomas
Wolfe* (TUSAS). This short book compresses an enormous amount
of reading and thought about Thomas Wolfe into a very compact
space and does it with disarming ease. Professor McElderry's emphasis on the part that Wolfe's dramas played in his career is relatively
new; the other materials generally have been expressed before but
seldom so succinctly and convincingly. Vardis Fisher, himself a novelist of some stature, assembled a number of his essays, reviews, and
speechs on Thomas Wolfe and on other subjects, chiefly his own
novels, in *Thomas Wolfe as I Knew Him, and Other Essays* (Denver,
Alan Swallow, 1963). The Wolfe essays have been printed in essentially the same form before, and Mr. Fisher's book contributes little
that is new to Wolfe scholarship.

Hans Helmcke, in "Die 'Thomas-Wolfe-Renaissance' in den Verei-
nigten Staaten" (*JA*, IX, 181-195), gives a detailed examination of
scholarship and critical attitudes toward Thomas Wolfe in the United
States in recent years and makes a convincing case that a Thomas
Wolfe revival is well on its way toward becoming a fact. Irvin Hal-
perin sees Thomas Wolfe "as a young Faust" in his search for ex-

perience and traces the way in which Wolfe's early love for Germany led to his intensified love for America ("Hunger for Life: Thomas Wolfe, a Young Faust," *AGR*, XXX, vi, 12-14, 31). C. Hugh Holman, in "Thomas Wolfe and the Stigma of Autobiography" (*VQR*, XL, 614-625), compares Wolfe and Ernest Hemingway in their use of material from their own lives and concludes that "autobiographical" is a pejorative term which is applied to Wolfe because of his failure to keep the time of action and the attitudes of his fictional characters separate from the time of composition of the novel and the attitudes of Wolfe as writer. Richard S. Kennedy views "Thomas Wolfe's *Look Homeward Angel* as a Novel of Development" (*SAQ*, LXIII, 218-226). He describes the novel as a *bildungsroman* which describes the ordeals through which the hero passes as initiation rites preliminary to manhood. Mr. Kennedy feels that Wolfe universalizes this theme by giving Eugene Gant a wide range of experience and by using a rich and rhetorical style to suggest a complex universe. Paschal Reeves, in "Thomas Wolfe and His Scottish Heritage" (*SFQ*, XXVIII, 134-141), asserts that Wolfe sees Scottish characteristics as the dominant and distinguishing traits of North Carolinians and regards the Scottish folk as the "finest people on earth." Nash K. Burger, in "A Story to Tell: Agee, Wolfe, Faulkner" (*SAQ*, LXIII, 32-43), finds that all three share a strong attachment to the southeastern region.

iii. Minor Authors

The authors of lesser stature during the first third of the century were dealt with in several book-length publications in 1964 and—with the exception of Katherine Anne Porter, whose long-promised novel *The Ship of Fools* (1963) precipitated a flurry of articles and notes—most of the significant work on these writers were in relatively brief critical-biographical studies.

George Ade, by Lee Coyle (TUSAS), is a study of an almost forgotten figure who seems to be having a minor revival.[3] Famous in his own time for *Fables in Slang* and for his successful plays, Ade is an excellent example of a talented writer influenced by the genteel tradition and hungry for the mass audience which he finally secured. Coyle's study does him justice as "a good, simple man with a magnificent gift which he packaged for the market place."

3. See "Fiction: 1900-1930" in *ALS*, 1963, p. 134, where a substantial amount of Ade's writing in reprinted volumes is discussed.

Also in the same series, *James Lane Allen,* by William K. Bottorff
(TUSAS), is another examination of a gifted minor novelist who is,
in a sense, an embodiment of the genteel tradition. Polished in style,
involved usually for the wrong reasons or on the wrong side in the
running war between realism and romance, Allen has passed almost
into the limbo of forgotten writers. Mr. Bottorff finds him interesting
in his concept of myth, would like to find him of greater value than he
is presently considered, and struggles valiantly for him but never finds
a solid vantage point from which to view him.

*Harry Leon Wilson: Some Account of the Triumphs and Tribula-
tions of an American Popular Writer,* by George Kummer (Cleveland, Western Reserve Univ. Press, 1963), is a study of one of the
genteel writers who succumbed to the sentimental formulas of the
mass market. Wilson is best known for comic romances like *Ruggles
of Red Gap* and for successful plays written in collaboration with
Booth Tarkington. Mr. Kummer's book is an essentially defensive
biographical sketch with a focus on Western humor as a reflection
of social values, but the end result is a portrayal of a standard *Saturday Evening Post* writer in the days when that magazine was almost
the official journal of the complacent middle class.

Louis Bromfield, by David D. Anderson (TUSAS), is a critical
study of a once promising writer of great talent and great success.
Mr. Anderson includes a great deal of plot summary and relatively
little biographical data. Although he is highly critical of much of
Bromfield's work, he still tends to overpraise him. He views *The
Farm* and *The Rains Came* as Bromfield's best novels, whereas most
critics would have chosen *Early Autumn, Possession, The Green Bay
Tree,* and *A Good Woman* as his major claims to fame. Mr. Anderson
praises Bromfield's "story telling" but seems not to recognize the intense, sexually oriented feminism which gave his early work strong
but unpleasant power. Bromfield's claim to fame is as a member of
the "Revolt from the Village," and his last years give us a feeling that
Sinclair Lewis has finally joined the Rotary Club, a self-betrayal
which Anderson does not see.

Bernard Grebanier's study, *Thornton Wilder* (UMPAW, No. 34,
Minneapolis, Univ. of Minn. Press), is essentially a truculent defense
of Wilder against his critics, both Marxist and scholarly. Mr. Grebanier gives us an accurate, brief biographical statement and some
valuable plot summaries, but his almost unqualified admiration for
Wilder will seem to many people too excessive. Wilder also was the

subject of two bibliographical studies. Jackson R. Bryer, in "Thornton Wilder and the Reviewers" (*PBSA*, LVIII, 35-49), lists over four hundred reviews of Wilder's novels and plays; and Heinz Kosok's "Thornton Wilder, Ein Literaturbericht" (*JA*, IX, 196-227) is a bibliographical description and evaluation of Wilder's work and present critical place.

William L. Nance, S. M., in *Katherine Anne Porter and the Art of Rejection* (Chapel Hill, Univ. of N. C. Press), makes a detailed, thoughtful, and extended examination in depth of Miss Porter's fiction. He finds that her work is centered upon the theme of the rejection of life and of love, and his final judgment of Miss Porter is unfriendly despite his admiration for her fictional skill. A similar treatment by Sister Mary Bride dealing with "Flowering Judas" ("Laura and the Unlit Lamp," *SSF*, I, 61-63) concludes that the heroine of this story in rejecting love also rejects life and that the theme is "the unlit lamp and the ungirt loin." Sam Bluefarb, taking a somewhat different view, examines "Loss of Innocence in 'Flowering Judas'" (*CLAJ*, VII, 256-262). Lodwick Hartley examines *The Ship of Fools* ("Dark Voyagers: A Study of Katherine Anne Porter's *Ship of Fools*," *UR*, XXX, 1963, 83-94) and finds the confusion and dark chaos in that book not an artistic failure but a successful projection of a pessimistic view of life. Sister M. Joselyn writes "On the Making of *The Ship of Fools*" (*SDR*, I, ii, 46-52), and Marjorie Ryan, in "Katherine Anne Porter: *Ship of Fools* and the Short Stories" (*BuR*, XII, i, 51-63), compares the novel and her short stories and finds the presence of recurrent themes but different styles. Sister M. Joselyn describes "'The Grave' as Lyrical Short Story" (*SSF*, I, 216-221) as opposed to mimetic stories; and Daniel Curley also selects "The Grave" for examination ("Treasure in 'The Grave,'" *MFS*, IX, 377-384) and concludes that "the mind of the writer is the grave of the past" and that despite her rebellion against Catholicism her fable is "indelibly stamped with the Christian names of Realities." His analysis of this story is penetrating.

Aside from these studies, other writers of this period received short shrift, usually in journals devoted to American studies or to bibliography. James H. Cassedy, in "Muckraking and Medicine: Samuel Hopkins Adams" (*AQ*, XVI, 85-99), examines Samuel H. Adams as muckraker and as a novelist on medical themes and on the fight against the evils of patented medicine. His article documents a minor but significant portion of the muckraking era. Shinji

Takuwa, in "The Method of Stein's *Three Lives*" (*Eigo Eibungaku Rouso*, No. 14, Jan.), describes Gertrude Stein's method of altering our sense of time through the use of the present tense. Maxwell Bloomfield, in "Dixon's *The Leopard's Spots*: A Study in Popular Racism" (*AQ*, XVI, 387-401), examines Thomas Dixon as a racist propagandist whose views are now being echoed in the statements of Southern segregationists. Kenny A. Jackson examines "Robert Herrick's Use of Chicago" (*MASJ*, V, i, 24-32) and finds that the novelist used the evils of Chicago to demonstrate "the price mankind must pay for commercialism and industrialism." A useful record of Herrick's Chicago fiction is given in this article. John E. Hart, in "Albert Halper's World of the Thirties" (*TCL*, IX, 185-195), finds that the novelist's primary concern was with subjective matters rather than with reform and concludes that his works are worthwhile for their style and symbolism. Robert L. Welker, in "Liebestod with a Southern Accent" (*Myth and Reality*, pp. 179-211), sketches the career of a neglected novelist and finds much—perhaps too much—to praise in Evelyn Scott's work.

Matthew J. Bruccoli in two bibliographical pieces ("Five Notes on Ring Lardner" and "Ring Lardner's First Book," *PBSA*, LVIII, 297-298, and LVIII, 34-35) contributes to the bibliographical description of six of Lardner's publications. William White, who has done three previous bibliographical listings dealing with John P. Marquand, in "A Treasury-Cavalcade of the Best of Marquand" (*ABC*, XIV, iv, 1963, 17-18), makes a chatty and incomplete listing of Marquand's stories and articles in collections of materials in magazine anthologies and a listing of reprints of the *Mr. Moto* stories. James J. Napier lists twenty-eight books and over ninety magazine stories in "Joseph Hergesheimer: A Selected Bibliography, 1913-1945" (*BB*, XXIV, Sept.-Dec., 1963, 46-48; 1964, 52, 69-70). Steven Foster explores the confused critical stances about Henry Miller in "A Critical Appraisal of Henry Miller's *Tropic of Cancer*" (*TCL*, IX, 196-208).

George Santayana was examined as a philosopher in several articles in various philosophical journals during the year, but William H. Marshall's essay "An Expanding Theme in *The Last Puritan*" (*Person*, XLV, 27-40) was the only serious treatment of Santayana's unique venture into the novel form. Mr. Marshall's essay traces the themes and symbols on which the tragedy of the last Puritan— that of being compelled on Puritan principles vainly to reject Puritanism—rests. A thoughtful and discriminating article about an important work of fiction, Mr. Marshall's essay is weakened only by his failure fully to connect Santayana's philosophical and symbolic position with the social world which he describes.

James T. Farrell, whose standing with present-day critics is ambiguous (I would regard him as a major writer although he is receiving very little attention), published *Selected Essays*, edited by Luna Wolf (New York, McGraw-Hill), a collection of pieces a number of which had been published earlier and a few of which are new, notably "Reflections at Sixty." T. G. Rosenthal, in "Studs Lonigan and the Search for an American Tragedy" (*BAASB*, No. 7, Dec., 1963, pp. 46-53), sees the Studs Lonigan trilogy as an important record of the disintegration of a society. Ashley Brown, in "The Novel as Christian Comedy" (*Reality and Myth*, pp. 161-178), describes Caroline Gordon's *The Malefactors* as a triumph of fictional technique in its rendering of the actual experience of religious conversion. Most readers will feel that he overpraises the novel, and a recognition of its *roman à clef* characteristics would probably have qualified some of Mr. Brown's judgments. John Pilkington, in "Stark Young at the Southern Literary Festival" (*UMSE*, V, 35-42), deals with Stark Young's last visit to the University of Mississippi and the address that he delivered then.

It is worthy of note that during 1964 *Dissertation Abstracts* recorded completed dissertations on Erskine Caldwell (XXIV, 4696-97), Willa Cather (XXIV, 2041 and 4699-4700), John Dos Passos (XXIV, 4693-94), James T. Farrell (XXIV, 5413), Henry B. Fuller (XXIV, 2039-40), Joseph Hergesheimer (XXIV, 2481-82), Sinclair Lewis (XXIV, 4692-93), and Thomas Wolfe (XXIV, 4195-96 and XXV, 1207). Clearly young scholars are at work in the largely unplowed field of American fiction during the first third of our century. And this is good, for much remains to be done: realism and naturalism need sharper definition; the popular taste of our century and its influence on artistic performance needs study; and informed and judicious biographical-critical studies are needed for a number of artistically minor but culturally significant writers. The early decades of the century are moving sufficiently into the past for their dispassionate examination to become increasingly possible and needed.

University of North Carolina

13. Fiction: 1930 to the Present

William T. Stafford

A brief introduction and a conclusion. The books covered in the survey that follows measure, when stacked together as they now are on the top of a file cabinet in my office, exactly one foot, six and one-quarter inches. The total number of items covered is 176. The total number of authors represented is 48. Twenty-two general items were written. The foregone conclusion: there was no dearth of attention to writers of modern American fiction during 1964. Further than that I am not sure I am willing to go.

i. General Studies

The most impressive single book to have been devoted exclusively to contemporary American fiction during 1964 is Marcus Klein's *After Alienation: American Novels in Mid-Century* (Cleveland, World). Limited by the fact that Klein surveys only five novelists (Bellow, Ellison, Baldwin, Morris, and Malamud), it is nonetheless the only book of the year that would bear a comparison (in critical insight, in range) with Eisinger's *Fiction of the Forties* (1963) or Hassan's *Radical Innocence: The Contemporary American Novel* (1961). Klein's central thesis is perhaps of less importance than his discussions of the five writers he covers, although the thesis itself, paradoxically enough, is viably relevant to a much wider range of contemporary writers of fiction than the handful he selects. "Alienation," Klein contends, has given way in American fiction to what he calls "accommodation," an uneasy word, never overly insisted upon, that nonetheless does suggest "a sentiment or an attitude or a motive" we find recognizable in broad stretches of modern fiction: the loss of identity that leads to a search for self; the search for self that leads to a sense of isolation; the sense of isolation that leads to a need for community; the accommodation to community that leads to a loss of identity; and around it goes. This is putting it badly, putting it baldly—something Klein never does—and one can, I think, learn a great deal from his individual chapters even if one rejects the "accommodation" thesis altogether. Klein's book, I feel, is a significant, illuminating study.

Of major significance in an entirely different way is Walter Allen's impressive *The Modern Novel in Britain and the United States* (New York, Dutton), although only two chapters of it are devoted to American fiction since 1930: "The Thirties: American" (pp. 138-187) and "War and Post War: American" (pp. 293-332). Its significance is in the calmness of Allen's perspective, in his sane views on how both periods are and should be characterized, and in his arrangement and selection of authors. His introduction to the American novelists of the 1930's is especially good. He delineates clearly the kind of special impact made on American writers of the time by the Depression (in contrast to that made on British ones); he sees how the now-considered best novels of the period "are precisely those least directly concerned with social questions of the time"; and he chronicles ways novels of World War I "conditioned" American literary views of the Depression. The writers he discusses in this chapter include Dos Passos and Farrell; Edward Dahlberg, Nelson Algren, and Richard Wright; Albert Halper and Robert Cantwell; Steinbeck; Nathanael West, Henry Roth, Daniel Fuchs, and Lionel Trilling; Djuna Barnes, Kay Boyle, and Henry Miller; O'Hara and John P. Marquand. His last chapter is somewhat less satisfactory, the material necessarily more amorphous, judgments necessarily more slippery. There are sections there on the novelists of World War II (Vidal, Burns, Mailer, Jones); on what he calls the "gothic" and, later, the "Southern" mode (Bowles, Capote, McCullers, Buechner, Styron, O'Connor); a somewhat odd conjunction of Salinger and Kerouac (but not Cheever, Updike, or Philip Roth); three off-beats (Edward Newhouse, Auchincloss, and Wright Morris); and, finally, two Negro writers (Ellison and Baldwin) in one grouping; three Jews (Bellow, Gold, and Malamud) in another. It is an impressive performance.

Three other works deserve mention in this grouping. Robert Detweiler's slim monograph, *Four Spiritual Crises in Mid-century American Fiction* (UFMH, No. 14, Gainesville, Univ. of Fla. Press), more limited in scope than Klein's book even while related to it in its thesis, is restricted to studies of single novels by Styron, Updike, Philip Roth, and Salinger. Detweiler views the "accommodation" themes of modern American novelists in broad religious terms with demonstrations of affinities between *Set This House on*

Fire and Tillich; *Rabbit, Run* and Niebuhr; *Letting Go* and Buber; and *Franny and Zooey* and a weak "amalgamation" of Christianity, Zen Buddhism, existential terminology, and Jewish tradition. Detweiler may well make some of these affinities too explicit, but generally speaking his little study is convincing and illuminating. Harry T. Moore edited *Contemporary American Novelists* (Carbondale, Southern Ill. Univ. Press), an uneven collection of new essays on various novelists by various critics. Moore's brief introduction is primarily a survey of "a few books on the recent American novel" after about 1950, and the two essays collected in the volume that treat the subject in a generic way—Norman Mailer's "Some Children of the Goddess" and John W. Aldridge's "The War Writers Ten Years Later" —are both reprints from earlier periodical publications. W. Tasker Witham's *The Adolescent in the American Novel: 1920-1960* (New York, Frederick Unger) is a strange content analysis of almost six hundred American novels depicting various aspects of the problems of adolescents. Of more value, I would say, to the sociologist than to the literary scholar, it does include as an appendix a twenty-page chronological list of American novels of adolescence, indicating author and title, locale, sex and age of its protagonist, the attitude of the author toward his material, and the kind of adolescent problem depicted in each novel.

Of four articles treating special aspects of contemporary American fiction, probably of least importance is Robert Conquest's "Science Fiction and Literature" (*CritQ*, V, 1963, 355-367). Mostly, but not exclusively, about British science-fiction writers, its simple point is that this special branch of "popular" fiction appears to be on the edge of being re-assimilated into general literature—a healthy service, Conquest contends, toward bringing "pleasure" back to fiction and helping to discredit overrated "psychological" fiction. Of more significance is Jerry J. Bryant's "The Last of the Social Protest Writers" (*ArQ*, XIX, 1963, 315-325), which ties the vigor and vitality of early novels of World War II—by Calmer, Shaw, Heym, Mailer, and Jones—to their having transferred to power structures in the military the old "villains" of the 1930's: the capitalist "bosses," the industrialists. Ihab Hassan's "Laughter in the Dark: The New Voice in American Fiction" (*ASch*, XXXIII, 636-640) is a much too brief survey of the comic in modern American fiction, contending that "the deflection [there] of laughter toward anguish" is perhaps "a common and powerful event of the modern imagination." But probably the most important of these articles is Morris Beja's "It Must Be Important: Negroes in Contemporary American Fiction" (*AR*, XXIV, 323-336). The Negro, Beja demonstrates, has never been used in American fiction without reference to his race—not by Melville or Twain or Faulkner; not by McCullers, Edward Lewis Wallant, Robert Groves, Philip Roth, Saul Bellow, or Norman Mailer; not even by Baldwin, Wright, Ellison, William Melvin Kelley, or John A. Williams. But this is perhaps as it should be, for race is itself still a conscious entity in American life, and fiction must reflect it while it is.

Two studies of the contemporary short story appeared in 1964. The most impressive is William Peden's *The American Short Story: Front Line in the National Defense of Literature* (Boston, Houghton Mifflin), which is a useful book, if I may make this kind of distinction, without being a good book. That is to say, it will serve well a felt need without, except in small stretches here and there, being very exciting or stimulating or provocative. Peden's opening chapter, "Backgrounds and Antecedents," is a defense of the short story (since about 1940) as the most congenial of the literary genres to the temper and temperament of our age, an age incidentally, which has seen the perfection of the genre in spite of all kinds of obstacles from book publishers, the decline of the "slicks," and so on. His second chapter, which had previously appeared elsewhere (*SSF*, I, 33-44), is a survey of the market place and a rather good history, mostly in the footnotes, of previous histories of the modern short story in America. His third chapter is primarily speculation about the forces in modern life that have contributed to the American short story's having "come completely of age." His next three chapters are the ones which contain his surveys of the writers: first, under a grouping he entitles "Jane Austens of Metropolis and Suburbia"; next, under "Sick in Mind and Body Both"; finally, under "Of War and Peace and Other Matters," which he breaks down into (1) "The War and the Short Story," (2) "There is No Revolutionary Situation in America," (3) "The Woods are Full of Regional Writers," and (4) "Spaceships, Aliens, and Bug-eyed Monsters." One finds in these various groups about what one would expect, three to five paragraphs of discussion of the major writers, one-paragraph treatments of others, and long lists of still others in footnotes. But there are surprises too—an extended and perceptive treatment of John Cheever's short fiction in the

first group and excellent accounts of the short fiction of Tennessee
Williams and James Purdy in the second. After a final chapter in
which he deplores the necessity for his own groupings, reminds us of
how varied these writers are, and predicts a better future for science
fiction and stories by Negroes, he appends a list of "One Hundred
Notable American Short Story Writers, 1940-1963: A Checklist." In
short, it is a volume we can surely use.

Maxwell Geismar's account, "The American Short Story Today"
(StL, IV, ii, 21-27), is precisely what one would have expected of the
author of *Henry James and the Jacobites*. He deplores the fiction of
Salinger, Roth, Updike, Malamud, J. F. Powers, and others; he deplores "the increasingly narrow range of its visions and content alike,
the lack of horizons, social, ideological, metaphysical, emotional—
and the stress on that intricate craftsmanship of 'the well-made story'
which even further limits the human and literary content." But there
is hope, he says, in the example of Zola (!)—and such writers as James
Jones, William Styron, John Hersey, Nelson Algren, and others. There
is no lack of provocation here.

A final grouping in this general section should include three remarkable autobiographical accounts: H. E. F. Donohue's *Conversations with Nelson Algren* (New York, Hill and Wang), Edward Dahlberg's *Because I Was Flesh* (Norfolk, Conn., New Directions, 1963),
and Thomas H. Moore's edition of *Henry Miller on Writing* (New
York, New Directions). Algren's "conversations" in effect are his life
story—and a strange and captivating life it is, too. It would be invaluable to anyone working with Algren's fiction. There is gossip and
comment on Hemingway, on Baldwin, on John O'Hara, Bellow,
Wright, Heller, and Mailer. It is good humored and frank, unpre-
tentious and engaging. Dahlberg's *Autobiography* is something entirely different. It is an intrinsic work of art. And although the life
story of this Swinburne from Kansas City will be, and has already
been, tied in with Dahlberg's novel *Bottom Dog* (which Walter Allen, interestingly enough, relates to the fiction of Algren), its ultimate
virtue is all self-contained. Finally, fans of Henry Miller and, indeed,
any students of Miller's work or of the period will appreciate this
anthology of the writer's comments on writing. Editorial apparatus
is practically non-existent, with a simple one-page preface by Moore
explaining his rationale for the four groupings he uses to organize
Miller's various comments: while Miller was first struggling to be a
writer, while he was finding his own voice, and while "at work" (with

some previously unpublished manuscript material). A final section
treats "Writing and Obscenity" in general.

ii. James Baldwin

Of the thirteen studies written on James Baldwin during 1964, by
far the most authoritative is the long chapter by Marcus Klein in his
After Alienation (pp. 147-195). It may well be, in addition, the best
essay on Baldwin yet written. Surveying essays and fiction, Klein
sees an almost steady degeneration: "As a Negro, Baldwin was society's victim. As a victim, he was alienated. As an alienatee, he presented himself with vast moral authority. In the space of a few years
the rhetoric and the authority have done him less and less service,
and he has been left to fall back on an iteration of the word 'love.'
Love in its demonstration has become, finally, a fantasy of innocence." But there are other perceptive observations, such as Baldwin's
use of essays to "evade the demands of fiction" and his writing essays
as fiction to "evade the demand of thorough ideas." Klein explores
the dilemmas of Baldwin's Negro-ness and its implications for his
writings: his need both to escape and present it. He sees the central
relation of music to all of Baldwin's work and his curious ties with
Henry James, whose relation to Europe has some startling affinities
with Baldwin's (unperceived) relations with the American South, the
ties of *Another Country* to *The Wings of the Dove*, the possible (unconscious) but revealing ties to America suggested by Baldwin's use
of "we." Another first-rate essay on Baldwin's total writing is that by
Robert Sayre, "James Baldwin's Other Country" (*Contemporary
American Novelists*, pp. 158-169). Sayre also ties in the essays with
the fiction, seeing the fiction rightly as perhaps more revealing of
Baldwin's real insights than his essays. But Sayre also sees that while
Baldwin "has learned the art of the novel" he has "taught the art of
the essay." In David Levin's "Baldwin's Autobiographical Essays:
The Problem of Negro Identity" (*MR*, V, 239-247), the writer is in-
structed to recognize and accept his place in the respectable Ameri-
can tradition "that begins with Bradford, Woolman, Franklin, Ed-
wards, Emerson and Thoreau" and to stop stratifying the American
Negro as "different." One brief article in French is concerned with
Baldwin in a general way, Michel Gresset's "Sur James Baldwin"
(*MdF*, CCCL, 653-655).
Four of the articles on Baldwin treat the man or his race with

little or no attention to his writing as writing. Into this category would fall Kay Boyle's brief "Introducing James Baldwin" (*Contemporary American Novelists*, pp. 155-157), in which she contends that what it means to be a Negro is what it means to be a man. Robert Coles, in "Baldwin's Burden" (*PR*, XXXI, 409-416), contends that Baldwin grossly oversimplifies the Negro problem by too often divorcing it from the human problem. Raymond A. Schroth, S.J., in "James Baldwin's Search" (*CathW*, CXCVIII, 288-294), uses Baldwin to discuss the race problem in America and the fact that he has made us aware that "the presence of the Negro excuses the white man from facing himself and dealing with his own vices." Finally, Marvin Elkoff, in "Everybody Knows His Name" (*Esquire*, LXII, ii, 59-64, 120-123), presents a readable current profile, *New Yorker* fashion, complete with photographs, and wonders if involvement with public issues, his "other self," is not destroying his "private self," the artist.

Studies of individual novels include George E. Kent's "Baldwin and the Problem of Being" (*CLAJ*, VII, 202-214), which, like most surveys of his fiction, sees Baldwin's first novel, *Go Tell It on the Mountain*, as his best. Only here was his distance, his perspective, equal to his imagination, his vision. Wallace Graves in the same journal views the same novel, in "The Question of Moral Energy in James Baldwin's *Go Tell It on the Mountain*" (*CLAJ*, VII, 215-223), and finds it not uniformly satisfying because of sentimentality in his portrait of Richard's parents and in his "protective irony toward Elizabeth." Perhaps the best of these explications is Eugenia W. Collier's close examination of *Another Country*, in "The Phrase Unbearably Repeated" (*Phylon*, XXV, 288-296), which pays little attention to the race issue and examines instead the novel's search for love and the way music is used in it as a technique to clarify its theme. The comparative study by C. B. Cox and A. R. Jones, "After the Tranquilized Fifties: Notes on Sylvia Plath and James Baldwin" (*CritQ*, VI, 107-122), uses Baldwin and Plath to defend the depiction in literature of "breakdown, neurosis, even suicide" as a "proper reaction to the human condition." Otherwise, they say "we are escaping from the truth." A final brief article is Dorothy N. Foote's "James Baldwin's 'Holler Books'" (*CEA*, XXV, viii, 1963, 8, 11), which accuses Baldwin, especially in *The Fire Next Time*, of advocating the exchange of black supremacy for white.

Clearly the important literary criticism on Baldwin during the year was that by Klein and Sayre, and possibly Levin.

iii. Saul Bellow

As is the case with Baldwin, the best article written on Bellow in 1964 was that by Marcus Klein, "Saul Bellow: A Discipline of Nobility" (*After Alienation,* pp. 33-70). Bellow is his almost "classic" case: "Accommodation has meant in all cases an impossible reconciliation, a learning to live with, and at the same time a learning to deny, what has been plainly there: the happy middling community of these years, the suffocating suburbs, the new wealth, the fat gods, the supermarket, the corporate conscience, and also one's own conscience." Klein traces the way protagonists, in novel after novel, move from isolation to affirmation of ordinary life in the world. He sees the "greater difficulty" Bellow faces—and solves—in his insistence on urban settings in contrast to rural ones. He neatly ties him in with the classic Redskins of American letters—and with the Pale Faces too. He can conclude that "fiction is only the jittery act of reaching [for moral certainty]. When the goal is sufficient, as in Bellow's fiction it has been, and when in spite of jitters the reach is serious and long and constant, and one can see that it is reaching, fiction becomes crucial. As in Bellow's case it has."

Two other general studies of Bellow's fiction are David D. Galloway's "The Absurd Man as Picaro: The Novels of Saul Bellow" (*TSLL,* VI, 226-254) and Frederick J. Hoffman's "The Fool of Experience: Saul Bellow's Fiction" (*Contemporary American Novelists,* pp. 80-94). Galloway's is an examination of the extensive ties and parallels—and differences—Bellow's fiction has with the novel of the absurd, especially with Camus' *The Stranger.* Hoffman's survey offers some cautious correctives: that Bellow is perhaps better with the controlled short piece than with the long. *Seize the Day* is the best thing he ever did. "The emphasis that critics have put upon his affirmation has sometimes been excessive." Bellow, Hoffman contends, has demonstrated that "one cannot, or should not, affirm superficially. But he [Bellow] *has* maintained that it is possible and necessary to affirm."

Studies of individual novels include Denis Donoghue's "Commitment and *The Dangling Man*" (*Studies,* LIII, 174-187), which sees Joseph of that novel as embodying the central situation in all of Bellow's fiction. William J. Handy, in "Saul Bellow and the Naturalistic Hero" (*TSLL,* V, 538-545), examines *Seize the Day* and its non-hero, Tommy Wilhelm, who is shown to be significantly unlike the natu-

ralistic heroes of Dreiser, Steinbeck, or Hemingway, but significantly like those of Salinger or Malamud. That is to say, the openness
of his grief in the end frees him from the phoniness around him, from
his own former phoniness. He recognizes his humanity.

iv. Bernard Malamud

Three excellent general articles appeared on Malamud during the
year. Charles A. Hoyt, in "Bernard Malamud and the New Romanticism" (*Contemporary American Novelists*, pp. 65-79), views recent
American fiction as the new Romanticism, following "athletic fatalism," "closed realism," and "chipped classicism." Malamud, Hoyt
contends, epitomizes this new force perfectly. And he states his thesis
succinctly: "Suffering is Malamud's theme, and upon it he works a
thousand variations: some comical, some menacing; some austere,
some grotesque; some imaginative, others classic." In "Bernard Malamud: The Sadness of Goodness" (*After Alienation*, pp. 247-293),
Marcus Klein has another fine chapter. Malamud, he says, escapes
accommodation only on the surface. He only *seems* to be a special
case. In fact, "for Malamud, too . . . the informing motive is the necessity of accommodation to this world, and the difference in the materials and in the manner is a difference primarily in his original
distance from the world." He goes on to point to parallels with Wright
Morris, to examine, minutely, the Homeric parallels of *The Natural*
to the folklore of baseball, and to look at *The Assistant* as "the apprenticeship of Frank Alpine . . . to the discipline of Jewish suffering." He
examines the short stories and *A New Life*, with the latter's ties with
both Stendhal (the movement from the capital *to* the provinces) and
Sinclair Lewis, as well as Levin's attempted engagements with the
West, nature, community, American history, and social forces. Marc
L. Ratner, in "Style and Humanity in Malamud's Fiction" (*MR*, V,
663-683), also has a thesis about recent American fiction. It most often
presents, he says, "a particular kind of asocial novel in which the
central figure is a twentieth century isolato, understandably preoc-
cupied with preserving his individuality from the abstract labels
which categorize him into invisibility." Malamud, however, has escaped some of the problems of others, Ratner contends, by avoiding
"the pitfalls of self-conscious sentimentality, sterile mythmaking or
limited topical reality." He then examines in some detail the works,
concluding that Malamud's "permanent value . . . lies in his poetic

sensitivity . . . and his belief in a moral humanistic code of behavior. . . ."

Two studies of individual works are less important. Sam Bluefarb presents a much too detailed examination of the stories in *The Magic Barrel* ("Bernard Malamud: The Scope of Caricature," *EJ*, LIII, 319-326, 335) wherein he shows Malamud's ties with the Jewish caricatures of Sholem Aleichem and his use as technique of a kind of "double-edged O. Henry-ism." Laurence Perrine's brief explication ("Malamud's 'Take Pity,'" *SSF*, II, 84-86) contends that the last scene of that story actually takes place in the afterworld.

v. Vladimir Nabokov

Nabokov was given short shrift in 1964. There were no general studies of his fiction, although L. L. Lee, in "Vladimir Nabokov's Great Spiral of Being" (*WHR*, XVIII, 225-236), presents an impressive explication of how the spiral informs one's understanding of not only *Pale Fire*, Lee's major subject, but also *Lolita* and, indeed, most of Nabokov's other fiction. In Carol T. Williams' " 'Web of Sense': *Pale Fire* in the Nabokov Canon" (*Crit*, VI, 1963, iii, 29-45), we also find an extensive analysis of how the Hegelian spiral is a useful concept in understanding and evaluating *Pale Fire*, and it, in turn, Nabokov's other fiction.

Of the four studies of *Lolita* easily the best humored is G. D. Josipovici's "*Lolita*: Parody and the Pursuit of Beauty" (*CritQ*, VI, 35-48). For Josipovici, the achievement of *Lolita* is beyond description in any place except the novel itself. Nabokov's antagonism to critical flim-flam is one of the "preoccupations of his novels"; thus, to look at *Lolita* as "an exercise in its own interpretation" may allow one to grasp its "essential nature." When Humbert "takes" Lolita, he destroys her worth as a symbol of the Beautiful; those who "take" the novel do the same. Hence, "to say that . . . [the novel] is 'about' anything, to try and abstract its 'theme,' or its 'message' is to be guilty of Humbert's initial error: it is to try and possess carnally what can only be possessed imaginatively." Charles Mitchell, in "Mythic Seriousness in *Lolita*" (*TSLL*, V, 1963, 329-343), provides another extensive analysis. *Lolita* presents, he says, "in mythical form [the Hegelian triad controls it], first the problem and then the solution to the existential despair of its narrator." Mitchell covers a great deal of the scholarship on the novel and works out much too seriously the patterned movement of the novel's three parts, the movement that de-

fines itself finally in Humbert's achievement of "self transcendence."
Elizabeth Eyber's translation of Herman Teirlinch's "Notes on Nabokov's *Lolita*" (*LitR*, VII, 439-442) probably should never have been
made, for it is in effect a charge that the novel is pornographic—and
on the grounds that Nabokov's knowledge of lewdness could only
have come from personal experience! Arthur E. DuBois's "Poe and
Lolita" (*CEA*, XXVI, vi, 1, 7) is not very significant: a recognition of
various allusions in the novel to Poe and his works.

vi. Flannery O'Connor

Although seven articles on Miss O'Connor appeared in 1964, none of
them is very extensive or impressive. Sister Rose Alice, S.S.J. ("Flannery O'Connor: Poet to the Outcast," *Ren*, XVI, 126-132) presents a
scattered survey contending that Miss O'Connor's recurrent themes
are Christian ones—not unlike those of Graham Greene's, even if her
subject matter and techniques are strikingly different. Ted R. Spivey
presents another over-all view of Miss O'Connor's work ("Flannery
O'Connor's View of God and Man," *SSF*, I, 200-206), seeing her
proper context as one with writers such as Kafka and Bernanos, perhaps Dostoievsky. However, she has a miraculous Christian strain
unique with her: "the hope of paradox and prophecy. . . . The
prophecy that through the motiveless criminal shall come a new man
free of the Devil . . . the sort of miracle that the secular mind . . .
finds . . . hard to accept." Brainard Cheney provides a brief tribute
and assessment ("Flannery O'Connor's Campaign for Her Country,"
SR, LXXII, 555-558). His major points: her continuing theme is "to
reflect her Christian vision to a secular world"; she had a rare talent
for the comic, wherein "the *means* is *violent*, but the end is [always]
Christian." Josephine Jacobsen, in "A Catholic Quartet" (*ChS*, XLVII,
139-154), compares her with Muriel Spark, Graham Greene, and J. F.
Powers. And there is one study of her in German, Rainulf Stelzmann,
"Der Stein des Anstosses: Die Romane und Erzählungen Flannery
O'Connors" (*SZ*, CLXXIV, 286-296).

   Two brief explications appeared. Sister Jeremy, C.S.J., in "*The
Violent Bear It Away*: A Linguistic Education" (*Ren.*, XVII, 11-16),
demonstrates how syntax and diction are clues to a meaningful reading of the story. Sister M. Joselyn, in "Thematic Centers in 'The Displaced Person'" (*SSF*, I, 85-92), examines the ways the final revelation in that story shows "that the displacer is the [truly] displaced."

vii. J. D. Salinger

Although studies continue to proliferate on Salinger, many of them are repetitious and unoriginal, leading again to the already often expressed wonder at how long this writing of more and more about less and less in Salinger can continue. Richard Rees, in "The Salinger Situation" (*Contemporary American Novelists*, pp. 95-105), attempts to come to grips with a single problem: can Salinger really be good when he is so widely and continuously popular? Is Salinger's appeal, as many critics have charged, simply an invitation into "a cozy club of tender and sympathetic souls who see themselves as the only 'real' people in a world full of pathetic phoneys"? His answers, of course, are yes (to question one), no (to question two). Along the way Rees sees affinities with Orwell and Ionesco and examines "Franny" in some detail as (with *Catcher*) Salinger's best tale. Two other general studies include Kenneth Hamilton's "One Way to Use the Bible: The Example of J. D. Salinger" (*ChS*, XLVII, 243-251), which details the uses of the New Testament in Salinger's works and concludes "that he uses it largely as a mirror to reflect light derived from other sources." O. Mannoni, in "Le Masque et la parole" (*TM*, XX, 930-942), sees the work up through *The Catcher* in the "American" tradition, but the various chronicles of the Glass family have more affinities with Kierkegaard, Kafka, Flaubert, and perhaps Sartre. Perhaps mention should also be made of the reprinting of Arthur Mizener's extended general study, "The American Hero as Poet: Seymour Glass," in his *The Sense of Life in the Modern Novel* (pp. 227-246).

Five more studies of *The Catcher in the Rye* appeared in 1964. Three of them are general studies of the novel. Jonathan Baumbach, in "The Saint as a Young Man: A Reappraisal of *The Catcher in the Rye*" (*MLQ*, XXV, 461-472), provides a long, detailed defense of the novel in terms of its "self-defining" structure and style. J. D. O'Hara, in "No Catcher in the Rye" (*MFS*, IX, 370-376), demonstrates again that the growth in the novel is from Holden's wanting to be a "catcher" to the discovery that one cannot be. Kermit Vanderbilt's "Symbolic Resolution in *The Catcher in the Rye*: The Cap, the Carousel and the American West" (*WHR*, XVII, 1963, 271-277) is yet another explication of how the three symbols in his (Vanderbilt's) title grace "Holden's first steps on the way to his discovery of a new life." Two notes on the novel include Patrick Costello's "Salinger and 'Honest Iago'" (*Ren*, XVI, 171-174), an attack on those who would read Mr. Antolini as a homosexual, seeing him instead as mis-read by both Holden and the novel's critics by the false values of the life around him (and them). Candadai K. Tirumalai, in "Salinger's *The Catcher in the Rye*" (*Expl*, XXII, Item 56), corrects a previous reading of the novel that did not see that the museum Holden rejects is the Museum of Natural History (death), instead of the Museum of Art.

Only two studies of the Glass family appeared. In a long, well-informed, better than average essay, Kenneth Hamilton ("J. D. Salinger's Happy Family," *QQ*, LXXI, 176-187) sees Salinger as a preacher of pure religious faith. Robert Detweiler demurs in "J. D. Salinger and the Quest for Sainthood" (*Four Spiritual Crises*, pp. 36-43), for although Franny's quest is unmistakably a religious one, the affirmation that results is only the substitution of one kind of phoniness for another. Salinger's religious answer, Detweiler contends, is neither Christian, Zen, nor existential, but a weak amalgamation "that loses in depth what it gains in breadth." His conclusion: "One is . . . doubly disappointed in a fictional attempt at depicting the religious crisis that is overwhelmed by its own religiosity."

Two notes on the stories include Dallas E. Wiebe's "Salinger's 'A Perfect Day for Bananafish'" (*Expl*, XXIII, Item 3), a spoof (?) on Seymour and the fact that the "sound of one hand clapping" is as possible and probable as the contention that Seymour has six toes on one of his feet, or a left hand with two thumbs—which, of course, one *could* hear clapping. Thomas Kranidas, in "Point of View in Salinger's 'Teddy'" (*SSF*, II, 89-91), defends the last ambiguous sentence of the tale as "crucially illuminative of the major theme of the story."

Salinger has also made the dissertation list: see John Michael Howell, "The Waste Land Tradition in the American Novel" (*DA*, XXIV, 3337), a study of *The Waste Land*'s influence on Fitzgerald, Hemingway, Faulkner, and Salinger.

viii. John Updike

John Updike, more talented than Salinger (in my opinion), has received far less attention. Of the three articles appearing on his work, probably the best survey is that by David D. Galloway, "The Absurd Man as Saint: The Novels of John Updike" (*MFS*, X, 111-127), which defines the religious quality of Updike's vision as man's desire to join together this world and his ideals of the next. For Galloway, Updike's technical adroitness serves him in good stead with his themes, for he is able to give convincingly man's significance even when man is seen as dead-beat or slob. William Van O'Connor's "John Updike and William Styron: The Burden of Talent" (*Contemporary American Novelists*, pp. 205-221) is in effect two separate essays that view Updike as a man with a subject who is steadily improving. And Robert Detweiler's "John Updike and the Indictment of Culture-Protestantism" (*Four Spiritual Crises*, pp. 14-24) utilizes Reinhold Niebuhr to examine *Rabbit, Run* and concludes that "the force of Updike's novel, like Niebuhr's theology, is in exposing a society which, because it will not come to terms with its evil, cannot find the redemption of love." Arthur Mizener's essay on Updike, "The American Hero as High-School Boy: Peter Caldwell," is reprinted in his *The Sense of Life in the Modern Novel* (pp. 247-266).

ix. Robert Penn Warren

Of all the contemporary writers covered in this chapter, Robert Penn Warren is the one whose stature at this date is the most clearly defined. Charles H. Bohner provides a fitting tribute to that achievement in his *Robert Penn Warren* (TUSAS) in what is clearly the best full-length study of Warren now available. Warren's life, his ties with the Fugitives, his criticism, his poetry, his fiction—and, most importantly, their relationship—are all tightly and judiciously organized into what strikes me as an eminently satisfying presentation. Bohner's last chapter, which covers Warren's work after *Band of Angels* (exclusive of *The Flood*), is a little less judicious than what comes before. For example, he overrates *The Wilderness*, it seems to me, at the expense of *The Cave*. Unfortunately, he was unable to include *The Flood* in his very competent study. Paul West's brief pamphlet, *Robert Penn Warren* (UMPAW, No. 44, Minneapolis, Univ. of Minn. Press), is also good. He too gives the poetry its due, the criticism and polemic no less than the drama and fiction. Things are necessarily slighted, but the touch is sure and convincing. Item: "We have only to read a random page of Warren's prose to see that experience 'enchants' him in the same measure as his desire to find meanings is urgent." Finally, one should mention here Marden J. Clark's now four-year-old study, "Religious Implications in the Novels of Robert Penn Warren" (*BYUS*, IV, 1961, 67-69), a good survey, up through *The Cave*, of the role of Christianity in Warren's art.

Students of *All the King's Men* will certainly want to see Warren's own account of the relation of Huey P. Long and Louisiana to the genesis of that novel ("The Matrix of Experience," *YR*, LIII, 161-167). And I should think that they would also want to see Robert J. and Ann Ray's "Time in *All the King's Men*: A Stylistic Analysis" (*TSLL*, V, 1963, 452-457), an able demonstration of how time—as revealed in both the flashbacks and verb tenses—moves Burden from "an absolute and . . . static concept of time into a new perspective," —into, that is, a concept of "dynamic time." John Edward Hardy's well-known study of the novel, "Robert Penn Warren: The Dialectic Self," is reprinted in his *Man in the Modern Novel* (Seattle, Univ. of Wash. Press, pp. 194-207).

Other studies of Warren include James B. Scott's "The Theme of Betrayal in Robert Penn Warren's Stories" (*Thoth*, V, 74-84), an examination of the related themes of betrayal—"some effected by people, and some by time"—in *The Circus in the Attic and other Stories*. Victor H. Strandberg, in "Theme and Metaphor in *Brother to Dragons*" (*PMLA*, LXXIX, 498-508), provides an extensive, detailed analysis of this narrative poem, concluding that the "mysterious, undefinable self, our collective unconscious, is the sole repository of all experience, and [thus] our sole hope, against 'naturalistic considerations,'" of transcending temporal limitations. The final significance of the poem's central beast metaphor: ". . . there is not only shame but hope in acknowledging oneself a brother to dragons." Winston Weathers, in " 'Blackberry Winter' and the Use of Archetypes" (*SSF*, I, 45-51), discerns in the setting, the major characters, and the action of this famous story a variety of archetypes. And Arthur Mizener, in "The Uncorrupted Consciousness" (*SR*, LXXII, 690-698), a long essay-review of *The Flood*, views Warren's latest novel as one of his best. Its style, its technique, and its structure are all examined; and its theme, "learning gradually to accept 'the secret and irrational life of man,'" does not exclude its rich "inclusiveness": ". . . nearly every important American way-station of the spirit is here."

x. Eudora Welty

The studies of Eudora Welty are almost all bits and pieces. Jo Allen Bradham, for example, in " 'A Visit of Charity': Menippean Satire" (*SSF*, I, 258-263), reveals the various techniques of Menippean satire —exaggeration, caricature, dramatic exchange, animal and mechanical diminution, and temporary exchange of worlds—that are operative in the story. Saralyn R. Daly, in "'A Worn Path' Retrod" (*SSF*, I, 133-139), contends that for Miss Welty "neither humanity nor heaven forsakes aspiration" and although "ultimate issues remain doubtful, the act elicits a response." W. U. McDonald, Jr., in "Welty's 'Keela': Irony, Ambiguity, and *The Ancient Mariner*" (*SSF*, I, 59-61), probably makes too much of the possibility that Little Lee Roy might mean the "Little King" and explores the uses of *The Ancient Mariner* in the story. And Melvin Delmar Palmer, in "Welty's 'A Visit of Charity'" (*Expl*, XXII, Item 69), shows how both "Little Red Riding Hood" and *Through the Looking Glass* are used in this story.

Somewhat more ambitious is Wendell V. Harris' "The Thematic Unity of Welty's *The Golden Apples*" (*TSLL*, VI, 92-95), whose title is indicative enough of its theme. According to Harris, time-enforced change, symbolized hope in allusions to the golden apples of myth, and numerous other mythological analogues tie the various stories in this collection into a unified whole. Marvin Felheim, in "Eudora Welty and Carson McCullers" (*Contemporary American Novelists*, pp. 41-53), views Miss Welty as steadily improving although not yet a master of the novel. He examines some of the stories, "A Piece of News," "A Still Moment," and others from *The Golden Apples* where myths, classical and literary, add dimension to her fiction. Loneliness, awareness, and love, says Felheim, constitute her themes. J. E. Hardy's important "*Delta Wedding*: Region and Symbol" is reprinted in his *Man in the Modern Novel* (pp. 175-193). And W. U. McDonald, Jr., has compiled "Eudora Welty Manuscripts: An Annotated Finding List" (*BB*, XXIV, 1963, 44-46).

xi. Other Novelists

James Agee is the subject of Jack Behar's dissertation, "James Agee: The World of His Work" (*DA*, XXIV, 4690), and of a comparative study by Nash K. Burger, "A Story to Tell: Agee, Wolfe, and Faulkner" (*SAQ*, LXIII, 32-43), which contends that Southern writers are successful only when returning to and writing about the South.

Louis Auchincloss' novels are surveyed by W. Gordon Milne in his "Auchincloss and the Novel of Manners" (*UKCR*, XXIX, 1963, 177-185). Milne sees Auchincloss' forte as satire; his world, the eastern seaboard of the well-to-do; his achievement, "offering a sense of society, a picture of the special attitudes, gestures, [and] conventional responses of characters belonging to a certain class."

The death of Hamilton Basso drew forth a brief memoir by Malcolm Cowley, "The Writer as Craftsman: The Literary Heroism of Hamilton Basso" (*SatR*, XLVII, June 27, 17-18), in which Cowley describes the writer as obsessed with typically Southern dilemmas: "deeply attached to the South and to the soil, yet repelled by . . . Southern Shintoism—while also being repelled by the coldness and impersonality of the North."

The ten novels of Gerald Warner Brace deserve much wider recognition contends C. Hugh Holman in his Introduction to *The Garretson Chronicle* (New York, Norton, pp. v-xviii). Brace's talent, says Holman, is one that would appeal to admirers of Santayana, Marquand, and Trollope. And the particular appeal of *The Garretson Chronicle* is in the fact that "its gallery of characters have the integrity of fact and still tease the mind into tentative and shifting views of the nature of reality."

"James Cain and the 'Pure' Novel" is the title used by David Madden in his two-part study of the fiction of Cain (*UR*, XXX, 1963, 143-148; XXX, 235-239), a writer, says Madden, with a style like Hemingway's, a vision like Faulkner's, but more akin to Flaubert than to either. He also sees affinities with Poe and Camus. Madden probably overrates Cain even if he does describe him as a writer "whose journalistic temperament has blurred his creative field of vision."

John Cheever comes very close to receiving the attention he deserves in George Garrett's "John Cheever and the Charms of Innocence: The Craft of *The Wapshot Scandal*" (*HC*, I, ii, 1-4, 6-12). This is a superb and important article, concerned not only with *The Wapshot Scandal* but also with the broad subject of the *New Yorker* magazine and its effect on the contemporary short story. Cheever, Garrett maintains, not only helped "form" the modern short story; he also has had something to do with changing it. He has gotten away from the single situation; "has introduced a new freedom in the form," releasing the writer-narrator through his mixtures of the "real" and the "fanciful," the farcical and the fantastic. As a novelist, Garrett continues, Cheever is in a range with Faulkner, for *The Wapshot Chronicle* has a relation to *The Scandal* not unlike that of *The Hamlet* to *The Town*. And it is the Wapshot books that Garrett examines affectionately, even as he keeps his distance about their shortcomings and failures.

Because I was Flesh: The Autobiography of Edward Dahlberg (mentioned above) is the occasion of two studies of this writer: Ihab Hassan's "The Sorrows of Edward Dahlberg" (*MR*, V, 457-461) and

Paul Carroll's "Sunt Lacrimae Rerum" (*SR*, LXXII, 527-530). Hassan presents a brief survey of Dahlberg's works, his high repute among a small group, and discusses his repudiation of proletarianism and his embrace of myth. *Can These Bones Live*, according to Hassan, was Dahlberg's turning point, but like everyone else he considers *Because I Was Flesh* the writer's masterpiece. Paul Carroll examines the use of myth in the autobiography's picture of Dahlberg's mother, Lizzie, and the way that book "performs the lonely trial of recalling to us the fact that grandeur may exist amid the chaos and hearty vulgarity of our pragmatic world."

The long, long chapter on Ralph Ellison in Marcus Klein's *After Alienation* (pp. 71-146) covers, with perhaps greater thoroughness than the subject deserves, everything Ellison has written, his journalism and early short stories as well as *The Invisible Man*. The point that he returns to again and again is Ellison's dilemma in terms of escaping from or exploiting into universality his "Negro-ness." Ellison's "accommodation" is indeed a special one, as is Baldwin's, and the first part of this chapter is a discussion of that problem for the Negro writer. "What they have written about constitutes exactly a special and interesting variant of that motion from alienation to accommodation that has occupied these years generally—the most interesting a motion in their case because their alienation has a longer and more complicated character, and because accommodation is the less available." Klein explores Ellison's involvement with the Negro cause and with communism during the late thirties and forties—and the way his stories are a necessary preparation for his novel. He examines influences on the writer, especially his learning to accommodate American folklore to his fiction and his feeling ultimately that he was in the main stream of nineteenth-century American literature. Then follows a forty-page, minute analysis of *The Invisible Man*, "a furious picaresque which . . . is *all* an initiation rite." Klein sees many perceptive things in the novel. For example, he sees that each incident, in part and in total, is a protest against the protest novel. He sees its final discovery to be the paradox of "otherness"—the underside of the seen and known, the beneath of whatever is up there. But his "down there" is paradoxically a home—and, more importantly (a point Klein does not clearly see), *not* to be seen, in a way, is to make the accommodation Rinehart's alienation makes him strive for. Even so, Klein has done it again; this is a beautiful essay.

Ellison himself made two important statements in 1964—in "On

Becoming a Writer" (*Commentary*, XXXVIII, iv, 57-60) and in
Allen Geller's "An Interview with Ralph Ellison" (*TamR*, No. 32,
pp. 3-24). The burden of both is his insistence upon the integrity of
his fiction, its strivings toward a condition of standing on its own
"unracial" feet. The former essay is an important account of his own
development as a writer. In the latter, he insists upon his ties to
classical American literature. He points out, for example, that Baldwin is as much Henry James as he is Negro, that Captain Ahab, for
another example, is as much his (that is, Ellison's) as he is Hemingway's.

In "The Fiction of Herbert Gold" (*Contemporary American
Novelists*, pp. 170-181), Harry T. Moore surveys the works and finds
their major weakness to be a too ready facility with rhetoric. Only
two works are praised, the stories of *Love and Like* and *The Man
Who Was Not With It*, Gold's only novel where the clever rhetoric
is organic rather than showy.

In "Albert Halper's World of the Thirties" (*TCL*, IX, 185-195),
John E. Hart resurrects *Union Square* (1933), *The Foundry* (1934),
and *The Chute* (1937). "Sticking close to the American scene, and
interpreting personal experience in terms of social history, he
[Halper] has created an authentic vision of our human predicament."

John Hawkes is lavishly but not convincingly praised in S. K.
Oberbeck's "John Hawkes, The Smile Slashed by a Razor" (*Contemporary American Novelists*, pp. 193-204). "Astonishing sympathy,
satanic humor, cold detachment: these playful postures best describe the experimental fiction of John Hawkes, who 'finds both wit
and blackness in the pit.'" A better job is that by Earl Rovit, "The
Fiction of John Hawkes: An Introductory View" (*MFS*, X, 150-162),
where Hawkes is seen as fulfilling the prediction (by Allen Tate and
others) that the modern novel will be personal, sentimentally objective, tough, and unsocial. Hawkes's world, says Rovit, is "intensely
personal," "aseptically objective." He sees well the difficulties
Hawkes's fiction offers the reader. But he sees too that while it will
never be widely read, it is important because it "does explore . . .
man's resistance to his own fate that is rarely touched in fiction."

In "Joseph Heller's *Catch-22*: Only Fools Walk in Darkness"
(*Contemporary American Novelists*, pp. 134-142), Frederick R. Karl
points out that the military in that novel is in effect a replica of any
modern organization, law firm, or university and that Yossarian is the
individual in such a world, the moral man "who acts in good faith,"

who "accepts absolute responsibility," and whose strike for Sweden is in fact a strike for the good life, Paradise, Yeats's Byzantium. The world of the war is the world of now, and "a good deal of the humor of the novel derives from Yossarian's very openness in a society closed to authenticity and good faith."

James Jones and Norman Mailer, who received little attention in 1964, were considered jointly in Edmond L. Volpe's "James Jones— Norman Mailer" (*Contemporary American Novelists*, pp. 106-119). In this comparative study, Jones is seen as realist, Mailer as Romantic, while both are in reaction to the same problem, the individual's reluctance to be lost in massive organization, be it in the army or something else. Volpe finds a steady development of this theme in *From Here to Eternity*, through the weak *Some Came Running*, to the superb *The Thin Red Line*, where the individual at last disappears into the organization. Mailer also received double billing with William Styron in Marvin Mudrick's "Mailer and Styron: Guests of the Establishment" (*HudR*, XVII, 346-366). The novels of Styron and Mailer, Mudrick contends, have steadily degenerated, for each has "shown an inclination to sink his talents into journalism and literary politics, each apparently bent on retiring . . . into public life." Volpe too sees degeneration in Mailer, finding in *Advertisements for Myself* and *The Presidential Papers* only further confusion between artistic and political power.

Styron, however, received attention in his own right in 1964. His two novels are the subject of Jonathan Baumbach's "Paradise Lost: The novels of William Styron" (*SAQ*, LXIII, 207-217). *Set This House on Fire*, Baumbach maintains, is not as bad as most critics have contended, and where it fails is in those parts wherein Styron allows "his didactic purpose . . . to govern and shape his book." "The suffering creature, refusing to relinquish its last painful breath to the hand of impotent and brutal mercy, is Styron's metaphor for existence." *Set This House on Fire* receives even more extended treatment in Robert Detweiler's "William Styron and the Courage to Be" (*Four Spiritual Crises*, pp. 6-13), wherein Tillich and Kierkegaard are found useful in exploring the meaning of the novel. Marvin Klotz provides a comparative study in "The Triumph Over Time: Narrative Form in William Faulkner and William Styron" (*MissQ*, XVII, 9-20). (See above for a comparative study of Styron and Updike.)

In "The Singular Worlds of Jack Kerouac" (*Contemporary American Novelists*, pp. 120-133), Howard W. Webb, Jr., documents the origin and development of the "Beats" as they relate to Jack Kerouac. His major point, however, is that Kerouac is not truly a Beat, that he always affirms two worlds, the world of Lowell, Massachusetts, where he grew up, and life "on the road." He sees them imagisticly in conjunction in *The Town and the City* and then shows how the values of the Beat (in Kerouac's fiction) are in fact the values of his young life in Lowell. But he also sees a dead-end for Kerouac who, unless he finds some new ways to continue to affirm "Lowell's" values, has no place to go.

In "John Knowles's Short Novels" (*SSF*, I, 107-112), Jay L. Halio summarizes *A Separate Peace* and *Morning in Antibes*, finding in the first the initiation theme; in the second, a sort of continuation, the discovery of self, of love. James Ellis also examines the first of these two novellas ("*A Separate Peace*: The Fall from Innocence," *EJ*, LII, 313-318) and recommends it highly for high-school students.

James C. Austin's "Legend, Myth, and Symbol in Frederick Manfred's *Lord Grizzly*" (*Crit*, VI, 1963, iii, 122-130) is self-explanatory but also includes a brief sketch of Manfred's writings and parts of many letters from the writer to Austin.

William March's (W.E.M. Campbell) *The Bad Seed* is the subject of two notes discussing the similarities of that novel to Holmes's *Elsie Venner* without suggesting influence. See Abigail Ann Hamblen, "*The Bad Seed*: A Modern *Elsie Venner*" (*WHR*, XVII, 1963, 361-363), and William T. Going, "A Footnote to "*The Bad Seed*: A Modern *Elsie Venner*" (*WHR*, XVIII, 175).

The most important study of Mary McCarthy's fiction in 1964 was a statement of her own, "Letter to a Translator: About *The Group*" (*Encounter*, XXIII, V, 69-71, 74-76), in the form of a reply to a series of questions about that novel from its Danish translator. In much more detail than one would have expected, Miss McCarthy "explains" her intention in the novel in terms of style, technique, and structure: the absence of any intended "spokesman" in the novel, a list of her major "devices," the uses of the first and last chapters as "choruses," and so on. It is a useful dissection of the novel's techniques. Paul Schlueter's "The Dissections of Mary McCarthy" (*Contemporary American Novelists*, pp. 54-64) is perhaps not so useful. A survey of her work which praises the short stories as superior to her novels, it views Miss McCarthy as "intellectual," as having "clarity of insight," a "satiric tongue," and "dispassionate wit." His conclusion: "dissection sometimes requires more than enthusiasm and a sharp knife." For Bruce Cook, Mary McCarthy is still a shocked school girl: ". . . a bit of a Jansenist . . . she has been frozen in the haughty moral posture of her Catholic girlhood, unable to take the world as she finds it, yet unable to leave it be" ("Mary McCarthy: One of Ours?" *CathW*, CXCIX, 34-42).

The uneven reputation of Carson McCullers, according to Oliver Evans in "The Case of Carson McCullers" (*GaR*, XVIII, 40-45), is a result of (1) her themes of isolation and loneliness, (2) her use of freakish characters for symbolic reasons, and (3) her brand of realism that obscures her allegories. Marvin Felheim, in his comparative study of Welty and McCullers (see above), also emphasizes Mrs. McCullers' themes of loneliness. And Robert S. Phillips, in "Dinesen's 'Monkey' and McCullers' 'Ballad': A Study in Literary Affinity" (*SSF*, I, 184-190), examines the many parallels between the two stories. Phillips also, in "The Gothic Architecture of *The Member of the Wedding*" (*Ren*, XVI, 59-72), presents a much too detailed examination of the gothic elements in Mrs. McCullers' fiction with a still more detailed analysis of how her most popular novel exemplifies this "gothicism."

My first reaction to *James A. Michener* by A. Grove Day (TUSAS) was shock at the author's apparent conviction that *Tales of the South Pacific* "is . . . the best novel to come out of the World War II conflict in the Pacific." A footnote judgment apparently affirming that "appreciation of . . . [Mailer's *The Naked and the Dead*] is greatly tarnished by the revelation that it is a Marxist allegory hewing to the party line"—and citing an unpublished MA thesis as support for the statement—did not give that shock much relief. But these reactions are not quite fair. Professor Day, a collaborator on one book with Michener and a friend for fifteen years, is simply critically in tune with his subject. He states candidly that Michener's "stance is closer to the soap box than to the laboratory of the social scientist, [that] he is 'highly moral' and confessedly optimistic, and is committed to a faith in progress and the rational improvability of man." He places Michener with writers such as London and Upton Sinclair. His book contains a useful bibliography.

Henry Miller, a nice juxtaposition to Michener, had more attention abroad during 1964 than at home. Other than Thomas H. Moore's edition of Miller's comments on his own writing (see above), only three articles appeared in the United States. Steven Foster, in "A Critical Appraisal of Henry Miller's *Tropic of Cancer*" (*TCL*, IX,

196-208), maintains that it is "the function of . . . [this] novel to transmit . . . anxiety to the reader, so that his encounter with the work amounts to a genuine existential predicament." Walter Lowenfels, in "Unpublished Preface to *Tropic of Cancer*" (*MR*, V, 481-491), presents a memoir of his acquaintance with Miller in Paris during the late twenties and early thirties together with two "prefaces" written for the novel that were never before published. Finally, Grace D. Yerbury, in "Of a City beside a River: Whitman, Eliot, Thomas, Miller" (*WWR*, X, 67-73), sees *Tropic of Cancer* schematically and structurally related to "Crossing Brooklyn Ferry," *The Waste Land*, and Dylan Thomas' "Prologue to an Adventure." One dissertation on Miller was abstracted, William Alexander Gordon's "Henry Miller and the Romantic Tradition" (*DA*, XXIV, 3335-36).

Wright Morris is the subject of another of Marcus Klein's remarkable surveys in his *After Alienation* ("Wright Morris: The American Territory," pp. 196-246). Morris fits Klein's "accommodation" thesis well enough without, however, getting in his way. He surveys fourteen of Morris' novels, seeing in the first five a discovery of America in a very special sense, one that takes the reader from country to city, from present to past, from west to east. Klein finds a relatedness in the works, not unlike Faulkner's, that results, in effect, in a sort of "middle-western Yoknapatawpha." He sees a change in the novels of the 1950's, but apparently not as radically different as Morris himself thought it, with a much surer control of the comic and a more sustained distance between Morris and his characters. In his most recent works, says Klein, the past, although "far more untrustworthy," does not blind him to the fact that "the present remains problematic." All of Morris' fiction oscillates between "audacity" and "practicality," and his best fiction "time and again capture[s] the tension, the magnetic field, between these two basic impulses of his characters."

David Madden's book-length study, *Wright Morris* (TUSAS), is far less satisfactory. It is so much bits and pieces, so exclusively explication (in spite of a few concluding paragraphs of evaluation) as to obscure the whole. Only Madden's chapter on *Man and Boy* is completely coherent, though his conclusion is perfectly lucid that Morris' achievement has been his ability "to project upon the literary firmament a many-faceted, serio-comic view of the American Dream, landscape, and character." There is no information here about Morris' life that is not included in his "Chronology," although the book does contain an extremely useful annotated bibliography of Morris' uncollected short stories, reviews, and articles.

J. F. Powers' short story, "Keystone," is the subject of John J. Kirvan's "Ostergothenburg Revisited" (*CathW*, CXCVIII, 308-313), a demonstration of Powers' satire on the secularization of the Catholic church.

In *Frederick Prokosch* (TUSAS), Radcliffe Squires presents a model study of a relatively prolific novelist far too little known in America. It is beautifully written and organized, judicious in its judgments (about both the poetry and the novels), and brings to bear the best kind of literary mind through a balanced perspective. His biographical information is informative and relevant to his thematic organization of the fiction. Squires never claims too much, yet, one feels, he certainly claims enough.

The tragedy of "loss of self and loss of human love and identity" is a central theme of James Purdy's two novels and short stories, according to Regina Pomeranz, "The Hell of Not Loving; Purdy's Modern Tragedy" (*Ren*, XVI, 149-153). Not too far from this same contention is Gerald Weales's belief that "the impossibility of being recognized is the subject of most of Purdy's work" ("No Face and No Exit: The Fiction of James Purdy and J. P. Donleavy," *Contemporary American Novelists*, pp. 143-154).

John Rechy and Robert Gover are compared by Terry Southern in "Rechy and Gover" (*Contemporary American Novelists*, pp. 222-227). Rechy is seen in terms of Whitman, Wolfe, Sandburg, and Henry Miller, that is, in the tradition of "Romantic Agony." Gover, "on the other side of the street," is seen as much too dependent on Faulkner but able nonetheless to keep his own feelings well out of his narratives.

Philip Roth's *Letting Go* is read by Robert Detweiler as a novel which "explores the human condition from an angle which tempers the Jewish heritage with the existential thought of Martin Buber" ("Philip Roth and the Test of the Dialogic Life," *Four Spiritual Crises*, pp. 25-35). Martin Buber's *I-Thou, I-It* concepts do seem to provide remarkable insight into this novel.

B. F. Skinner's *Walden Two* is tied in with the tradition of utopian literature by Robert L. Stilwell in "Literature and Utopia: B. F. Skinner's *Walden Two*" (*WHR*, XVIII, 331-341).

A much more important study is that of the short stories of Jesse Stuart in Ruel E. Foster's "Jesse Stuart, Short Story Writer" (*Reality and Myth*, pp. 145-160), a detailed, authoritative, and convincing survey of Stuart's short fiction. Stuart "has a feeling for the life of things . . . and lets the universal shine through." He is seen to be in the tradition of Wolfe, of the southwestern humorists, of Mark Twain—seen, like Joyce's Molly Bloom, to be a Yes, Yes man—but one not blind to the evils and horrors of which man is capable.

In "Harvey Swados: Private Stories and Public Fiction" (*Contemporary American Authors*, pp. 182-192), Charles Shapiro pleads for recognition of novels of social criticism, citing Swados as proof enough that this kind of novel is still very much alive.

In *James Thurber* (TUSAS), Robert Morsberger gives us much too much of the obvious. *The Male Animal*, for example, simply will not withstand ten pages of close analysis. Yet Morsberger is very good on Thurber's language, and there is a happy phrase here and there: "Thurber combined Tom Sawyer's romantic Mitty syndrome with Huck Finn's horse sense and then added a Jamesian ambiguity for appropriate occasions."

Lionell Trilling's use of *The Ancient Mariner* and "Kubla Khan" is the subject of Burton S. Kendle's note, "Trilling's 'Of This Time, of That Place' " (*Expl*, XXII, Item 61).

Jessamyn West's use of the wind is explicated by Christopher G. Katope in "West's 'Love, Death, and the Ladies' Drill Team' " (*Expl*, XXIII, Item 27).

Victor Comerchero's *Nathanael West: The Ironic Prophet* (Syracuse, Syracuse Univ. Press) is a fine tribute to the novelist. The first full-length study of West's fiction, it analyzes the four slim novels in detail, yet is also able, in introductory chapters, to discuss West's "tensions" and "self" and, in the concluding ones, to generalize convincingly about West's "image of man" and to give to West's total fiction some meaningful classifications. Comerchero approaches his subject from many angles—Freudian psychology, mythic waste lands, sociological derivatives, literary history—and yet, in a sense, rejects them all. West's work, he concludes, is "prismatic"; he is "a visionary" whose best two novels "are his visionary nightmares." And the "afterglow" that follows "is an enduring one." In David D. Galloway's "A Picaresque Apprenticeship: Nathanael West's *The Dream Life of Balso Snell* and *A Cool Million*" (*WSCL*, V, 110-126), a point is made that Comerchero also makes: the apprenticeship of these two lesser works, in their "opportunity [for West] to detour, practice, and sample . . . bore [rich] fruit" in his other two novels.

Purdue University

14. Poetry: 1910-1930

Ann Stanford

The period 1910-1930 is just remote enough from our own that it has fallen into an era of reminiscence. With its chief poets aging or gone, those who knew them are in a mood to remember or to bring out letters that represent a kind of memory. And there is reassessment, too, of some of the major and minor figures who have not yet fallen into solid literary niches.

i. Robert Frost

The literature on Frost, especially, is undergoing a time of laud with general articles celebrating the poet, accounts of special phases of his life, a book-length biography, and a collection of letters. There are articles on his ideas and techniques as well, but these are not numerous in proportion to the total volume of work on Frost.

By far the year's most important addition to Frost scholarship is the publication of *Selected Letters of Robert Frost*, edited by Lawrance Thompson (New York, Holt, Rinehart and Winston). The book contains 466 letters from Frost besides nearly 100 from others to or about the poet. These were chosen, Mr. Thompson tells us, after examination of over 1,500 letters, as those which would give us the most rounded portrait of Frost the man. This broader view is especially needed, since the books of letters published in 1963 show Frost in more limited roles—those to Untermeyer revealing Frost in his reaction to the literary scene and those to Bartlett presenting him as a thoughtful friend. Besides the letters, Mr. Thompson has provided a lengthy chronological table and a full index. Each of the ten sections of the book is preceded by a brief biographical survey of the years covered by the letters.

These letters help to reveal the Frost who lay under the public character he created in his poetry. They reveal his gloominess and suspicions, his doubts of himself as artist, and the conflict of the artist and family man. His own experience taught him to know the destructive forces within one's personality and the need to keep these under control. In his own art he did not talk about himself, as he told Untermeyer. And he wrote to Cox: "A subject has to be held clear outside of me with struts and as it were set up for an object." Like the poems, the letters are not always as straightforward as they appear. Frost warns of this several times: "I have written to keep the over curious out of the secret places of my mind both in my verse and in my letters to such as you."

The purpose of Jean Gould's biography of Frost, *Robert Frost: The Aim Was Song* (New York, Dodd, Mead), is to offer "tribute to his courage, his indomitable will to overcome the obstacles in his path during the long struggle for recognition, and above all, to his song." Accordingly, Miss Gould deals with the places Frost went, the things he did, the friends he made. Though she obtained material from Frost himself regarding his early life in San Francisco, Lawrence, and Derry, the lack of documentation leaves it unavailable to the scholar. The almost fictional impression of familiarity with the domesticity of the Frosts and the presence of value-connotations ("Ezra was a sharp little man, with beady black eyes. . . .") mark the book as aimed for a wide, rather than scholarly, audience.

Two other books give a closer look at the poet during short periods of his life. *Robert Frost in Russia*, by F. D. Reeve (Boston, Little, Brown), describes Frost's two-week visit to Russia under a cultural-exchange arrangement in 1962. Two men accompanied him on this visit—Frederick B. Adams, Jr., director of the Pierpont Morgan Library, an old friend of Frost's, and Professor F. D. Reeve, who went "to help with arrangements and the language." Adams' account of the trip was published earlier (*To Russia with Frost*, Boston, Club of Odd Volumes, 1963). Reeve gives a day-by-day account of Frost's mission, describing how his first suspicions were allayed and his troubles in understanding and being understood were gradually overcome. Frost was acclaimed in Russia, but his self-appointed mission was greater than spreading a feeling for the best in American culture. He aimed to see Khrushchev himself and to discuss with him his ideas. Frost thought there was a continual drawing closer of the capitalist and planned economies, the one moving toward more socialism, the other becoming more humane. He pictured a magnanimous rivalry as a possibility between the two powers in sports, science, art, and in democracy itself. A great nation must

be magnanimous, Frost believed, and he attempted to get Khrushchev to solve the Berlin crisis by allowing the reuniting of the two
halves of Berlin.

Giving another close picture of Frost, this time in his early years
as a farmer, is *Robert Frost: Farm-Poultryman*, edited by Edward
Connery Lathem and Lawrance Thompson (Hanover, N. H., Dartmouth, 1963). During his career at Derry, Frost undertook to write
for the poultry journals—not the usual descriptions of methods of interest to poultrymen, but semifictional pieces displaying the wry
humor often found in his poems. Eleven essays are collected here,
all that appeared in *The Eastern Poultryman* and *Farm-Poultry* from
February, 1903, to December, 1905; some of these may well find their
way into the prose anthologies. Frost knew his subject firsthand; he
moved into the Derry farm in 1900 with a flock of three hundred
Wyandottes, though his interest in poultry-raising waned after he
began to teach in Derry's Pinkerton Academy. The introduction describes Frost's career in the raising of poultry and presents some of
Frost's friends, notably Dr. Charlemagne Bricault, producer of "bred-
to-lay" Wyandottes, and John A. Hall, who grew prize poultry by
"judicious neglect." The criticism that Frost received after he wrote
that Hall's geese roosted in trees even in the winter may have been
one reason he gave up writing for the poultry magazines.

In one of his letters Frost wrote: "Anyone who has achieved the
least form to be sure of it, is lost to the larger excruciations." For him
art was a means of imposing form on the chaos against which man
stood. It is this idea of the value of form that Anna K. Juhnke finds in
"Religion in Robert Frost's Poetry: The Play for Self-Possession"
(*AL*, XXXVI, 153-164). She finds in Frost's poetry an ambiguous attitude toward religion, which is reflected in a "play" with religious
matters. Such play moves between impulses either to reject religion
or to commit oneself to it. The uncommitted poet creates his forms for
self-protection and his own kind of salvation. If God is not a human
projection, he must speak and tell where he is. Such revelation is
most likely to be found in nature, where the stars, especially, provide
a figure for ambiguous affirmation and denial. Although a theory of
forms implies limits—of landscape, social relationships, language,
and poetic shape—such limits are not ultimate barriers to risk. However, Frost is unable to make a commitment to larger religious implications. *A Masque of Reason* ends without answering its deepest

questions, and *A Masque of Mercy* dismisses the possibility of losing oneself in order to find oneself. Frost returns to salvation through keeping the forms he makes.

Frost's emphasis on form is part of the classicism which Conrad Pendleton finds in "The Classic Dimensions of Robert Frost" (*PrS*, XXXVIII, 76-87), a subject explored last year by Reuben Brower and John Frederick Nims. According to Pendleton, Frost, like the ancient Greeks, believed that under the variety of nature lies a basic law and harmony directed by a system of cosmic control. Pendleton finds classicism also in Frost's simplicity and intensity, and in his "Sophoclean insights . . . which affirmed the wisdom and courage of the human race." Frost's poetry embodies an expression of positive values, restraint, and suggestions of universals through particulars. Mainly in the form of pastorals, Frost's poetry combines the Theocritan idyl in its details of country life with the Virgilian eclogue's revelation of character. To the latter Frost added more drama and a shaping of the regional language into one which also showed universal qualities in American speech. Frost once stated that he believed in "what the Greeks called synecdoche: the philosophy of the part for the whole," and he believed too in the middle way. It was the middle region of man between God and nature that he described; he saw things finite and infinite without confusing the two. He found a balance between man and nature, though not "a calm elevation of perfect beauty"—rather, he gave equal weight to each in "moods and subject matter." And classically too, his was a disciplined art. Though Frost acknowledged his debt to Theocritus and Virgil, he made few classical allusions. Rather he adjusted his poetry, putting it into the regional culture of the America of today.

Gorham Munson ("The Classicism of Robert Frost," *ModA*, VIII 291-305) as early as 1924 had referred to Frost as "the purest classical poet in America today," noting Virgil and Horace as his sources. Frost, says Munson, is classical in his rejection of the Romantic pathetic fallacy, acknowledging the line between man and nature, and in the choice of the central, broad areas of experience common to mankind as his subject.

Though Frost is so often said to have chosen the middle way, Mildred E. Hartsock contends that he actually took a position of courage ("Robert Frost: Poet of Risk," *Person*, XLV, 157-175). He accepted nature as involved in a process of evolving that seems brutal to thinking man, and he accepted the findings of science, but he held that man must go ahead and take the risks of action, even on incomplete knowledge. He did not retreat from society or science, but knew the need of our time is to reassert the self.

Frost in his assertion of the self usually follows a typical pattern of progression says Ruthe T. Sheffey in "From Delight to Wisdom: Thematic Progression in the Poetry of Robert Frost" (*CLAJ*, VIII, 51-59). She quotes Frost himself to show that the poem "begins in delight . . . and ends in a clarification of life." The delight often takes the form of a "passionate" observation, a remembered feeling. The poem begins in the upper world, but typically has a turn in the second half, where the poet comes to terms with the material world and the beginning delight yields to an austere denouement.

An example of the movement from a high point to the ordinary day is found in "Nothing Gold Can Stay" as explicated by Charles R. Anderson (*Expl*, XXII, Item 63). The couple in "The Draft Horse" are shown by Frederick L. Gwynn to accept even the horror of a ritual of sacrifice ("Analysis and Synthesis of Frost's 'The Draft Horse,'" *CE*, XXVI, 223-225). Another kind of sacrifice, that of the human psyche to a culture which represses affection and human needs, is described by Stuart B. James in "The Home's Tyranny: Robert Frost's 'A Servant to Servants' and Andrew Wyeth's 'Christina's World'" (*SDR*, I, ii, 3-15). Both the poet and the painter have not hesitated in much of their best work to portray the American home as a dark place of guilt and death, which may cripple the spirits of its inhabitants.

Several general articles on Frost have appeared. Louis Untermeyer's lecture, *Robert Frost: A Backward Look* (Washington, Lib. of Congress), refers to several of Frost's ideas—his regard for the importance of the creative impulse in teaching and learning, his sense of play, his sense of poetry as truth. The pamphlet includes a partial bibliography of Frost manuscripts, books, recordings, and motion pictures in the Library of Congress. Alfred Kazin ("The Strength of Robert Frost," *Com*, XXXVIII, vi, 49-52) found Frost a "figure of perilous balances" with a "fierce self-regard" who fought for his reputation and for his mastery of the human and technical aspects of his poems.

ii. Ezra Pound

In 1935 T. S. Eliot remarked that "the *point de repere* usually and conveniently taken, as the starting-point of modern poetry, is the group denominated 'imagist' in London about 1910." Affirming Eliot's belief in the historical importance of the Imagists, William Pratt has edited an anthology, *the imagist poem: modern poetry in miniature* (New York, E. P. Dutton). Pratt's introduction defends the originality of the Imagist poem and the importance of Imagist theory as a basis of much of the major poetry written since the beginning of the movement. The Imagist movement itself was not sustained, but occupied a few "creative moments." After these periods, during which the rules of Imagism were developed, Pratt finds that Imagism was no longer a movement, but a tool to be used by each poet as he wished. The addition of a new cadence to the repertoire of English poets and the turning of the symbol back toward the literal and concrete are two germinal accomplishments of Imagism, says Pratt, even though Imagist poetry itself lacked what William Carlos Williams called "structural necessity." A further endowment for poetry was "a diction that would leave the image unclouded by rhetoric or sentiment."

Of the Imagists, Pound was perhaps the most active in the search for a new kind of poetry. Two excellent books discuss his career and his work. Noel Stock's *Poet in Exile: Ezra Pound* (New York, Barnes & Noble) aims to cut through the tangle of opinions and prejudices regarding the career of Pound so that the reader can come to the work itself free of these. Mr. Stock explicates Pound's career from his education in the United States through the writing of the last *Cantos*.

In the United States, Pound had established his goal of being a poet and one who knew "more about poetry than any man living." Before he left this country he was already striving to get hardness and precision into his poetry. In London, Ford Madox Ford was a germinal influence on Pound's use of precision and his use of "the living tongue." Stock describes the impact of Fenollosa on Pound's work in 1914 as confirming his idea of the importance of concrete reality in poetry, the use of "*res* not *verba*," and discusses the work of Pound and Eliot in evolving a poetic language in which the intermediary explanation—which Pound considered the province of prose—was left out. Stock discriminates between Pound's roles as poet and as entrepreneur for the works of other writers and finds his judgment of the writers he helped introduce between 1913 and 1922 was extremely good. However, as Pound grew more interested in monetary theory and politics, he lost touch with the main stream of literature, and the quality of his prose declined. Contributing to the decline was his belief in the juxtaposition of concrete elements rather than in connective thought. Both in his poetry and his prose Pound represents the mind of modern man freed from restraint, incomplete, with nothing to rest on. Altogether Mr. Stock has done a valuable and readable study of the complex of influences and attitudes that moved Pound at various stages of his career.

Donald Davie, in *Ezra Pound: Poet as Sculptor* (New York, Oxford Univ. Press), explores Pound's poetry chronologically and in detail, an investigation for which Mr. Davie is exceptionally well-qualified. Central is the idea that Pound's approach to styles and the joining of styles goes beyond technique to an attitude toward human affairs in general. A major theme is that Pound was interested in sculpture and sculptural form. Though he is generally recognized as a man with a superb ear for the cadence of poetry, he at the same time experimented with poetry as a spatial art like sculpture—an art which approaches the infinite by formal perfection, which carves out what is already there—rather than a successive art like music.

In "Ezra Pound and Rabindranath Tagore" (*AL*, XXXVI, 53-63), Harold M. Hurwitz discusses the changing attitude of Pound toward the Indian poet between the years 1912, when Tagore came to London, and 1917. From an excited sense of discovery of the man and his work, Pound developed an antagonism, caused partly, Hurwitz thinks, by the decline in the quality of Tagore's work and partly by a change in Pound himself.

Several articles discuss portions of Pound's work. Max Halperen, in "Old Men & New Tools: The Chinese Cantos of Pound" (*Trace*, No. 52, pp. 1-8), finds that although the whole series is set within the framework of Chinese history, the clue to the meaning of each is not necessarily drawn from De Mailla's *Historie Generale de la Chine*, which Pound used as his major source. The *Cantos* are carefully related individual poems, each with its own thematic arrangement. Halperen traces the major themes of these *Cantos* (LII-LXI) and the particular design of each. LoisAnn Oakes discusses Pound's use of musical structure and his references to music in "An Explication of

'Canto LXXV' by Ezra Pound" (*WSCL*, V, 105-109), and George Knox looks at imagery connected with "Glaucus in 'Hugh Selwyn Mauberley' " (*ES*, XLV, 236-237).

There are two reminiscences involving Pound. One, an address given by John Espey at the Second Annual Conference in the Study of Twentieth-Century Literature held at Michigan State University, spring, 1962, and published in its "Proceedings" (*Approaches to the Study of Twentieth-Century Literature*, East Lansing, Mich. State Univ. Press), is an account of how he became a Pound scholar. The second, by Brigid Patmore, describes her meetings with the young poet ("Ezra Pound in England," *TQ*, VII, iii, 69-81). The incidents that Miss Patmore describes corroborate comments by Hurwitz that Pound changed during the years in England, and Yeats's sad exclamation later at Rapallo, "How do you account for Ezra?" reinforces the critical studies of Davie and Stock regarding the decline in Pound's awareness of the central movement of literature. Miss Patmore shows Pound in a favorable light in his early London days, both as a man of impressive literary acumen and as a loyal friend.

An attempt is made to distinguish between "The Aesthetic and the Intellectual Analyses of Literature" by James P. Dougherty (*JAAC*, XXII, 315-324). Dougherty sets forth the many problems involved in assessing the aesthetic and intellectual harmonies of a work, using the Pound controversy as an example. Careful to show that the final judgment is a complex one, Dougherty finds that in some works the reader must pass from an aesthetic judgment to an intellectual one "and weigh the writer's experience against his own, the writer's attitudes against his own."

The continuance of active interest in Pound and his influence to the present day is indicated in "Robert Creeley in Conversation with Charles Tomlinson" (*Review*, No. 10, pp. 24-35), in the course of which Creeley comments on the continuing importance of the work of Pound and H. D. for the (William Carlos) "Williamsite" group of American poets. Recent books have been published on Pound in such divergent places as Chile, the Netherlands, and South Africa.

iii. E. E. Cummings

In *e. e. cummings: The Growth of a Writer* (Carbondale, Southern Ill. Univ. Press), Norman Friedman traces the development of Cummings' vision and techniques book by book. For Friedman, Cummings belongs with the Romantic tradition in seeing natural order as superior to man-made orders and nature itself as process rather than product. Believing that the intuitive or imaginative faculty in man can perceive the essence of nature directly, Cummings is a Transcendentalist who values the immediate confrontation of experience, an attitude which underlies much of his impressionism. For him everyday perception is ruled by habit and lies like a film over the true world of spontaneity and concrete life. This first-hand world is revealed by the poet, who can see, not what a camera sees, but the "actual crisp organic squirm" itself. If rationalists object that this is a world of disorder, the answer is that the timeless, intuitively perceived world has an order of its own. But the Transcendental vision is not simple; the ideal needs the ordinary as the place in which to fulfil itself. Ideally, for Cummings, moral choice is based on the image one has of what he is and wants to become. To know, one should respond directly and spontaneously. An individualist, Cummings does not understand how people can live creatively in a community; for him all institutions are wrong. Instead of institutions, Cummings emphasizes love, not merely erotic romance, but giving without thought of return.

To embody such attitudes, Cummings has shaped an aesthetic in which art imitates a nature which is dynamic and spontaneous. Intelligence is not abandoned, but functions at "intuitional velocity." Though his work is in many ways conventional, Cummings attempts by technique to strip the film of familiarity from the language, in order to take it from the world itself and to create freshness and motion. Though his non-rational, experiential attitude has been present in much literature since Blake, like many Romantics he has cared too little for reason, and he has criticized all institutions in his eagerness to attack evil ones.

Friedman's thesis is coherent and well-stated, though the relation to the thesis of the various works and parts of works that he describes in the body of the book is not always clearly drawn. A briefer account of the ideas developed in this book is given in Friedman's article, "E. E. Cummings and His Critics" (*Criticism*, VI, 114-133), as the basis for his comments on the critical reception given Cummings' work since the 1920's. Friedman finds that both Cummings' detractors and his admirers have often failed to understand the real basis of his art in the Romantic organic view of nature and art. In the twenties the concern of the critics was with his techniques. In the thirties they

emphasized his individualism, either defending him as a Roman-
ticist protesting the social system or attacking him as an anarchist.
They did not recognize that Cummings' individualism does not fit
into the political category at all. In the forties and fifties his central
Transcendental view of life was beginning to be recognized. Though
they often mistake his Transcendental position, according to Friedman, the critics of Cummings have been more favorable than not.
The article contains a lengthy list of reviews, divided by decades.

Another book, *E. E. Cummings* by Barry A. Marks (TUSAS),
moves from a consideration of individual poems to influences and
tendencies in Cummings' work as a whole. For Marks, Cummings
needs to be looked at against a background of modernism in music,
painting, sculpture, and architecture. Cummings was aware of the
relationships among the various media and believed that art was
needed to restore the "vital impulse of life." Though describing the
interest in organic vitality that Friedman characterizes as "Romantic,"
Marks calls it a "realistic impulse," an impulse of the artist to show
what he really sees "rather than a combination of what he saw *and*
what he remembered, and thought." This kind of realism, Marks says,
involves looking at what is ugly and what is fragmented. It also involves getting motion into the poem, since the world is in motion.
Art must be a process of "unthinking."

Cummings, like others of his generation, was a formalist in that
he saw art as a reorganization of the chaos of nature. In language, he
added a plastic approach which involved not only a visual element,
but an exploitation of all the properties of language. But realism and
formalism were contradictory in Cummings' aesthetic. The realistic
view of the world presumes that the world, if seen clearly, is har-
monious. The formalist view bases its forms on the belief that the
world is chaos. Cummings did not reconcile these views, except in
the dualistic idea that the unconscious is the best part of existence.
Man can achieve fulfilment, but it is difficult. So his poems show
a contrast—some emphasize being open to the sensuous and per-
ceivable—the daylight, springtime poems; others emphasize putting
this aside to be open to the spiritual essence of things. Marks also
finds Cummings a characteristically American poet in his frustration
over the slowness of attaining the vision of what might be. This
involves an intensity growing out of the idea that "a new start . . .
is to be made neither in a new place nor in a new time but here and
now."

Both books illustrate the possibilities and dangers in writing about Cummings. Both present cogent arguments for the seriousness of his poetry and indicate the rich material available for comment. Both also show the difficulty of explicating the individual poems. So much is unsaid in a Cummings poem, and the meanings may be extended so far, that to state the farthest connotations, though they are really there, is to make the outer reaches of the poem bear almost too much weight.

Still the risk must be taken. Robert C. Walsh finds that "Anyone Lived in a Pretty How Town" (*Expl*, XXII, Item 72) describes the death of the child in man as he grows into adulthood. This contrasts with Marks's interpretation, which is more convincing, that *anyone* and *noone* are individualists who live and die among the ordinary people, people who strive for money and status, of the town. Paul O. William notes of "kind)" that night and even death are "mightily alive" in comparison to the dull scientific talk described in the poem (*Expl*, XXIII, Item 4). David R. Clark (*Expl*, XXII, Item 48) gives a valuable insight into the poet's careful technique in his presentation of two versions of a Cummings poem, "it's / so damn sweet when Anybody—." The revised poem is improved and made more typically a Cummings poem by the shifting of a few words.

iv. Hart Crane

The assessment of Crane's importance in American poetry continues. The change in attitude since the thirties is documented by Judith Bloomingdale in "Three Decades in Periodical Criticism of Hart Crane's 'The Bridge'" (*PBSA*, LVII, 1963, 360-371). She finds that Yvor Winters' and Allen Tate's early reviews, which appeared in 1930, set the pattern for calling the poem "a magnificent failure" for the next two decades. The voices favoring the magnificence of the poem began to prevail in the fifties, culminating in Lawrence C. Dembo's book-length study. G. Thomas Tanselle, in "A Further Note on Hart Crane's Critics" (*PBSA*, LVIII, 180-181), adds a few items to Bloomingdale's periodical bibliography, while William White, in "Hart Crane: Bibliographical Addenda" (*BB*, XXIV, 1963, 35), supplements that given in Samuel Hazo's *Hart Crane: An Introduction and Interpretation* (1963).

Deena Posy Metzger continues the exploration of the meaning of "The Bridge" in "Hart Crane's *Bridge*: The Myth Active" (*ArQ*,

XX, 36-46). Devoting her attention primarily to "The Dance" section, Mrs. Metzger finds two middle American myths which provide unity and development. One is the myth of the serpent and the eagle, involved in the founding of Tenochtitlán; the other, the myth of the Toltec god of civilization, Quetzalcoatl, who is traditionally represented as a plumed serpent. In Crane's poem, the eagle is associated with space, power, knowledge, industrialization—the European influence; the serpent is equated with time and the indigenous qualities of America. Crane associated the idea of white men coming in the guise of gods with the mystic and messianic possibilities of America which must be achieved through the fusion of European and Indian elements. Robert Joseph Andreach, in "The Spiritual Life in Hopkins, Joyce, Eliot, and Hart Crane" (*DA*, XXV, 467), also finds that "The Bridge" is concerned with the evolution of a religious myth and the possibility of a religious life for twentieth-century man.

A fusion, this time of portraits, occurs also in Hart Crane's poem on Shakespeare, according to Jean Guiguet ("*To Shakespeare* de Hart Crane," *EA*, XVII, 586-590). The poet, in describing Shakespeare, selected the qualities that most resembled Crane himself. Guiguet finds words and phrases in other poems and letters of Crane which refer to himself and closely parallel the language of this sonnet.

v. Conrad Aiken

Reuel Denney has produced a short but perceptive study of the work of Conrad Aiken (*Conrad Aiken*, UMPAW, No. 38, Minneapolis, Univ. of Minn. Press). Though Aiken's *The Jig of Forslin* is contemporary with Pound's "Hugh Selwyn Mauberley" and Eliot's "The Love Song of J. Alfred Prufrock" and though the central figure in each resembles the others in being out of tune with his time, Aiken followed different aesthetic influences and developed a different attitude from the other two. Aiken's style may be described as "impressionistic." He attempts to follow a musical form in catching the temperaments of his characters in a sequence of variations. He is more concerned with the motives of his characters than their actions. While he achieves power from this in the rendering of certain character types whose actions and thoughts flow into each other, it is hard for him to move into the narrative poem.

In his early "symphonies" he developed a technique suitable to his purpose, a series of subsections in which a cluster of sensuous impressions were formed and in which he made use of synesthesia. But this style could become cloying and was unsuited to narrative. Where it is appropriate, his use of a luxuriant style, full of repetition and decoration, has helped to keep alive an important stylistic tradition in opposition to the spare poetic line of his contemporaries. Denney finds too that Aiken's view of man is consistent and vital in showing man learning to enjoy and realize himself.

However, E. P. Bollier finds that Aiken's skepticism is an unsatisfactory basis for poetry ("From Scepticism to Poetry: A Note on Conrad Aiken and T. S. Eliot," *TSE*, XIII, 1963, 95-104). Aiken began by being influenced by Eliot's views derived from F. H. Bradley. Bradley and Eliot assumed that all knowledge begins in immediate experience and that the world that begins in a "finite center," the individual, is the only reality the finite self can know. The world depends on the self for reality, and the self depends on the world it knows for identity. Both Aiken and Eliot dramatized the impermanent self in their early poetry. Aiken strove to make his consciousness articulate. However, Eliot did not deny the possibility that there was a truth outside the individual, and that such truth would be found by human minds, not by an individual; hence the vision of the poet includes such a collective formulation. Aiken did not reach this point; he has not separated the functions of poet and philosopher. Hence, according to Bollier, Aiken's poetry has been strained by the need of showing that things as they are "must be so, not only for Aiken, but for everyone."

V. L. O. Chittick too asserts that Aiken attempted in the early prose and verse to find out who he really was. Discussing the relationship between Aiken and Lowry (*"Ushant's* Malcolm Lowry," *QQ*, LXXI, 67-75) Chittick comments briefly on Aiken's philosophy as shown in *Ushant*.

vi. Carl Sandburg

In *Carl Sandburg* (TUSAS), Richard Crowder gives a balanced treatment to the works and career of the midwestern poet. Admitting the flaws of diffuseness, cataloguing, and excessive use of anecdotes, Crowder finds enough of color, suggestion, and melodic variety to make Sandburg's work an individual and permanent contribution to American literature. Crowder admits that some critics have found Sandburg's work minor or beneath notice; on the other hand, responsible critics have praised it. The complaint that Sandburg writes always of the Midwest and has therefore been called a provincial, Crowder says, is not a valid one, since other acceptable writers have represented a single area as the basis of their universal concepts. More justified are criticisms that Sandburg's ardor and enthusiasm for democracy have led to uncritical optimism and that in longer pieces he tends to pile up details rather than organize them.

Jerome Green ("Carl Sandburg as Poet: A Study of the Criticism and Other Factors Contributing to His Reputation as a Poet through 1960," *DA*, XXV, 1209-10) finds that Sandburg's choice of subject matter, his bias for common people, and his language and free verse are the qualities most singled out for praise or blame. The initial reviews of his books of poetry showed a preponderance of favorable reaction, though some reviewers denied the value of his work. A smaller number of critical articles on Sandburg appeared after the 1920's, indicating both the indifference of some critics and the turning to other forms by the poet himself as he took on the role of literary celebrity.

vii. Moody, Bishop, Masters, Millay, Robinson, Stein

An attempt is made to revive the reputation of William Vaughn Moody in Martin Halpern's *William Vaughn Moody* (TUSAS). Moody was the great new voice of the 1890's, a shade too early to be a part of the movement toward a new poetry, and his poetry retains the generalities and formal structure against which the modern revolt was directed. At times, however, the work of Moody did reflect new movements, particularly that of Symbolism. Moody's greatest strength and claim to remembrance, according to Halpern, lies in the plays, both the verse drama and those prose dramas most successful on the stage. Unfortunately Moody died before he could combine his ability in good verse dialogue with his demonstrated power to write a producible play.

"John Peale Bishop: A Celebration" (*Reality and Myth*, pp. 80-97), by Eugene Haun, calls attention to Bishop as a poet whose fame should be greater. Bishop's art was ordered, balanced, objective to the point of being politely detached. The earlier poems, though accomplished, give evidence of his sources; Bishop's own voice comes through most definitely in the dramatic monologues and in his elegy on F. Scott Fitzgerald. S. C. Moore ("Variations on a

Theme: The Poetry and Criticism of John Peale Bishop," *DA*, XXIV, 1963, 2482) finds that Bishop's work was imitative and that he was hampered by his constant search for a tradition. An explication of "Bishop's 'Ballet'" (*Expl*, XXIII, Item 12) by the same writer shows Bishop's indebtedness to works of art; "Ballet" includes quite literal descriptions of certain of Chirico's paintings.

In "Edgar Lee Masters, Political Essayist" (*ISHSJ*, LVII, 249-260), Lois Hartley describes Masters' intense enthusiasm for Jeffersonian democracy, including states' rights, his belief in constitutional government, and his interest in labor—all of which are background for his poetry and fiction. A short letter by Robinson appeared in 1964 with a commentary by Robert Liddell Lowe ("A Letter of Edwin Arlington Robinson to James Barstow," *NEQ*, XXXVII, 390-392), but next year will be a better one for Robinson, with at least two books forthcoming. A reminiscence of a romance with Edna St. Vincent Millay is the subject of "My Friend Edna St. Vincent Millay" (*MTJ*, XII, ii, 1-3) by Floyd Dell. He found the young poet was haunted by her belief in "the impermanence of love." Gertrude Stein discusses her book of poetry, *Tender Buttons*, in an interview recorded stenographically and reported by Robert Bartlett Haas ("Gertrude Stein Talking—A Trans-Atlantic Interview," *Uclan Review*, IX, i, 1963, 40-48).

We have been looking at the fragments of an era—here a reminiscence or a letter, there a critical commentary on a major writer. Perhaps the best synthesis of the age can come from the dialogue of two poets who flourished in the twenties, who are still writing, still talking of their art and the world. Their informal conversation is caught in *The Dialogues of Archibald MacLeish and Mark Van Doren* (ed. Warren V. Bush, New York, E. P. Dutton). For two days a crew with camera and sound-recorder followed the poets around MacLeish's Uphill Farm, while they talked over a wide range of subjects—poetry (they were first attracted by its music), their plays (*J.B.* and *The Last Days of Lincoln*), the American temper, their ways of writing, their teaching, their friends. From the view of biography this is a valuable portrait of two men and their time.

Poetry for them is related to the world; it can make things happen through its revelation, because, as MacLeish puts it, it helps one come "to know what you already know, to know it alive in the heart instead of knowing it up here dead in the head," and it makes "a sort of pattern of meaninglessness . . . to deal with tragic meaninglessness." And as Van Doren says, "Poetry makes an immense difference in the world, if only that it makes everybody who reads it better; better in the sense of being deeper and more delicate, and more generous in his understanding."

San Fernando Valley State College

15. Poetry: 1930 to the Present

Oliver Evans

i. General

Only one substantial book concerned specifically with the current scene in American poetry appeared in 1964, but it is of the first importance: *National Poetry Festival Proceedings* (Washington, Library of Congress), a detailed report of the meetings held in Washington from October 22 to October 24, 1962, and attended by some of the most important poets (including the late Robert Frost and William Carlos Williams) in the United States. In addition to formal readings of poems and essays, only some of which had appeared previously in print, the Festival featured numerous impromptu speeches and informal discussions and debates; they are all faithfully set down here, and the volume, though long overdue, is as unique as it is indispensable.

Three of the longer speeches were published as essays in 1963 and were discussed in this volume last year: Randall Jarrell's "Fifty Years of American Poetry," Allen Tate's "Shadow: a Parable and a Polemic," and J. V. Cunningham's "The Problem of Form." The principal topics under discussion at the Festival were the present status of poetry magazines, the relation of the American poet to his public, and the concept of poetic form. Morton Dauwen Zabel, in "The Poetry Journal in Our Time" (pp. 17-27), states that the publishing of any literary magazine presupposes both dedication and persistence on the part of the editor, who must take the long view and resist "personal whim or coterie privilege." In "The Role of the Poetry Journal" (pp. 29-33), Louise Bogan notes with satisfaction the lessening, in some of the smaller magazines, of regional emphasis in favor of a more international tone and warns that publications whose main interest is "the projection of shock for shock's sake" are doomed to early failure. According to Stanley Kunitz ("The Role of the Poetry Journal," pp. 35-38), one of the most important tasks of an editor is to recognize and to promote the prevailing style of his time; he cannot *create* the style, but he can and should clarify it "so that its outlines become unmistakable." *Poetry*, he claims, is the only literary magazine in English that has been fully conscious of its responsibility in this respect.

In the haranguing style characteristic of his latter-day criticism, Karl Shapiro, in an essay entitled "What Is a Public?" (pp. 161-164), denies that the American poet has one. Poetry is the only art in the United States, he asserts, without a substantial public, and the reason for this is not that the public has a "blind spot," but that there simply isn't much American poetry. (The keyword here is *American*: Mr. Shapiro does not deny that lots of good poetry is being written in America, but he contends it is the product of a European rather than an American tradition and thus has little reality for American readers.) *Poetry*, he declares, became almost from its founding an "Anglo-American review." He finds promising symptoms of Anglophobia in the newest generation of poets, however, and suggests hopefully that a genuine American poetry may now, for the first time since Whitman, be in the making: "We are in our Beowulf years. That is why it seems absurd to me for our poets to pretend they are the jaded heirs of prosody and culture. We would look much better to paint our bodies blue and butter our hair." Babette Deutsch, however ("The Poet and His Public," pp. 145-152), maintains that the public must share some of the blame for the fact that poetry is not more widely read in this country. Comparing the situation here with that in the Soviet Union, where Mayakovsky and Evtushenko enjoy huge popular audiences, she charges that the American public has not "provided for the poet" with the result that a "reciprocal contempt" characterizes their relationship. Howard Nemerov ("The Poet's Interest," pp. 153-158) refuses to be depressed; the poet's attention, he says, must be on his poem rather than on his public, which in any case he has no means of estimating accurately. This is not to say that poetry is ineffectual: "Without meaning to, perhaps without especially wanting to, poetry changes the mind of the world. The Muse's interest . . . is not a practical interest. . . . We write, at last, because life is hopeless and beautiful."

In a style whose extreme compactness borders on the eccentric, Léonie Adams ("The Problem of Form," pp. 275-280) discusses the concept of organic form, which she says (citing Sir Herbert Read) is realized by "fusing in one vital unity both form and content." Not a *prescription* in the sense that it can be compounded by ready-made formulas, it is rather a *description* of something which, once it has been achieved, is unmistakable. Using a worksheet of Yeats's "Wild Swans at Coole," she shows how Yeats, after repeated efforts, objectified this concept of form.

Sir Herbert Read, the only Britisher participating importantly in the Festival, makes a number of miscellaneous observations, in "American Bards and British Reviewers" (pp. 347-366), on Anglo-American literary relations. Without naming Mr. Shapiro, he attacks his theory of a national poetry. It is diction, he claims, and not idiom, that determines genuine poetry: "The idiom of Donne differs from the idiom of Milton, a vast difference, but they speak the same language." Rejecting the idea that poetry can be the expression of "some undefined and undefinable national ethos," he warns that the attempt of certain American poets to "steer a separate course" is ill-advised: "We have most dignity, whatever our origins, if we acknowledge the long and vital tradition of our common language and strive, not to speak with a wayward accent, but as purely as our individual sensibility will allow. That, I believe, is what the best American poets have done."

The Library of Congress publication, as has been said, was the only substantial critical work to appear in book form; prefatory essays, however, introduced a number of anthologies concerned both with modern poetry generally (Walter Lowenfels, *Poets of Today*, New York, International Publishers, and Jascha Kessler, *American Poems*, Carbondale, Southern Ill. Univ. Press) and with special types and aspects of it (William Pratt, *The Imagist Poem*, New York, Dutton; Langston Hughes, *New Negro Poets*, Bloomington, Ind. Univ. Press; Edwin Glikes and Paul Schwaber, *Of Poetry and Power*, New York, Basic Books). Mr. Lowenfels' collection is more representative than Mr. Kessler's; actually it is something of a hodgepodge (from which, however, such "academic" poets as Wilbur and Snodgrass have been carefully excluded) in which Ferlinghetti, represented by the dreadful "Tentative Description of a Dinner Given to Promote the Impeachment of President Eisenhower," keeps uneasy company with Eve Merriam. Karl Shapiro, oddly enough, is not represented. Mr. Kessler's collection includes only sixteen poets (one reason for this is that he set forty, rather arbitrarily, as his age limit), but they are for the most part well-chosen. Of the special collections, Mr. Pratt's is probably the most impressive: his introduction is distinguished, and among the moderns whom he classifies as Imagists are Stevens, Moore, and, of course, Williams. Mr. Hughes's anthology is prefaced by Gwendolyn Brooks, who says, reasonably: "At the present time, poets who happen also to be Negroes are twice-tried. They have to write poetry, and they have to remember that they are Negroes." His contributors, among whom are Mari Evans and LeRoi Jones, do both, and their work is generally of good quality. *Of Poetry and Power* collects poems which in some way concern the late John F. Kennedy, either the living man or his memory, and to read it is to realize the astonishing *rapport* which existed between this president (more than any other with the possible exception of Lincoln) and the tiny minority who write poetry in this country. Among the more prominent names represented are Auden, Berryman, Eberhart, Miles, and Swenson, but Ginsberg and Corso are here too. As Arthur Schlesinger, Jr., says in his Introduction: "So many of the writers identify themselves with him . . . and they do so because they perceived in him, not just another American president, but *mon semblable, mon frère*, who, as much as the poets themselves, felt the terror of the age, and, in striving to master both terror and himself, challenged the self-pitying notion so cherished in our nuclear epoch of the abjectness of the individual in the face of history."

James Dickey's *The Suspect in Poetry* (Madison, Minn., Odin House) turns out to be mainly a collection of previously published book reviews and is not concerned primarily with major poets; there is, however, a perceptive essay on Randall Jarrell. As his title might imply, Mr. Dickey is intent on exterminating certain heresies, the most dangerous of which, as he sees it, is the notion that poetry can separate itself successfully from ordinary experience: Wallace Stevens, he suggests, must be a failure in this sense.

Actually, Mr. Dickey's thesis is typical of a very large number of articles that appeared in 1964. In fact, as one surveys the total scene, it becomes immediately apparent that what continues to dominate it is the war which has been raging for some years now between the champions of "academic" and esoteric poetry (and formalistic criticism) and the defenders, of whom Mr. Shapiro is probably the most militant, of the new democratic faith. In this struggle the New Critics are, of course, importantly involved: they and the poets they admire and explicate are referred to as the Establishment (though the term is ambiguous, having also commercial literary connotations of the *Saturday Review* variety) by the democrats and the demagogues, among which last must be included some of the noisier members of the Beat persuasion. It would perhaps be more accurate to refer to the academicians as neoclassicists, since in the last analysis the New Criticism, with its emphasis on form, was a corrective against the criticism of "feeling" (or, in Eliot's term, of "appreciation") and was to that extent antiromantic. We associate the New Critics with the Apollonian rather than the Dionysian view of art and life, with the Aristotelian rather than the Platonic, or, to employ a political terminology, with the literary Right rather than the Left. (According to this terminology the Beat poets and critics would comprise the extreme Left Wing.)

Thus having defined our battle lines, we find that both forces are about equally armed and equally numerous, though perhaps the ranks of the democrats have increased somewhat since 1963. And the Leftists are clearly the aggressors: thus, out of fourteen articles concerned specifically with this struggle, only three defend the Rightist point of view. But these figures are misleading, for the Apollonians do not always choose to fight. Surely no one who contemplates the rapidly growing list of essays (and books and doctoral dissertations) devoted to Stevens, Moore, and Ransom will make the mistake of underestimating the solid power of the Establishment. And the attacks upon it are sometimes rather puerile. When Gil Sorrentino, praising Rexroth's last two books, says approvingly (*Poetry*, CIV, 179-181) that he has never been a "word-man," we remember Mallarmé's reply to a friend who told him he had a "marvelous idea" for a poem: "Poems are not made with ideas but with words."

Reviewing some of the more belligerent activity on the Left, we cannot overlook a powerful bomb which exploded in the very center of the academic camp—Karl Shapiro's "Is Poetry an American Art?" (*CE*, XXV, 395-405), which, in addition to repeating Mr. Shapiro's thesis at the Poetry Festival (that American poetry is a European transplant that refuses to take local root), makes two further points: (1) prose, not poetry, is the medium best suited to the American genius; (2) the fact that the Beat movement, the only genuine effort to create an American poetry since Whitman, seems already to have exhausted itself is proof that there is no future for poetry in this country. Quoting Whitman to the effect that the American muse tends to soar to the "freer, vast, diviner heaven of prose," he claims that our most influential poets (Pound, Eliot, Williams) "moved as far in the direction of prose as they were able" and that the literary form with the greatest future is the novel: "I am sometimes inclined to think that literature itself gave up the poem when the novel was invented." American poetry, he maintains, received its death blow from Poe, who "had no self" but was instead mere "potting soil": "Poe is the author of the uncontaminated poem, which I refer to as the laboratory poem." Nowadays, he argues, it is the New Critics whose influence is responsible for these "marvelous mechanical poems": "I am not trying to be witty when I say that the average graduate student who works a little at it can write a poem as well as Yeats. My opinion of Yeats has suffered considerably from this discovery. Was Yeats a graduate student?"

Mr. Shapiro dropped two other bombs during the year. In "What Is Creative Writing? or Playing Footsie with the Philistines" (*Descant*, VIII, iii, 2-18), he asserts: "Poetry and all creativity will perhaps become natural in this country and at long last, because of the ultimate rout of Hicult. . . . The poet will shortly accept Masscult as his natural medium and in whatever form it takes, T.V., Broadway, the films, advertising, journalism, comic book, Beat manifesto, or *Playboy*. Everything at the bottom, and everything in the mass, belongs to the artist. It is his medium and his birthright. It seems to me that poetry is about to be born in this country." Remembering that in *CE* he predicted its certain demise and conceded the failure of the Beat movement, we rub our eyes. Both articles appeared the same year; it is impossible to know which was written first, and perhaps it does not greatly matter, for Mr. Shapiro's critical pieces should obviously be read as poems—as such, they can be quite effective, and the right of a poet to alternate his moods in rapid succession is universally acknowledged. (Mr. Shapiro is perhaps his own best example of the peculiar advantages of mixing poetry with prose, "creative" writing with expository.)

Finally, the entire summer issue of *Carleton Miscellany* consisted of a series of six lectures which Mr. Shapiro recently delivered at Carleton College. The series is entitled "A Malebolge of 1400 Books"; he arranged his material (random comments on a wide variety of authors) alphabetically, so that the six lectures "cover" these authors as follows: Aristotle-Dante, Coleridge-Eliot, Frost-Lawrence, Lautréamont-Robert W. Service, Shakespeare-Yeats. (The last lecture is entitled "Henry Miller and Myself.") The tongue-in-cheek tone scarcely permits a serious approach: this is rather sly of Shapiro, for there is no question that he is often in deadly earnest—and never more so than when he is endorsing the great democratic fallacy that the merit of a poem is in direct ratio to its popularity. It is possible, up

to a point, to sympathize with his hatred of pretense in literary matters, but is there not, in the very intensity with which this hatred is
expressed, something that is itself a bit pretentious? (As there is also
in the case of the writer he so greatly admires, Henry Miller.)

Somewhat sounder, if less colorful, criticisms of the Establishment were made by Alfred Owen Aldridge ("Biography in the Interpretation of Poetry," *CE*, XXV, 412-420), Aida Mastrangelo ("Bene-
detto Croce and the New Critics," *SA*, IX, 1963, 455-465), Edwin
Nierenberg ("Poetry and Belief: the Dancer and the Dance," *Person*,
XLV, 385-398), and Stephen Spender ("How to Identify the Poet,"
SatR, XLVII, Aug. 8, 15-17). Mr. Aldridge, deploring the effect of
Crocean aesthetics on recent criticism, maintains that Eliot, Brooks,
and Warren have been the chief offenders in separating criticism
from biography. Their attitude, he argues, "closely conforms to the
twentieth-century tendency in music, painting and other arts to place
highest value on the abstract and impersonal." A weakness of his
article is that he does not sufficiently distinguish among the New
Critics; thus, Kenneth Burke, who is commonly thought of as a New
Critic, would almost certainly agree with Aldridge's statement that
"In a very literal sense the style is the man—and knowing the whole
man helps us to understand any part of his esthetic expression." (Mr.
Burke has in fact stated the same idea in only slightly different
words.) Miss Mastrangelo denies that the New Critics *did* practice
Croce's aesthetics. She will not involve him in their disgrace: the
notion that a poem is a sort of "experimental mouse," she says, is inconsistent with Croce's thesis that it brings into activity "the whole
soul of man." Mr. Nierenberg regrets the tendency of the New Criticism to separate the "values of poetry" from "life values." He asks,
"How believe in idealism or formalism in a poem, and not in life?"—
which might perhaps be answered by saying that the poem has a
life of its own. Throughout his article Mr. Nierenberg tends to con-
fuse issues of general (or private) morality with religious orthodoxy.
It is perfectly proper for him to write, "I cannot think of a major modern writer whose work, through its subject or its treatment of its subject, does not connect with the spiritual life of modern man," but
this is very different from saying (what is implied throughout), "I
cannot think of a major modern writer who does not write out of the
conviction of one religious faith or another." (Camus did not, among
others.) Mr. Spender's attack is better reasoned. He blames the Establishment for creating an image of the poet that makes him indis-

tinguishable from a businessman. Prior to the thirties, he states, poets were thought of with a certain affection as vague, impractical, and frequently zany creatures, but Eliot, the bank clerk with his Prufrockian attire, changed all that: "In his pronouncements this new type of poet emphasized that he did not think writing poetry was different from exercising any other talent. . . . They wrote a kind of poetry for which they themselves provided rules proving that it was the only poetry possible to write today." There is much truth in this, and the essay is one of the best on our list. He concludes, wisely and wittily: "It seems to me that poets should be practicing schizophrenics. They should cultivate the idea that whatever they do publicly, whatever they do as ordinary men rather than as poets, is a pose and that for them the reality has nothing to do with pretending to be real and accepted professional persons."

Oblique defences of the Establishment were made by Howard Nemerov ("The Difficulty of Difficult Poetry," *CM*, V, ii, 35-51) and Ann Stanford ("Les Jeunes Poètes Américains," *Iô*, No. 3, pp. 21-26), and a defense of criticism generally was offered by Murray Krieger ("The Poet and His Work—the Role of Criticism," *CE*, XXV, 405-412). Mr. Nemerov reminds us that difficulty is not a monopoly of modern poetry: Johnson found Milton difficult, and *The Rime of the Ancient Mariner* baffled many nineteenth-century critics. Moreover, what seems difficult to one age may be clear to another. The second half of his article classifies, *à la* Burke, the forms such difficulty usually assumes. Miss Stanford, in a translation for French readers of an article which she has not as yet, unfortunately, published in this country, traces the history of the current schism and correctly observes: "Vocal as they are, and definitely on the scene, the antiacademics are far from representative. . . . The more conservative poets, working with more traditional forms and more concerned with logical and contemplative content, hold more of the important journals." Mr. Krieger takes issue with the view expressed some years ago by Karl Shapiro that criticism is meaningless because the critic is forced to use rational discourse to explain the non-rational. For rational and non-rational Mr. Krieger substitutes the terms propositional and contextual, and while conceding that the critic does indeed have a considerable problem, he does not think it altogether unsolvable: "The critic must try to grasp the contextual within the terms of the propositional while trying to avoid the generic, conceptual world of experience to which this discourse, as propositional, must lead."

He cannot do this *absolutely*, but he can hope for a partial success: "The procedure is muddy and self-defeating, but it *does* proceed." Shapiro, he suggests, has been enticed into the Crocean cul-de-sac which declares the poem to be totally inaccessible to the critic.

A neutral position is taken up by Samuel Hazo ("The Poets of Retreat," *CathW*, CXCVIII, 33-39). Accepting Maritain's definition of poetry as a "divination of the spiritual in the things of sense, which expresses itself in the things of sense," Mr. Hazo views as equally dangerous the retreat into craftsmanship and the retreat into a "self-created isolationism."

Of the few miscellaneous articles which do not directly concern themselves with the schism, the most interesting are probably Leslie Fiedler's "A Kind of Solution: the Situation of Poetry Now" (*KR*, XXVI, 54-79), Denis Donoghue's "The Good Old Complex Fate" (*HudR*, XVII, 267-278), and Laura Riding's "Further on Poetry" (*Chelsea*, No. 14, pp. 38-48). Mr. Fiedler offers lively but frequently eccentric judgments of Auden, Stevens, Ransom, Williams, Shapiro, Roethke, Lowell, Wilbur, and Ginsberg. He asserts that Auden, whose work he says is becoming increasingly Americanized, is the "most eminent poet producing work in America" and suggests that Ginsberg is not really the Attila that, Cavafy-like, many of us (Fiedler included) long to see "at the gates." Mr. Fiedler's essay is marred by its too-personal tone and by its overemphasis on sex: the references to Ginsberg's acknowledged homosexuality are irrelevant and in dubious taste, and he seems to take for granted the "fact" that Whitman was a deviate. How some modern poets solve the problem of being an American is the somewhat tenuous theme connecting a series of reviews by Mr. Donoghue: the poet is lucky who can ignore the problem, he states, for it continues to vex him at his peril. Laura Riding's extraordinary essay (an excerpt from her forthcoming book entitled *The Failure of Poetry*) continues the project of learned subversion which she began in 1933 in *Poet, a Lying Word* (London, Barker). Because of the "sanctified status" of poetry in our society, she claims, poets and public have been duped into thinking it something better than the shoddy reality-substitute which it "really" is. "The poetic process," she writes, "seems too grand a thing to be judged simply as a language-process—though it cannot be judged with rational seriousness except as that. More than a thing of words, poetry is conceived as the harboring-place of a blessed weakness, merely to be possessed of which has a divine quality of achievement. And, indeed, in it certain infirmities of the human spirit are magnificently institutionalized—and made to count sentimentally as strengths."

ii. Individual Poets

a. **Wallace Stevens.** As in 1963, the most active scholarship concerned Wallace Stevens, the list of these items more than doubling that of his closest rival in this respect, William Carlos Williams. There were two important books: Henry W. Wells's *Introduction to Wallace Stevens* (Bloomington, Ind. Univ. Press) and John J. Enck's *Wallace Stevens: Images and Judgments* (Carbondale, Southern Ill. Univ. Press). If Mr. Wells's book is not the definitive work on Stevens —Samuel French Morse's monumental critical biography, we hear, is now nearing completion—it is probably the closest thing to it yet in print. It does what has not yet been done, even in Mr. Enck's excellent book, and that is to treat Stevens' work in all its numerous aspects. There is a certain sacrifice where the explication of individual poems is concerned, and many readers will disagree with specific interpretations (such as that of "Postcard from a Volcano"), but these are inevitable; on the whole, we could scarcely wish, while awaiting the *magnum opus*, for a better companion to Wallace Stevens, which is what this sets out to be and, within its limits, succeeds in being. Mr. Enck's emphasis is somewhat different; he seems primarily interested in the relation of Stevens' poetry to its general cultural context, and he displays both learning and ingenuity in defining the matrix and the milieu of particular poems. His comparisons of Stevens' work to that of certain modern painters are sensitive and intelligent; his genius, however, is not for explication (as witness his interpretation of "The Emperor of Ice Cream"), and the book is inadequately indexed. There is a fine Preface by the general editor of the Crosscurrents Modern Critiques Series, Harry T. Moore, who has been responsible for the publication of some of the best contemporary criticism in America.

Two of the more interesting essays on Stevens are by John Crowe Ransom ("The Planetary Poet," *KR*, XXVI, 233-264) and William Bevis ("Metaphor in Wallace Stevens," *Shen*, XV, ii, 35-48). Ransom, who published some of Stevens' best poems in *KR*, observes that, of the three areas of men's lives (the practical, the aesthetic, and the religious) in which it is possible for them to achieve success, Stevens distinguished himself as a businessman in the first and as a poet in the second. For some years he feuded with the church, but abandoned this struggle late in life—which is not to say, of course, that he capitulated. Of the various "hymns" which he wrote celebrating the finality of death, "Sunday Morning," according to Mr. Ransom, is his greatest, but "Notes toward a Supreme Fiction" remains his masterpiece "as a philosophical poem." Stevens' peculiar distinction, he suggests, lies in his blending of the philosophic and poetic strategies: "Never less than prodigal in the evocation of spectacular images or situations, he develops them in extended passages of almost pure poetry scarcely soiled by argumentative terms; all the same, they embody and objectify the argument." Ransom's brilliant essay is marred by his pointless comparison of Stevens to Whitman, in which the latter (as might be expected from a critic who prefers Donne's poetry to Shakespeare's on the ground that Donne had "more learning") is the loser. Mr. Bevis defines three categories of reality in Stevens' poetry: the *res*, or physical external world; the imagination, which fuses this world with the self; and the *Ding an sich*, a transcendent reality located, like the first, in the external world and independent of ourselves. Stevens uses metaphor, he maintains, only when he is concerned with the second category and rejects it when he desires direct contact with the other two "because such a desire attempts to transcend consciousness, imagination, and all the mental characteristics of the ego."

The entire spring issue of *ELH* (XXX, i) consisted of appreciations of Stevens by Samuel French Morse, Michel Benamou, Roy Harvey Pearce, J. Hillis Miller, and Joseph N. Riddell. In "Wallace Stevens, Bergson, Pater" (pp. 1-34), Morse discusses the influence of Bergson's theory of comedy on the poems written between 1915 and 1921 and declares that Stevens in his own life sought to realize the Pateresque ideal of burning with a "hard, gem-like flame": he was one of the several artists who rescued this ideal from the disrepute into which it fell after World War I. Among other good things, Morse's essay contains a valuable explication of "The Comedian as the Letter C." Benamou's essay, "Wallace Stevens and the Symbolist Imagination" (pp. 35-63), compares Stevens with Baudelaire and Mallarmé. During the late twenties, he claims, Stevens' imagery changed radically: he abandoned the feminine "night constellation" (Moon-Woman, summer and the south, vegetation, music, etc.) for the masculine "day constellation" (men, winter and the north, mud, violence, etc.); the change in his choice of symbols was accompanied by a change in his style, which became increasingly abstract after the manner of Mallarmé. Pearce, in "Wallace Stevens: the Last Lesson of the Master" (pp. 64-85), suggests that Stevens, despite his frequent insistence that "God is a postulate of the ego," came increasingly to believe in an "all-suffusing incorporeality" and cites as evidence "The Region November" and "As You Leave the Room." He makes a convincing case, and his essay is an object lesson in the type of speculative criticism that he practices so skilfully. Miller, in "Wallace Stevens' Poetry of Being" (pp. 86-105), asserts that at the heart of every Stevens poem there is a "precise metaphysical experience": "Or rather, this experience is beyond metaphysics, since the tradition of metaphysics is based on a dualism putting ultimate being in some transcendent realm, above and beyond what men can see. Being, for Stevens, is within things as they are, here and now." And though it can be apprehended, it cannot be described; to describe it would be to fix it, and to fix it would be to lose it. In "The Contours of Stevens' Criticism" (pp. 106-138), Riddell discusses the treatment this poet has received from such critics as Kermode, Bloom, Pearce, Hoffman, Tindall, Baird, and Martz. In the thirties and forties Stevens' reputation, except in academic circles, suffered a decline, and Riddell credits Roy Harvey Pearce with having turned the tide. Now, he maintains, it bids fair to overshadow Eliot's and even, possibly, Yeats's.

b. **William Carlos Williams.** Most important in the list of Williams items is Linda Welshimer Wagner's *Poems of William Carlos Williams* (Middletown, Wesleyan Univ. Press), a serious and scholarly book which honestly faces the problem of explication. Mrs. Wagner maintains that Williams' best work is contained in his last books, *The Desert Music* (1954), *Journey to Love* (1955), and *Pictures from Breughel* (1962), and that this "proves the truth of his statements about life and art, that success 'comes after a lifetime's efforts' and that the artist 'has to live and live long *in* this world.'" Refuting Karl Shapiro's contention that Williams abandoned metaphor in favor of a common idiom, she asserts that on the contrary he used it "with increasing frequency and with increasing skilfulness." With Williams, she explains, metaphor was not merely a matter of content but a principle of organization as well: "Indeed it is probably because Williams did think of figurative speech as a structural device as well as a verbal one that critics could ignore it in his poetry: integral to the poem as a whole, it is relatively inconspicuous." With abundant examples, she shows the structural importance of metaphors used as late as 1962. Of *Paterson* she says that "Not only is the entire poem a single metaphor, but it also depends for much of its structure on symbolic and transitional metaphors." If Mrs. Wagner's own style is something less than felicitous, her occasional analyses of Williams' prosody—a complicated business—are extremely accomplished, and the book contains a good index and bibliography. Unfortunately it is dominated by an air of hero worship, and her determination to prove Williams a literary saint sometimes causes her to slight other poets, as when she says that Stevens' reputation "appears to have already reached its zenith," a statement for which there is little if any evidence.

In "William Carlos Williams: An Italian View" (*PrS*, XXXVIII, 307-316), Vittorio Sereno, who has translated this poet into Italian, states that his work is not "a poetry of ideas, but poetry that begets ideas out of things." He renders objects not only as they are, but, by developing their potential, reveals all that can be "dug" from them. "Every Williams poem," he declares, "is a self-sufficient fact . . . an *autonomous living organism*." David Ignatow, "Williams' Influence: Some Social Aspects" (*Chelsea*, No. 14, pp. 154-161), contends that Williams is the most powerful influence in American poetry today. Among those he names who have felt this influence most strongly are Zukofsky, Olson, Levertov, and Ginsberg. Beyond making these fairly obvious points, Mr. Ignatow's article is not particularly illuminating, and his suggestion that Ginsberg may be to our day what Eliot was to his will cause readers on both sides of the Atlantic to raise their brows.

c. Marianne Moore. It is rather astonishing that Bernard F. Engel's *Marianne Moore* (TUSAS) should be the first book-length critical study of a poet whose prestige has been almost universally acknowledged for at least a quarter of a century. Mr. Engel shrewdly accounts for the prevalence of paradox in her work by saying that, as a moralist, she "wishes to advocate a set of values, yet as an artist and as a person she adheres to principles that enjoin caution in assertion." The values she endorses are those that lead to a sense of personal honor and civic decency, and they "include courage, independence, responsibility, genuineness, and a certain ardor in the conduct of one's life." But she does not make the mistake of endorsing these overtly or abstractly; mindful, Engel says, of Blake's dictum, "To Generalize is to be an Idiot, To particularize is the Alone Distinction of Merit," Miss Moore prefers the method of implication through selection of significant detail: the method, that is, of Objectivism. "Concern with both ethics and 'things,'" he observes, "has made Miss Moore frequently a poet of the analogy: she presents the 'thing' in order to suggest or assert a point of ethics." But not content with mere suggestion or assertion, the poems, he claims, "usually also are suffused throughout with attitudes of approval or distaste reinforcing that point." (Fortunately this is not true of Miss Moore's best work, and his apology for "In Distrust of Merits" is unconvincing.)

An article (in Italian) which appeared in SA ("Marianne Moore," by Lina Unali, IX, 1963, 377-424) explains Miss Moore's Objectivism not as ethical strategy but as a "need" to correct her lyric impulse and to control the emotion of which, she implies, this poet has always been somewhat wary: "Where emotion is concerned, there is a certain reserve." Emphasis on objects, rather than on the emotions produced by the objects, sometimes leads to a "zig-zag" effect which can make for difficulties in reading and comprehension; on the other hand, Miss Unali maintains, if the poems were "too clear" they would lose much of their admirable terseness and something, perhaps, of their mysterious power. That Miss Moore suppresses her emotions is also the opinion of A. K. Weatherhead, who, in "Two Kinds of Vision in Marianne Moore" (ELH, XXXI, 482-496), states: "With some of her poems one feels that Miss Moore is more content to conceal the message of the poem than to run the risk of being carried away by her feeling, and overstating it."

d. **John Crowe Ransom.**   Karl F. Knight's *The Poetry of John Crowe Ransom* (The Hague, Mouton & Co.) is also the first book-length study of another very considerable modern. Mr. Knight analyzes three aspects of Ransom's work: diction, metaphor, and symbol. This poet's frequently criticized use of pedantic and archaic language accomplishes, he argues, three purposes: elevation of tone, functional incongruity, and irony. Ransom's major themes are dissociation of sensibility and mutability, particularly the former, which he believes is the consequence of the specialization of modern life: "Ransom believes that man's originally coherent relationship to nature has been perverted by the abstractionism which is the concomitant of the scientific method. And thus images and figures and events which are perverted, distorted, or dulled come to symbolize the curse of modernism: the dissociation of sensibility or the fragmentation of personality." He is saved from naturalism by his faith in a world of classical order and balance, "a world which at times man has realized," and by his belief in the essential nobility of man.

An original, if controversial, view of Ransom's characteristic attitudes (wit, urbanity, irony) is offered by Thornton H. Parsons in "The Civilized Poetry of John Crowe Ransom" (*Per*, XIII, 244-262). Civilized individuals, he argues, are torn between the positive desire for emotional poise and the negative fear of naïveté. And civilized poets are "likely to cultivate the literary traits of urbanity, wit, irony, tact, tone—to be, in short, highly self-conscious about emotion and at the same time intensely alert to conceal their seriousness." Ransom's poems on the subject of death, he says, expose the central struggle: "proper gentility and chivalric politeness are at war with his desire to be cruelly witty on subjects that have been treated too reverently or too sentimentally, subjects that have been off bounds for lightness and humor." The trouble with this theory is that it does not sufficiently respect the influence on Ransom of the metaphysical poets he so greatly admires and whose reputations he has done so much to resuscitate. It is hard to think of Donne as being "civilized" in this sense: would Donne have been afraid of appearing naïve?

***e*. Tate and Shapiro.**   Allen Tate is the subject of the most recent of Minnesota Pamphlets on American Writers (George Hemphill, *Allen Tate*, UMPAW, No. 39, Minneapolis, Univ. of Minn. Press). It is overshadowed by the publication in 1963 of R. K. Meiners' more ambitious study of Tate, *The Last Alternatives*, mentioned in last year's volume, but it is admirably compact and informative and evaluates Tate not merely as poet, but also as critic and as novelist. Conceding that there is very little "sweetness" in Tate's early work, Hemphill suggests, and rightly, that it was in "Sonnets at Christmas" that this poet came into his own. "Seasons of the Soul," however, he regards as his finest achievement to date, and he quarrels with Meiners' interpretation of this poem. (Meiners' book, incidentally, is reviewed— on the whole favorably—by Kermode in *SR*, LXXII, 124-131.) Carol Johnson, in "The Heroism of the Rational: the Poetry of Allen Tate" (*Ren*, XVII, 89-96), claims that Tate's poems, in which the formal element looms so large, are dominated by the "jurisdiction of reason"; the point would scarcely seem to require proving. Miss Johnson praises "The Mediterranan" as a "nearly perfect poem" and asserts that no living poet in English "has come more closely or more expertly to grips with the problems engendered by his analytic-creative purpose and the obstinate immateriality of the medium than Allen Tate."

Karl Shapiro's new book of poems, *The Bourgeois Poet* (New York, Random House), is reviewed by Louis D. Rubin, Jr., in "The Search for Lost Innocence: Karl Shapiro's *The Bourgeois Poet*" (*HC*, I, v, 1-16). Rubin argues that Shapiro's abandonment of traditional form was the consequence of his disillusioning experience as a member of the Establishment (it was the least productive period, poetically, of his career) and that it was entirely predictable. But though he appears sympathetic to some of Shapiro's recent theories about life and poetry, and the relations between them, he turns in a verdict on *The Bourgeois Poet* that is largely negative. "The real difficulty," he says, "is that Shapiro isn't a mystic, however much he tries to be one by dabbling in Zen Buddhism, Wilhelm Reich, Jung, Ouspensky, and 'cosmic consciousness.' He is essentially a rationalist." As for his technique, "no-form is not the answer," and it remains for him, if he rejects traditional forms, to discover one which will display his undeniable talent to best advantage. One thing, Rubin says, is certain: he is *not* going to stop writing poems, as he has threatened. This is the most charitable view of Shapiro that it is perhaps possible to take at this point, and Rubin's review is as sensible as it is kind, though in his discussion of Shapiro's latter-day influences he does not do sufficient justice to Henry Miller. *The Bourgeois Poet* is also the subject of a literary round-table (*Oberlin Quarterly*, I, ii, 5-32) which is as lively as it is amusing, with Shapiro stubbornly insisting on the validity of the prose-poem form.

A vigorous defense of Shapiro by Sam Bradley appeared this year: "Shapiro Strikes Back at the Establishment" (*UR*, XXIX, 275-279). Bradley contends that Shapiro's fight for the "natural man" has been "misunderstood" in academic quarters, but that his position is essentially humanistic. The article is in large part a praise of the cult of personality: "Modern civilization allows men to be noncreative; efficient in their positions in a robot-rigid culture, men tend to grow timid, stupefied by fat and barrier day-dreams, eager for authority outside themselves." When he quotes Shapiro's statement, I would sacrifice every great book ever written, including the Bible and Plato, for the psychological well-being and the cultural skepticism of one child," we are reminded at once of Faulkner's saying (which Shapiro may possibly have had in mind) that the *Ode on a Grecian Urn* is worth "any number of old ladies."

f. **Eberhart and Lowell.** The achievement of Richard Eberhart is the subject of another *HC* monograph ("Hunting a Master Image: The Poetry of Richard Eberhart," I, iv, 1-12), this one by Daniel Hoffman, and the occasion is the publication of Eberhart's new book, *The Quarry.* "What comes after a poet's Collected Poems?" Hoffman asks rhetorically, and the answer, in this case, is apparently "Plenty." Reviewing this poet's career, Hoffman notes that he has always been a "stubborn individualist" who belonged to "no popular movement"; for this, of course, he paid a price, but the increasing excellence of his work is proof that the payment was worthwhile. Notwithstanding Eberhart's own statements ("An Interview with Richard Eberhart," by Denis Donoghue, *Shen,* XV, iv, 8-29) that he regards a poem as a "gift from the gods" and that he thinks of himself primarily as an intuitive poet, Hoffman claims that the rational element looms very large in his work, which at its best unites "the contrary claims of intuition and intellect, of heart and head." A second article dealing with this poet, "Reflections on Richard Eberhart," by Ralph J. Mills, Jr., appeared in *ChiR* (XV, 1962, iv, 81-99). Mills takes Eberhart at his own evaluation of himself as a daemonic poet and accounts in this way for the unevenness of his production: unlike Thomas, with whom he is sometimes compared, he does not revise his work a great deal; he does not recollect his emotions in tranquillity. The uniqueness of his best poems is that, whatever the grammatical tense, the experience is somehow made to occur in a "timeless *now.*"

Robert Lowell's entire literary career is reviewed by Neville Braybrooke in "The Poetry of Robert Lowell" (*CathW,* CXCVIII, 230-237). Braybrooke notes that the religious imagery upon which this poet relied so heavily in the forties was abandoned, for the most part, in the fifties. The essay is valuable for its use of biographical information to illuminate some of Lowell's poems, such as "The Mill of the Kavanaghs," in which, according to Braybrooke, he identified with both Anne and Harry Kavanagh. In a joint review of *Imitations* and Hugh Staples' *Robert Lowell: the First Twenty Years* (discussed in last year's volume), Richard Fein ("The Trying-Out of Robert Lowell," *SR,* LXXII, 131-139) declares Lowell's book a success; the

poet has advanced, he says, "from a religiously charged and traditionally formed poetry to an unrelenting secular search for the self
in terms of a language that clamps into place like a razor blade."
Staples' book, he finds, does not sufficiently stress this change. An
interesting article by A. K. Weatherhead, "Imagination and Fancy:
Robert Lowell and Marianne Moore" (*TSLL*, VI, 188-199), compares
these two poets in terms of the famous distinction proposed by Coleridge, who regarded the imagination as superior. According to
Weatherhead, *Lord Weary's Castle*, more than any other modern
book, illustrates the working of the imagination as Coleridge conceived it. Moore, on the other hand, operates primarily in the world
of fancy: the images exist "in and for themselves." Oddly enough, in
his article, "Two Kinds of Vision in Marianne Moore," referred to previously, Weatherhead himself distinguishes between two kinds of
images in Miss Moore's work, and his conclusions in that essay would
tend to discredit the comparison with Lowell.

g. Theodore Roethke *et al.*   Theodore Roethke's increasing prestige
may be measured by the appearance of four items published this
year—and one, in Italian, in 1963: "Theodore Roethke," by Mariolina
Meliadò (*SA*, IX, 1963, 425-454). Noting the influence of Blake on
this poet's work, Miss Meliadò claims that Roethke's interest in "cosmic consciousness" and his inexhaustible capacity for "sensual enjoy-
ment" place him in the tradition not only of Blake but also of the
"life poetry" of Whitman, Lawrence, and Thomas. William Meredith,
in an important article ("A Steady Storm of Correspondences:
Theodore Roethke's Long Journey Out of the Self," *Shen*, XVI, i, 41-
54), states that while Roethke's early poems order experience, his
later ones "attend on experience with the conviction that there is
order in it." Admitting that the influence of Yeats was perhaps too
strong, he nevertheless proclaims Roethke's work to be as "finished
and distinct" as any of his generation, matched only by Lowell's and
Berryman's. "Only a very large and assured artist," he says, "can retain his sense of self while deferring to created order." Peter Levi,
S.J., finds ("Theodore Roethke," *Agenda*, III, iv, 11-14) that Roethke's
early work was difficult and mannered and prefers the "marvelous
final poems." Levi praises his individuality and claims that no other
modern has excelled him technically. Ian Hamilton ("Theodore
Roethke," *Agenda*, III, iv, 5-10) prefers the early work; he regards
Praise to the End! as a "very bad book." Praising the greenhouse

imagery of the early poems, he claims that when Roethke attempts to make his plants and animals symbolize his "inner turmoils" he "runs into trouble." An interesting personal memoir of Roethke by Robert B. Heilman, who knew him intimately and who found him "witty, imaginative, sometimes troublesome," appears in *Shen* ("Theodore Roethke, Personal Notes," XVI, i, 55-64).

Miscellaneous items include two pieces on John Berryman, a comment on Louis Zukofsky by William Carlos Williams, and an article on Yvor Winters with a peppery rejoinder from the latter. Carol Johnson, in "John Berryman and Mistress Bradstreet: A Relation of Reason" (*EIC*, XIV, 389-396), maintains that "Homage to Mistress Bradstreet" is a finer poem than *The Bridge*, which she claims (citing Winters) is relatively incoherent. Berryman's poem, she says, is "among the few distinguished efforts of substantial length in its period." Arthur and Catherine Evans, in "Pieter Breughel and John Berryman, Two Winter Landscapes" (*TSLL*, V, 1963, 310-318), state that Berryman, in "Winter Landscape," attempted to produce in words a response similar to that which the painter created in *Hunter in the Snow*, which inspired the poem. It is an extremely interesting essay. "An evident artistic rapport," they declare, "can be argued between a visual sequence in painting and a narrative tempo in poetry." The similarity in effect of these two masterpieces, they suggest, implies a "secret friendship" which exists among the arts. Praising the work of his disciple Louis Zukofsky, William Carlos Williams, in a brief preface which must have been among the last things he wrote (*Agenda*, III, vi, 1-4), states that this poet's concern has always been with "the spiritual unity of the world of ideas"; the poems, he says, "are grammatical units intent on making a meaning *unrelated* to a mere pictorial image." Reviewing Yvor Winters' *Collected Poems*, a former student of his, Alan Stephens, had the temerity to suggest (*TCL*, IX, 1963, 127-139) that Winters' best work is the product of his middle period, to which Winters replied testily, "Stephens is in no position to judge many of my poems because he simply doesn't know what they are about" ("By Way of Clarification," *TCL*, X, 130-135). On this note of "clarification" we close our survey.

San Fernando Valley State College

16. Drama

Malcolm Goldstein

i. Texts

By the end of 1964 the Indiana University Press had published five double volumes of reissues of the "America's Lost Plays" series, including (in addition to works reported last year) plays by John Howard Payne, James A. Herne, Charles Hoyt, Bronson Howard, and a group of melodramas, among which are such famous titles as *From Rags to Riches* by Charles A. Taylor, and *No Mother to Guide Her* by Lillian Mortimer. Questions of literary quality are of course irrelevant to a consideration of the series, which sets before us a substantial part of the record of our early theater.

The value of the series to scholars is matched by the *Autobiography* of Joseph Jefferson, the celebrated nineteenth-century actor. A new edition prepared by Alan S. Downer (Cambridge, Mass., Harvard Univ. Press, Belknap) makes this lively book available in an elegant format. In his introduction Downer gives a resumé of Jefferson's seventy-one years on the stage and discusses the sources and development of his famous vehicle, *Rip Van Winkle*. Unintrusive notes identify for present-day readers the persons and places whose names Jefferson casually dropped into his text.

It is more difficult to estimate the value of the only other notable dramatic texts of the year: Eugene O'Neill's *Ten "Lost" Plays* (New York, Random House) and *More Stately Mansions*, ed. Donald Gallup (New Haven, Yale Univ. Press). With the publication of these volumes all of O'Neill's dramatic writing to survive destruction in manuscript is now available, unless, as seems unlikely, unrecorded manuscripts are discovered. The eighteenth-century physician John Arbuthnot once remarked of the outrageous biographies of recently deceased worthies published by Edmund Curll that they added a new terror to death; just such a fear is elicited by the present volumes of very feeble plays. None will enhance the playwright's reputation, and it is virtually certain that he would not have approved plans to issue them. Nevertheless, there is some justification for letting them appear. All the "lost" plays have long been available: *Thirst, The Web, Warnings, Fog,* and *Recklessness* were first printed in an authorized volume of 1914; *Abortion, The Movie Man, The Sniper, A Wife for a Life,* and *Servitude,* in an unauthorized volume of 1950. *More Stately Mansions,* intended to be the fourth play of the cycle "A Tale of Possessors Self-Possessed," escaped the famous burning of manuscripts at Tao House in 1943. With the permission of Mrs. Carlotta Monterey O'Neill, a version prepared by Karl Ragnar Gierow was produced in 1962 at the Swedish Royal Dramatic Theatre; scholars, therefore, despite whatever misgivings they may have about the play, are obliged to take account of it. The printed text is a product of the combined effort of Gierow, who edited O'Neill's draft to make a producible drama, and Donald Gallup, who collated Gierow's Swedish translation with the manuscript to arrive at an English version which changes no more than a dozen of O'Neill's own words. Gallup also provides a "Prefatory Note" on the provenance of the manuscript and the method of arriving at the text.

ii. Criticism and Scholarship

a. Nineteenth century.   Francis Hodge's *Yankee Theatre: The Image of America on the Stage, 1825-1850* (Austin, Univ. of Tex. Press) is a welcome contribution to the history of American drama and a pleasure to read. A writer whose enthusiasm for his subject never flags, Hodge describes in his first chapters the busy life of the early nineteenth-century theater as it was viewed by English visitors and native Americans. He then treats the development of the stage Yankee, a shrewd, plain-dealing member of the lower classes who prides himself on his independence and is not to be outwitted: indeed, as Hodge labels him, a symbol of America. The pages devoted to the delineation of this character make up a brief history of American comedy in its formative years and freshly illuminate the nation's popular culture. In the central sections of the book Hodge takes up the careers of four admired impersonators of the Yankee: James H. Hackett, George H. Hill, Dan Marble, and Joshua Silsbee, with the major share of attention falling, appropriately, to Hackett. Hodge's studies have enabled him to visualize clearly the stage presences of these performers and—a difficult feat—to re-create them on paper. The book is not, however, a study of actors and acting only. It is a detailed report on a body of drama whose authors explored the

216   Drama

American character both lovingly and belligerently and whose influence is detectable in plays written at least as late as the first two
decades of the present century.

A quite different variety of drama is the subject of Walter J.
Meserve's "American Drama and the Rise of Realism" (*JA*, IX, 152-
159). Observing that the development of realistic drama paralleled
the development of realistic fiction in the late nineteenth century,
Meserve discusses the local-color plays of the time, the efforts of
eminent novelists to write for the stage (Howells, Twain, Harte,
Crane, James), and the beginnings of the influence of Ibsen. The
chief value of the essay lies in Meserve's comments on Herne, whom
he sees as the chief American imitator of Ibsen and whose *Margaret
Fleming* (1890) he believes represents the climax in American dramatic realism, as the term applies to the period under discussion.

James, perennially a playwright *manqué*, receives additional attention in Michael J. Mendelsohn's "'Drop a Tear . . .': Henry James
Dramatizes *Daisy Miller*" (*MD*, VII, 60-64). The play which James
made out of his novella was published in his lifetime but not produced. Mendelsohn indicates that it is melodramatic, padded with
unnecessary and poorly conceived characters, and cheapened by a
happy ending. Despite his expressions of snobbish disdain for theatrical producers, James quite clearly was willing to concede all for
a popular success.

b. **Twentieth century.** Reasonably enough, O'Neill remains the
most discussed American playwright of the century. In addition to
the run of biographical, evaluative, and source-hunting books and essays, papers on the quality of his thought have begun to appear. The
cycle of critical opinion is still in the upswing; in the year's work no
essay of any merit whatever offers an attack.

The only book-length study of the year is Frederick I. Carpenter's
Eugene O'Neill (TUSAS). Although it cannot have been the most
agreeable of assignments to supply the O'Neill volume for the Twayne
United States Authors Series, Carpenter carries it out effectively. He
follows a substantial biographical chapter with a general essay on the
pattern of the tragedies, whose recurrent theme he identifies as the
"dream of an impossible beauty beyond the horizon." Since it would
be difficult to examine all the works in O'Neill's canon in the limited
space allowed, he considers only twenty of the plays individually.
Obviously, however, this is a fair number. Readers familiar with the

work of the Gelbs, Doris V. Falk, and Doris Alexander will not need this book, but it should prove useful to students as an introduction.

O'Neill: A Collection of Critical Essays, ed. John Gassner (Englewood Cliffs, N. J., Prentice-Hall), brings together fifteen papers by various hands, of which thirteen are reprints. Gassner's introduction places O'Neill in his time and profession and, in brief, reviews the kinds of responses he has drawn from critics. The contributors of the collection's two new essays are John Henry Raleigh and Travis Bogard. In *"Anna Christie: Her Fall and Rise,"* Bogard discusses the development of the play from *Chris Christophersen* to *The Ole Davil* to demonstrate O'Neill's regard for the natural force of the sea as a source of power, happiness, and peace. Raleigh's "Eugene O'Neill and the Escape from the Chateau d'If" is a study of the impact of *The Count of Monte Cristo*, James O'Neill's immensely popular melodrama, on the playwright's work.

As the O'Neill enthusiasts continue their search for sources and influences, the results of their labor are not always of the first importance. Horst Frenz, in "Eugene O'Neill's *Desire Under the Elms* and Henrik Ibsen's *Rosmersholm"* (*JA*, IX, 160-165), notes that our knowledge of the influence of Strindberg on O'Neill has made it difficult to observe the influence of Ibsen, which nevertheless is present in the plays. Yet the comparison of *Desire* and *Rosmersholm* which he offers as evidence of the influence depends too much on general matters of plot to be convincing. In "A Literary Source for O'Neill's *In the Zone"* (*AL*, XXXV, 530-534), William Goldhurst suggests that Arthur Conan Doyle's "The Little Square Box" provides some of the material for O'Neill's one-act. Grant H. Redford, in "Dramatic Art vs. Autobiography: A Look at *Long Day's Journey into Night"* (*CE*, XXV, 527-535), deplores—perhaps gratuitously—the tendency of critics to examine the tragedy as autobiography only, inasmuch as it is a carefully shaped work of dramatic art.

Two essays by William R. Brashear demonstrate O'Neill's familiarity with Schopenhauer and Nietzsche. In "O'Neill's Schopenhauer Interlude" (*Criticism*, VI, 256-265), he concludes that the philosopher's system of thought provides the "intellectual framework" of *Strange Interlude*. As he interprets the play, Nina's "God the Father" is Schopenhauer's "will to live," the force which prescribes action for man which man thinks he is undertaking on his own. At the conclusion of the play it is apparent that the characters are "worn out from willing" in their efforts to live. Brashear finds a kind of humorous detachment in the play as the characters encounter problems in their attempts to exercise wills of their own. His "The Wisdom of Silenus in O'Neill's *Iceman*" (*AL*, XXXVI, 180-188) reminds the reader that in Nietzsche's *The Birth of Tragedy* the wisdom of Silenus is that it would be best not to be born, second best to die soon. This notion is present in the lines from Heine which Larry Slade quotes to Parritt.

Essays on O'Neill's intellectual capacity are offered by James P. Pettegrove and Edwin A. Engel. Pettegrove, in "Eugene O'Neill as Thinker" (*MuK*, X, 617-624), attempts to refute the repeated charge that O'Neill's intelligence was not of a high order. Examining the plays to that end, he finds evidence of the dramatist's humanism and of his striving to make a penetrating investigation of religion. Engel's "Ideas in the Plays of Eugene O'Neill" (*Ideas in the Drama: Selected Papers from the English Institute*, ed. John Gassner, New York, Columbia Univ. Press) provides what may be described as a brief introduction to O'Neill for mature readers. His thesis is that the ideas and emotions which O'Neill developed in adolescence were of abiding importance to him throughout his career. His preference was for the "big ideas" of man, life, death, love, and hate, and his treatment of them accords with his learning and experience in youth. His attitudes toward religion were, according to Engel, initially linked to his attitudes toward his father, but after *Dynamo* the role of the mother becomes increasingly complex, and associated with her are not only love and peace, but guilt and sin. Engel points out that with *The Iceman* love becomes something to be shunned, a dangerous pipe dream. Yet, as he demonstrates, with *Long Day's Journey* O'Neill effected a reversal of attitude, no longer demanding love, and absolving himself and his family for their inability to supply it. Among the year's studies in O'Neill this essay is unquestionably the most rewarding.

One of the playwright's earliest theatrical associates receives homage in Arthur E. Waterman's "Susan Glaspell and the Provincetown" (*MD*, VII, 174-184). The essay is an appraisal of Glaspell's plays to 1922, when she left the Provincetown. Waterman finds them courageous as expressions of unpopular social views. He relates the plays to the spirit of the company, which favored experimentation but never lost sight of traditional American realism.

The New Playwrights' Theatre, another of the Greenwich Village organizations of the past, is the subject of George A. Knox and Herbert M. Stahl's *Dos Passos and the "Revolting Playwrights"* (Upsala, Lundequistska Bokhandeln). Founded in 1927 by Michael Gold, Em Jo Basshe, John Howard Lawson, Francis Edwards Faragoh, and John Dos Passos, with the assistance of Otto H. Kahn, the company dedicated itself to the production of radical antinaturalistic plays. Too passionate to spot the weaknesses in their writing and too contentious to agree on policy, the dramatist-founders were unable to attract either the intelligentsia or the working class. Knox and Stahl have chosen to relate the history of the New Playwrights with particular emphasis on Dos Passos, the leading literary figure among them. Their approach is somewhat misleading since Dos Passos was less important to the company's activities than Gold or Basshe, whose quirky but apparently engaging personalities initially sparked Kahn's interest. Nor are they as forthright as they might be on the efforts of some members to draw the company into the orbit of the Communist party. Another doubt of the present reviewer, who has studied the primary sources of the book, concerns the extent to which the company was associated with the productions of Faragoh's *Pinwheel* and Gold's *Fiesta*. But, these matters aside, the authors offer an entertaining account of the careers of all five playwrights within a comprehensive view of the theater of the 1920's.

Among other writers to come to the fore in the post-World War I years, Robert E. Sherwood is currently among the most highly regarded. His debt to Bernard Shaw is investigated by Anne N. Lausch in two articles: "The Road to Rome by Way of Alexandria and Tavazzano" and "Robert Sherwood's 'Heartbreak Houses'" (*ShawR*, VI, 1963, 2-12, 42-50). The first, on reflections of *Caesar and Cleopatra* in *The Road to Rome*, presents some interesting parallels; the second, however, on *Heartbreak House* and *The Petrified Forest*, is unconvincing. R. Baird Shuman's *Robert E. Sherwood* (TUSAS) stays within the now familiar pattern of the Twayne series in offering a biographical chapter and detailed summaries of the playwright's work. As with many volumes in this astonishingly uneven series, the documentation of the biographical material is inadequate. Moreover, the chapters on Sherwood's writing include too few interpretative comments to balance their weight of plot incidents. One may also note some curiosities of judgment—for example, Shuman's observation that *The Petrified Forest*, actually one of the most provocative plays of the Depression, depends for its effect upon "hokum" and is "thoughtful escape drama" (p. 29). Probably what is needed is more careful editorial assistance.

Two quite different but equally useful essays of the year span the decades of the twentieth century. John T. Flanagan, in "The Folk Hero in Modern American Drama" (*MD*, VI, 402-416), comments perceptively on three types of dramatic folk hero: the genuinely mythical hero (John Henry, Paul Bunyan), the actual figure rendered superhuman by the playwright (Joe Hill, Jesse Jones), and the celebrity (Lincoln, among many others). Readers of Francis Hodge's *Yankee Theatre* will find this an instructive afterpiece. In "Myth and the American Dream: O'Neill to Albee" (*MD*, VII, 190-198), Jordan Y. Miller offers observations on the success myth—the American notion that success *must* come to energetic youth—as dramatized by four playwrights, including Williams and Miller as well as those mentioned in the title.

It is an obvious fact that the success myth was the principal theme of American dramatists of the 1930's. The Depression decade provides material for Gerald Rabkin in *Drama and Commitment: Politics in the American Theatre of the Thirties* (Bloomington, Ind. Univ. Press). Rabkin's mature study, the best-written book in drama for 1964, will inevitably be compared to Morgan Y. Himelstein's *Drama Was a Weapon*, to the disfavor of the latter. After two preliminary chapters, the first a somewhat overlong definition of the term "commitment" and the second a general account of the influence of politics on drama through the decade, the author continues with three chapters on the major purveyors of social drama—Theatre Union, the Group Theatre, and the Federal Theatre—and chapters on the work of John Howard Lawson, Clifford Odets, S. N. Behrman, Elmer Rice, and Maxwell Anderson. Rabkin is less interested in the specific social and political concerns of the period than in the general upheaval as reflected in drama and very much less interested in the history of the three companies singled out than in the tone and social aims of each, which he describes. His primary interest is literature, as he demonstrates well in his studies in the five playwrights, each a balanced combination of summary and commentary. That he concludes with Anderson is unfortunate, since the result is something of an anticlimax, but this is surely a minor quibble.

Two of the playwrights given special attention by Rabkin are the subjects of short articles. In "*Winterset*: A Modern Revenge Tragedy" (*MD*, VII, 185-189), Francis E. Abernethy examines Anderson's play with the purpose of relating it to Renaissance blood tragedy, with particular reference to *Hamlet*. Michael J. Mendelsohn's "Clifford Odets: The Artist's Commitment" (*Literature and Society: Nineteen Essays by Germaine Brée and Others*, ed. Beatrice Slote, Lincoln, Univ. of Nebr. Press) is a discussion of the playwright as an idealist who held to the belief throughout his career that society is capable of improvement—in short, an optimist, despite (as Mendelsohn points out) his profound disapproval of the term.

Bernard Grebanier's *Thornton Wilder* (UMPAW, No. 34, Minneapolis, Univ. of Minn. Press) is a brief, appreciative commentary on the sum of Wilder's fiction and drama. Pointing out that Wilder's preference in literature is for the classics, the author believes that he is nevertheless a Romantic at heart. Grebanier expresses his opinions mildly and evenly throughout, but if the amount of space given to individual works has any meaning, he would seem to admire Wilder's novels more than his plays and among the plays to prefer *The Skin of Our Teeth* to *Our Town*, which receives a mere two pages. A virtue of the pamphlet is that it provides the first mature criticism of the recent *Plays for Bleecker Street*, a group of three one-acts.

Of the dramatists who have gained prominence since World War II, Tennessee Williams and Arthur Miller continue to hold the leading position. The recent successes of Edward Albee, however, have resulted in the establishment of a third favorite of nearly equal allure; it is a safe enough wager that at the present moment a good half-dozen essays on the themes of sterility and materialism in *Tiny Alice* are in preparation.

Williams' work is now sufficiently voluminous to justify the writing of books about it. Unfortunately, the year's sole book-length critical study of the playwright, Francis Donahue's *The Dramatic World of Tennessee Williams* (New York, Ungar), is not a success. Although it contains some biographical material and, at the close, an evaluative chapter, its bulk is made up of plot summaries. Another sort of book is the work of Edwina D. Williams, the playwright's mother, "as told to Lucy Freeman": *Remember Me to Tom* (New York, Putnam's). The title would suggest that Mrs. Williams is estranged from her son, but such is not true. In general, her book is a chatty piece of rosy reminiscence. If one makes the necessary allowance for a mother's exaggeration, the biographical material which she offers may have value for the serious student. An interesting article is Roger B. Stein's "*The Glass Menagerie* Revisited: Catastrophe Without Violence" (*WHR*, XVIII, 141-153). The author finds the themes of illusion and frustration, as they are developed in the life of the Wingfields, to have particular importance to the time of the play—the late 1930's—when the suffering of the nation as a whole was akin to that of the family. Stein sees much Christian symbolism in the play, but believes that the characters cannot expect help from God, for in Williams' universe man is abandoned by his creator.

The year's studies of the plays of Miller are more stimulating as well as more plentiful. Arvin B. Wells, in "The Living and the Dead in *All My Sons*" (*MD*, VII, 46-51), finds the play to be more complex than have most other critics. In his opinion it is not merely a "social thesis play," but a plea for mercy in our judgment of character and behavior, since Joe Keller, ignoble though he may be, is in part a victim of the society whose questionable values he has adopted. In "The Right Dream in Miller's *Death of a Salesman*" (*CE*, XXV, 547-549), Stephen A. Lawrence takes a new position on an old problem: the stature of Willy Loman. As he views the play, the fact that Willy believes in love means that he is not a petty man, but one whom society has undervalued. Henry Popkin, in "Arthur Miller's *The Crucible*" (*CE*, XXVI, 139-146), gives a detailed analysis of the play and its protagonist. He observes that the congressional hearings of the McCarthy period do not provide exact parallels to the situation in Salem, because of the complexity of the problems which gave rise to them. John Proctor, according to Popkin, is an Aristotelian hero spotted by his adultery, which is a greater trouble to him in the defense of his name than the charge of witchcraft. Interestingly, he notes a curious similarity in the lives of Proctor, Eddie Carbone in *A View from the Bridge*, and Quentin in *After the Fall*: all three are driven to child-women by cold wives. Arthur Ganz, in "Arthur Miller: After the Silence" (*DramS*, III, 520-530), discusses *After the Fall*, Miller's most controversial play to date. Ganz finds it imperfect, but not easy to dismiss. His objections center in the characterization of Quentin, whose sense of guilt does not quite ring true. Yet because Miller is now beginning to recognize "the complexities of guilt," Ganz finds in the play a promise of better work to come. (On the other hand, one may add that in *Incident in Vichy*, produced after the publication of this essay, Miller continues to explore the springs of guilt without adding to his stature as a dramatist.) In "Arthur Miller and the Common Man's Language" (*MD*, VII, 52-59), Leonard Moss analyzes the playwright's rhetoric to demonstrate how Miller at his best expresses "inward urgency" through colloquial speech. In *Arthur Miller* (UMPAW, No. 40, Minneapolis, Univ. of Minn. Press), a well-written, informative pamphlet, Robert Hogan treats the entire body of Miller's work through *After the Fall*. Especially noteworthy are the twelve pages on the dramatist's early writing up to *All My Sons*, most of which is relatively unfamiliar; equally useful are the sections on the adaptation of Ibsen's *An Enemy of the People* and *The Misfits*.

Critics of Edward Albee have made the most of what is still a small body of work. A touch of querulousness is occasionally evident in their comments, but it is evident that he is a writer who provokes thought. Kenneth Hamilton, in "Mr. Albee's Dream" (*QQ*, LXX, 1963, 393-399), charges the playwright with childishness in *The American Dream*. Woman, as exemplified by Mommy in the play, would appear to be a boy's notion of a threat to masculine solidarity. Commenting on "Morality, Absurdity, and Albee" (*SWR*, XLIX, 249-256), Wendell V. Harris finds *Who's Afraid of Virginia Woolf?* impressive because it is hopeful, whereas *The American Dream* and *The Sandbox* satirize the irremediable, and *The Death of Bessie Smith* and *The Zoo Story* are attacks on humanity. Daniel McDonald, in "Truth and Illusion in *Who's Afraid of Virginia Wolfe?*" (*Ren*, XVII, 63-69), deplores the tendency of critics to dwell on the play's symbolism, since, as he interprets it, it is about "real people and their illusions"—specifically, the breakdown of youthful illusion. He admits, however, that it is possible to find a Christian allegory in the play. In "Absurdity in *The Death of Bessie Smith*" (*CLAJ*, VIII, 76-80), Walter C. Daniel sees in the Negro orderly, held down by racism yet confident and proud, a reflection of the ridiculousness of American optimism—indeed, a concrete example of the absurdity of existence. A comprehensive view of all the plays through the 1963-1964 season is offered by Allan Lewis in "The Fun and Games of Edward Albee" (*ETJ*, XVI, 29-39). In a detailed examination, Lewis justifies his assertion that all are paeans to impotence. Yet, like most readers and theatergoers, he admires *Virginia Woolf* for its lack of compromise with truth, its exciting rhythms, and its vigor.

It is appropriate to conclude with mention of an essay on the youngest among our current playwrights of undoubted seriousness, Jack Gelber. Stanley G. Eskin, in "Theatricality in the Avant-Garde Drama: A Reconsideration of a Theme in the Light of *The Balcony* and *The Connection*" (*MD*, VII, 213-222), discusses the importance of role-playing in the development of character in the work of Pirandello, Genet, and Gelber. In his analysis of *The Connection*, Eskin observes that the characters are unwilling to assume their roles in the play, but that on doing so at the request of the producer who is to make a film on drug-addiction, they emerge from their torpor to reveal their personalities and form a kind of connection with the audience through sympathy. Thus by deliberate theatricality, reminding the audience that it is witnessing a play, Gelber provides for the acceptance of the addict as a human being. But one may add, with no intention of belittling Gelber's talent, that O'Neill found it possible to give his audience the same understanding of such a person through the most familiar, non-absurd, naturalistic techniques.

Queens College

Index

American Literary Scholarship, 1963

Partly in response to the first readers of the 1963 volume, this index is designed to increase for many years the usefulness of the essays contained in the annual. Like the essays themselves, it, too, can serve scholars as a measurement of literary activity.

The index is primarily an index of authors of critical works and of the authors who are their subjects. A movement or genre is indexed only if the work under discussion is significantly on that subject. Hence, an incidental reference to the Gothic novel would not be indexed, but if, for example, an article were about the influence of the Gothic novel on Faulkner, *Gothic novel* would be an index entry. However, the index does attempt complete coverage of literary figures referred to throughout the book. Works are cited only under authors who have at least a chapter devoted to them (i. e., those in Part I).

Joseph M. Flora

Duberman, Martin B., 125-126
Dukore, Bernard F., 206
Duneka, Frederick A., 63
Dunlap, William, 198
Dunne, Finley Peter, 56
Dunne, Philip, 56
Dupee, F. W., 65
Durham, Philip, 157-158
Dusenberry, Winifred L., 208
Duskis, Henry, 55
Dutton, Geoffry, 49
Duvall, Severn, 107
Dwight, Timothy, 99, 102
Dworkin, Martin S., 187-188
Dyson, A. E., 88

Eastman, Max, 212
Eaton, Clement, 140
Eberhart, Richard, 8, 191
Eble, Kenneth, 87, 88
Eckley, Wilton, 51
Eckstorm, Fanny, 13
Edel, Leon, 64-65, 76
Edmonds, Walter P., 139
Edwards, John, 172
Edwards, Jonathan, 97, 102-103
Eggleston, Edward, 111-112
Eisinger, Chester E., 3, 133, 144-145
Elby, Cecil D., 36
Eliot, George, 68
Eliot, T. S., 76, 78, 80, 90, 139, 166,
    167, 172, 173, 176, 178, 179, 181,
    183, 184, 185, 191, 196
Elliot, George P., 176-177
Ellison, Ralph, 159, 216, 220
Emanuel, James A., 217
Emerson, Charles Chauncey, 4
Emerson, Ralph Waldo, 3, 4-9, 13, 15,
    24, 27, 39, 40, 44, 46, 51, 165 n.,
    168, 169, 191, 218, 220, 221
Emerson, Ralph Waldo, *works*
    "American Scholar," 7
    "Brahma," 8
    "Days," 8
    "Hamatreya," 8
    Journals and Miscellaneous Note-
        books of Ralph Waldo Emerson,
        Vol. III, *1826-1832,* 4
    Nature, 6, 7, 123, 218, 221
    "Poet, The," 51
    "Right Hand of Fellowship," 5
    "Sphinx, The," 39
    "Una," 8
    "Uriel," 5

Emery, Clark, 174
Emig, Janet A., 108
Engle, Bernard F., 194
Evanson, Philip, 104
Ezell, John Samuel, 214

Falk, Doris V., 202
Falk, Robert, 218
Fannin, James Walker, 12
Farrell, James T., 133, 134, 141
Fast, Howard, 134
Faulkner, John, 74
Faulkner, William, 7, 72-80, 90, 102,
    109, 132, 144, 145, 214, 215, 219,
    223
Faulkner, William, *works*
    Absalom, Absalom!, 75, 76, 77, 78
    As I Lay Dying, 74, 79, 80
    "Bear, The," 61, 76, 79
    "Divorce in Naples," 76
    Fable, A, 76
    Hamlet, The, 75
    Mosquitoes, 76
    "Old Man," 61
    Requiem for a Nun, 77
    Sanctuary, 73, 76, 77, 78
    Sartoris, 73, 76, 80
    Sound and the Fury, The, 76, 77
Feldges, Alfred, 142
Fenton, Charles, 89
Ferguson, Alfred R., 4
Ferguson, DeLancey, 58
Fergusson, Francis, 194-195
Ferry, David, 165 n.
Fiedler, Leslie, 62
Fields, James T., 16
Fiene, Donald M., 148
Filler, Louis, 182, 212
Finkelstein, Dorothee Metlitsky, 31-
    32, 35
Finn, James, 151
Fisher, Richard E., 80
Fisher, Vardis, 159
Fitzgerald, F. Scott, 81-91, 132, 148,
    163, 223
Fitzgerald, F. Scott, *works*
    Great Gatsby, The, 82, 88, 165
    Last Tycoon, 163
    Letters, 86-87
    Pat Hobby Stories, The, 82, 86
    Tender Is the Night, 82
Fitzhugh, William, 98
Fletcher, John Gould, 166, 187
Flint, Timothy, 38

Index

American Literary Scholarship, 1964

The index for the 1964 volume is guided by the same principles as the 1963 index, which also appears in this volume. Coverage is mainly for authors of criticism and authors as subjects. Works are cited only for authors who appear in chapter titles in Part I. A movement or genre is noted when articles are significantly on that subject.

Joseph M. Flora